Just
Enough
Requirements
Management

Also Available from Dorset House Publishing

Agile Software Development in the Large:
Diving Into the Deep
by Jutta Eckstein
ISBN: 0-932633-57-9 Copyright © 2004 248 pages, softcover

The Deadline: A Novel About Project Management
by Tom DeMarco
ISBN: 0-932633-39-0 Copyright © 1997 320 pages, softcover

Five Core Metrics: The Intelligence Behind Successful Software Management
by Lawrence H. Putnam and Ware Myers
ISBN: 0-932633-55-2 Copyright © 2003 328 pages, softcover

Hiring the Best Knowledge Workers, Techies & Nerds:
The Secrets & Science of Hiring Technical People
by Johanna Rothman   foreword by Gerald M. Weinberg
ISBN: 0-932633-59-5 Copyright © 2004 352 pages, softcover

Peopleware: Productive Projects and Teams, 2nd ed.
by Tom DeMarco and Timothy Lister
ISBN: 0-932633-43-9 Copyright © 1999 264 pages, softcover

Project Retrospectives: A Handbook for Team Reviews
by Norman L. Kerth   foreword by Gerald M. Weinberg
ISBN: 0-932633-44-7 Copyright © 2001 288 pages, softcover

Software Endgames:
Eliminating Defects, Controlling Change, and the Countdown to On-Time Delivery
by Robert Galen
ISBN: 0-932633-62-5 Copyright © 2005 328 pages, softcover

Waltzing with Bears: Managing Risk on Software Projects
by Tom DeMarco and Timothy Lister
ISBN: 0-932633-60-9 Copyright © 2003 208 pages, softcover

For More Information

✔ Contact us for prices, shipping options, availability, and more.

✔ Visit Dorsethouse.com for excerpts, reviews, downloads, and more.

DORSET HOUSE PUBLISHING
An Independent Publisher of Books on
Systems and Software Development and Management. Since 1984.
3143 Broadway, Suite 2B New York, NY 10027 USA
1-800-DH-BOOKS 1-800-342-6657
212-620-4053 fax: 212-727-1044
info@dorsethouse.com www.dorsethouse.com

Just Enough Requirements Management

Where Software Development Meets Marketing

ALAN M. DAVIS

DORSET HOUSE PUBLISHING
3143 BROADWAY, SUITE 2B
NEW YORK, NEW YORK 10027

Library of Congress Cataloging-in-Publication Data

Davis, Alan Mark.
  Just enough requirements management : where software development meets
marketing / Alan M. Davis.
      p. cm.
  Includes bibliographical references and index.
  ISBN 0-932633-64-1
  1. Computer software industry. 2. Computer software--Development. 3.
Computer software--Marketing. I. Title.
  HD9696.63.A2D38 2005
  005'.068'5--dc22
                                    2004028999

Cover Design: Nuno Andrade

Distributed in the English language in Singapore, the Philippines, and Southeast
Asia by Alkem Company (S) Pte. Ltd., Singapore; in the English language in India,
Bangladesh, Sri Lanka, Nepal, and Mauritius by Prism Books Pvt., Ltd., Bangalore,
India; and in the English language in Japan by Toppan Co., Ltd., Tokyo, Japan.

Printed in the United States of America

Library of Congress Catalog Number: 2004028999

ISBN: 0-932633-64-1   12 11 10 9 8 7 6 5 4

Acknowledgments

I would like to thank Wendy Eakin of Dorset House, who quickly shared my vision to produce a "good enough requirements" book. Also deserving of thanks are the approximately 6,000 students to whom I have had the opportunity to teach requirements management over the years. Although I was officially the teacher, I feel I have learned so much from all of them and their experiences. My personal evolution as a requirements manager has progressed for the most part as the result of interacting with them.

I would also like to thank all of the colleagues I have worked with over the past 34 years, in both academe and industry. They too have been instrumental in shaping my thoughts and opinions.

I thank two universities for their contributions to this work: the University of Colorado at Colorado Springs, for granting me a sabbatical so I could devote time to writing, and the University of the Western Cape, South Africa, for providing me with a stimulating environment during my sabbatical.

But, above all, I want to thank my family for being with me always: my beloved wife of 27 years, Ginny; my wonderful children, Marsha and Michael; and my parents, Barney and Hannah.

Contents

Preface

When I first started studying requirements specifications and teaching classes on them in the late 1970's, I recognized that writing good requirements is very difficult. I worked hard to remove and help others to remove every trace of ambiguity from each and every requirement. I was convinced back then that a polished, word-processed requirements document was the only right way to record requirements. As I gained more and more experience, though, I started to realize that ambiguity can never be entirely removed from a requirements document that is written in natural language. So, I started to explore alternate ways of documenting requirements.

By the mid 1980's, my solution to the problem of ambiguity in requirements was to use more and more formalism. Formalism allows requirements writers to remove some of the ambiguity by replacing natural language with notations that possess unambiguous semantics. By 1990, I had written *Software Requirements,* a book that explored many of these rich notations.

By the mid 1990's, I was experiencing more and more push-back from customers. Computer-science-savvy customers embraced the notations. Of course, the software engineers loved the formalisms, such as finite state machines, decision tables, Petri nets, statecharts, and so on. However, a very large majority of the customers I was meeting were not computer-science-savvy and had no interest in becoming so. What they wanted was very simple: to have their real-world problems solved.

Around the turn of the millennium, I realized why we communicate on a day-to-day basis in natural language: It works. One secret to writing good requirements, then, is to write them primarily in the language of the customers. For example, consider these customers:

- a hospital administrator looking for a new patient records system
- a military officer interested in procuring a new weapon control system
- a marketing person looking for a new way to build a Website quickly
- an employee in an operating division of any company

What language is spoken and understood by these customers? Answer: natural language.

However, the days of large, word-processed requirements documents are over. These days, there are too many things that a manager needs to do quickly—more quickly than a word-processed document can provide. For example, a manager needs to know the following:

- How many requirements are there in Release 2.0?
- How many high-priority requirements have been delayed until Release 3.0?
- What percentage of the requirements for Release 2.0 are low-priority?
- Which requirements in Release 2.0 are high-priority, are being built for Customer X, and are the responsibility of Sally?

It was the need for quick answers to questions like these that helped me conclude that the only way to record requirements when pressed for time is to *list* the discrete requirements, annotating each with multiple attributes.

Having a list of requirements solves many problems, but it misses a major purpose of creating requirements in the first place.

We create requirements to address needs, or markets. Without a thorough understanding of those needs, we are wasting our time. What good are "perfect" requirements—ones that are nicely worded and neatly laid out in a table—if they fail to address the customers' needs?

This book is all about how to discover, prune, and document requirements when you are subjected to tight schedule constraints. If you are in an environment with unlimited resources and unlimited time, then you need not read this book.

March 2005   A.M.D.
Colorado Springs, Colorado

Just Enough Requirements Management

ONE

Introduction

REQUIREMENTS

It is a good idea to decide what you want to build before you build it. This is true for any human endeavor in which the person using an item is different from the person building it. This principle is especially true in software development, because software requires such a high degree of precision and coordination among team members in order to achieve acceptable levels of quality. If we did not seek agreement up front about what to build, we would likely end up with many more unsatisfactory systems, many more unhappy customers, and more software systems that fail because of assumptions that are incompatible with users' needs.

That is the primary reason that we write requirements: to document a common understanding of what system is to be built.

> A requirement *is an externally observable characteristic of a desired system.*

A candidate requirement must pass two tests to be considered valid: (1) the satisfaction of the requirement must be observable from a point of view that's external to the system, and (2) the requirement must help satisfy some need of the potential customer or other stakeholder.

Contrast the above with this more common definition: "A requirement defines what a system is supposed to do, without defining how it is to do it." This popular "what, not how" definition is fraught with difficulties [DAV93].

Let's say we are a group of analysts, and a hotel manager contacts us to help him. We ask him what he wants, and he responds with, "I want a telephone system." We could congratulate him on defining a requirement very well, for he clearly defined *what* he wants (a telephone system), not how it is to work ("push this button to make an outside call").

However, if we ask the hotel manager *why* he wants the telephone system, he might respond, "Well, I guess what I really want is a means of communication for all the guests; I don't really need a telephone system *per se.*" Now, we could argue that the *what* is a communication system and the *how* is a telephone system.

If we ask the hotel manager why he wants a communication system, he might respond, "I want to keep the guests happy." Now, we could argue that the *what* is keeping guests happy and the *how* is a communication system. If we ask the hotel manager why he wants to keep the guests happy, he might respond, "I want the guests to come back." Now, we could argue that the *what* is getting the guests to return and the *how* is keeping guests happy. We could continue this questioning process and eventually get to Abraham Maslow's hierarchy of needs [MAS70]. As you can see, every time we ask *why*, the previous answer suddenly becomes the *what,* and what we thought was a requirement suddenly looks like a *how*— not a requirement.

Yet another popular definition of a requirement is, "A requirement defines a problem of the customer without reference to any solution to that problem." This definition provides a nice theoretical basis, but as we saw above, the customer's problem might be that he or she wants a *specific* system. There is no precise line between problem and solution. We have in every case a continuum of issues ranging from the most problem-like ("I want to make money") to the most solution-like ("I want to make long-distance calls with the press of just one button").

Returning to the proposed definition of a requirement (an externally observable characteristic of a desired system), let's look at some examples and determine if they are in fact valid requirements. Let's imagine that we are at a company in the 1980's and we want to define requirements for the first remote mouse. Somebody suggests,

The system shall have three buttons.

To determine if that is a valid requirement, we need to consider the two tests:

- *Externally observable:* Yes. Clearly, when the mouse is built, we will easily observe (with our eyes, in this case) that the mouse does or does not have three buttons.
- *Desired:* To determine this, we need to ask the customers or users. It is possible that the customer would be satisfied with *any* method of moving slides forward, moving slides backward, and displaying a menu, in which case, having three buttons is not a requirement; the right requirement would be,

The system shall provide a means to enable users to move slides forward, move slides backward, and display a menu.

On the other hand, the customer may actually want three buttons! In that case, the original statement of the requirement is valid.

Next, somebody suggests,

One of the system's three buttons shall be 2" long, ± .1"; .5" wide, ±.0125"; and .0625" tall, ±.00001".

To determine if this a valid requirement, we need to look at the same two tests:

- *Externally observable:* Yes. Clearly, when the mouse is built, we can easily observe (in this case, using a linear measuring device) that a mouse button does or does not have these dimensions.
- *Desired:* To determine this, we need to ask the customers or users. If the user was planning to use a thumb to push the button, then this level of detail seems too restrictive. On the other hand, the customer may actually need these dimensions. For example, the plan might be for the button

to be pressed by a robotic finger, already built, that has precisely the accuracy indicated in this requirement! In this case, the statement of the requirement is valid, and nothing less specific will do.

What we see from the above examples is that nobody but the customers or users can determine whether or not a candidate requirement is valid. Furthermore, *it is impossible for a consultant to walk into your office, examine a requirement, and tell you that it is either too detailed or too vague. The correct level of detail is completely dependent on the needs of the customers.*

REQUIREMENTS MANAGEMENT

Requirements management is the set of activities that consists of gathering requirements, identifying the "right" ones to satisfy, and documenting them. There are three important subsets of requirements management activities:

- *Requirements elicitation* deals with gathering candidate requirements from customers, users, subject-matter experts, and other stakeholders.
- *Requirements triage* deals with determining which requirements should be satisfied when analyzed within the context of available development resources, time to market, revenue goals, and return on investment.
- *Requirements specification* deals with documenting the external behavior of the desired system.

Requirements management is an ongoing activity. Although it is the first activity to be initiated (as shown in Figure 1-1), it is more than just the first phase of software development. In the beginning, you are actively listening to customers, perhaps stimulating them with questions, conducting brainstorming sessions, and the like. During this time, lots of candidate requirements will be "coming at you." Some of these might express a general need, such as,

We need to reduce our billing error rates by at least 50 percent.

Some might express an abstract description of a possible solution:

The system needs to look similar to what we are familiar with.

And some might be very specific:

The system needs to display reports in this *format.*

After doing this for a while, you may start to envision a system that could solve some of the customers' needs. When this happens, you should start accumulating a list of candidate features of the solution system. As requirements elicitation continues, the length of the list of candidate features increases and requirements triage is used to hone the list down to those candidates that can be constructed with acceptable levels of risk. Much iteration occurs, and the candidate features are annotated to reflect your understanding of their relative importance, relative risk, and relative difficulty of satisfaction. Finally, triage selects the features, which you then flesh out and document as a list of requirements for the system to be built. After this is done, you should spawn a development effort as shown in Figure 1-1.

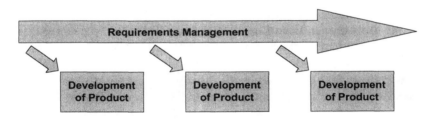

Figure 1-1: Ongoing Requirements Management
Spawns Software Developments.

During development, you cannot afford to stop listening to your customers and the other stakeholders. Throughout the development effort, new candidate features will arise and existing, approved requirements will change or be rendered unnecessary. Each time such an incident occurs, you must reexamine the triage decision. Consider the alternatives:

- add the new requirements
- delete other requirements
- change a previously approved requirement
- redirect the development staff
- initiate a parallel development effort to satisfy the new requirements

- extend the schedule
- cancel the current effort entirely

JUST ENOUGH

Before the Capability Maturity Model (CMM) [PAU93] became popular, software companies had no yardstick for measuring how mature their software development process was. Although far from perfect, the CMM does at least give us that yardstick. And its use has become fairly widespread. Through level 3 of CMM,[1] an organization strives to make its software process more repeatable and more measurable, through the documentation and institutionalization of specific process improvements. Although CMM does not demand that the institutionalized process be "heavy,"[2] many companies on the CMM path (and many CMM assessors) seem to think that it does. The result is that organizations are both gaining (from improved repeatability and measurability) and losing (by adopting excessively slow and tedious methods). In a time-to-market economy, this can be deadly.

At the other extreme, since the mid 1990's, many companies have reverted to the practices of the 1960's, in which little or no process is employed. Initiated by the dot-coms, these organizations believe that Internet-based applications, such as e-commerce, Websites, and portals, are somehow above even the most basic principles of software engineering learned over thirty years [DAV95]. Many factors led to the dot-com crash at the turn of the millennium, but one factor certainly was the lack of intelligent requirements management.

Symptomatic of such a lack is the wanton and random inclusion of requirements by coders, with no thought about how such changes affect product quality, product usability, customer satisfaction, or the probability of completing on schedule or within budget. A variant of this is agile development [COC02, HIG01], in which requirements are rarely documented but are instead imparted in real time, by the customer to the developer, as needed. There are many problems with this:

---

[1]There are five levels of maturity in the CMM, numbered 1 to 5, in ascending order of maturity.

[2]I use the term "heavy" to mean cumbersome, slow, overly methodical, with many reviews, carefully orchestrated to enable measurements to occur, and so on.

- The customer has his or her own job to perform and cannot be at the beck and call of the development team.
- Customer representatives come and go, and if all the contracts are oral, havoc and disappointment can result.
- One customer cannot be expected to be able to speak for all stakeholders, except under the most trivial of circumstances.
- Developers come and go, so expectations and agreements must be written.

As shown in Figure 1-2, neither of these two extremes represents the *right* amount of requirements process for all companies, or even for all projects within any one company. The right place on this scale for your project depends on many factors, including the corporate culture, time-to-market pressure, the criticality of the application, and so on. The right place on the scale is where you have *just enough* process to minimize your risks sufficiently while still achieving desired outcomes.

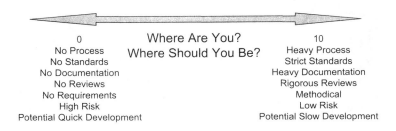

Figure 1-2: The Range of Rigor in Requirements Processes.

A few years ago, I was delivering a lecture at Boeing, in Seattle, and I had Figure 1-2 projected on the screen. A gentleman in the back of the room raised his hand and asked, "Where on that spectrum should I be?" I asked what his job was. He responded that he managed the flight control software development for the Boeing 777. My answer was easy: "As far to the right side of the diagram as possible."

On one hand, my answer was motivated by the fact that I am a frequent flyer. On the other hand, software whose failure can result in a significant loss of life must be held to the highest possible standards of quality.

Of course, any company producing software could claim the same for *its* application; after all, if its software fails to meet expectations, the company could fail. Every company must make a reasonable trade-off between quality, time-to-market, risks, meeting the right requirements, and so on. But the right place to be on the scale of Figure 1-2 must be driven by the implications of a product failing to meet its intended users' needs, not just whether its failure to meet a market could result in the failure of the company producing or distributing the product.

Documenting requirements is a lot like purchasing insurance. If you do not buy enough, you can end up with disastrous consequences. If you buy too much, you can waste vast quantities of money. If you do not pay enough attention to requirements, you endanger the project's success by introducing too much risk. If you pay too much attention to requirements, you overburden the project and raise the likelihood of being late and over-budget (see Figure 1-3).

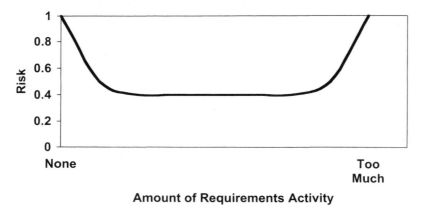

Figure 1-3: Too Much Requirements Can Be as Dangerous as Too Little.

THE CONTEXT OF REQUIREMENTS

Performing requirements activities is not a goal; it is a means to an end. To understand the end, we must first understand the context in which we are trying to identify and document requirements. That context differs significantly among general classes of environments, including the following:

Custom Software Development: This is the most straightforward environment and the one most requirements books address. In this situation, there is *one* customer with a specific problem he or she wants solved with a software-only solution. The customer has contacted a software development company to build a solution to that problem. Sometimes, multiple software development companies are involved, all competing for the right to do business with the customer.

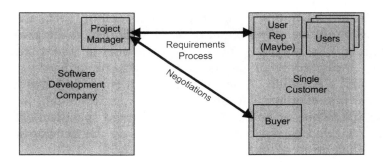

Figure 1-4: Custom Software Development.

Figure 1-4 shows the relationships involved in custom software development. The actors in the play that is software requirements usually include a buyer for the customer, who negotiates the terms of a contract, including cost, delivery date, and functionality; the employees of the customer, who will eventually use the software solution; representatives of these users, who attempt to speak for the company with a single voice; and the project manager, who represents the development organization in the negotiation. These players together ascertain what the needs are and agree to a set of requirements, a price, and a schedule. In general, the steps are as follows:

1. The customer states in general terms what he or she wants and issues a request for proposal (RFP).
2. The software development company creates a proposal outlining its approach, perhaps with a preliminary list of requirements, a proposed schedule, and a proposed budget.
3. The customer selects the best proposal and awards its authors a contract.
4. The software company prepares a requirements document and presents it to the customer.
5. Whenever the customer conceives of new requirements, negotiations ensue and requirements triage is almost always needed.

6. If the development team finds that it is going to exceed the budget or deliver late, negotiation and triage are performed once again.

Custom Embedded System Builders: In this situation, there is one customer with a specific problem he or she wants solved with a system, typically one composed of both custom software and custom hardware. This situation is quite similar to the previous one, except the players generally agree to a set of *system* requirements (independent of media, such as software or hardware), a price, and a schedule. After this agreement is reached, the development organization allocates the system requirements to software, hardware, or both. These more refined specifications are often reviewed by the customer to make sure the developers are proceeding on an adequate path (see Figure 1-5).

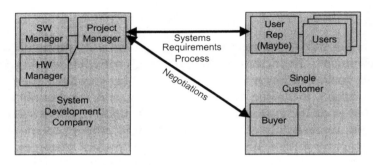

Figure 1-5: Custom System Development.

In general, the steps of custom system development include the following:

1. The customer issues a request for proposal (RFP) and often includes a system-level requirements document.
2. The system development company creates a proposal outlining its approach, a preliminary allocation of requirements to software and hardware, a proposed schedule, and a proposed budget.
3. The customer selects the best proposal and awards its authors a contract.
4. One of the first deliverables to the customer is a more detailed systems requirements document.

5. Subsequent deliverables include a detailed software requirements document and hardware requirements document.
6. Whenever the customer conceives of new requirements, more negotiation ensues and requirements triage is almost always needed.
7. If the development team realizes that it is going to exceed the budget or deliver late, negotiation and triage are performed once again.

Independent Software Vendors (ISVs): In this case, a company wants to produce software that it intends to sell many times within a market. It is often difficult, if not impossible, to find customers to talk with during the early stages. Instead, needs are identified through market research, demographic studies, sales force feedback, and the like. The primary spokesperson for the customers is the marketing organization within the development company (see Figure 1-6).

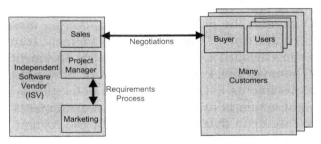

Figure 1-6: Independent Software Vendors.

In the case of independent software vendors, many factors influence the decision to enter a market. In general, the steps are

1. Decide what business you are in.
2. Select a target market.
3. Do market research to determine if the market is large enough for you to achieve your revenue goals. If it is already well-penetrated by competitors, determine who the customers are within that market, and whether the pain felt by these individuals is great enough to warrant your entry. Determine whether an appropriate marketing message exists that will help you capture an acceptable share of the

market. If your market research identifies any of these factors as a problem, return to step 2 and refine the market into a subset (a vertical market) or find another market altogether. In general, a narrow vertical market is far easier to get a foothold in than a larger, more diffuse market [MOO91].

4. If the market conditions are positive, then it is time to draft a list of very high-level features for the product. This is generally written by marketing and packaged in a Market Requirements Document (MRD). The contents of the MRD, the desired price, and the desired date of product introduction are then analyzed for compatibility. If not compatible, the requirements are triaged. If you cannot reach closure on this, return to step 2 and select a different market.

5. If triage is completed successfully, then you need to verify that a price point exists where the product can be successfully sold. Also, is there a marketing message that would be effective for these features, in this market, at this price, and so on?

6. Only after the price point and marketing message have been determined should the development team begin to write a detailed software requirements document.

7. Whenever marketing conceives of new requirements, requirements triage is needed to determine whether the right action is to defer the new requirements to a later release or to delay the delivery of the current release to accommodate the new requirements.

8. If the development project realizes that it is going to exceed the budget or deliver late, negotiation and triage should be performed once again.

Mass Marketed Embedded System Builders: In this case, a company wants to produce a hardware system (usually with software embedded within it) that it intends to sell many times within a market. Here, the same steps as the previous scenario are performed (see Figure 1-7).

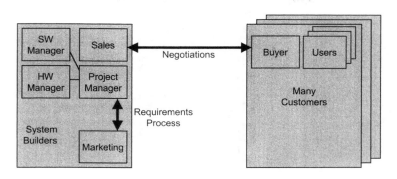

Figure 1-7: Mass Marketed Embedded System Builders.

Internal IT Organizations: In most large companies, the day-to-day information technology (IT) needs of employees, middle managers, and executives are satisfied by an internal IT organization. In theory, it should be easier to negotiate a set of requirements when the customers and developers are within the same company. However, this is not the case. Politics and power games are even more prevalent in this situation than when multiple companies are involved. The players in this scenario include the customers who have the problems, the developers within the IT shop who have been hired to solve those problems, analysts who are working between these two groups to help each party better understand the language and concerns of the other, and third parties who would love to enter the company if it chooses to outsource the work to them. In general, the steps are as follows:

1. The employees become aware of a problem. This is often inspired by a need to increase revenue, decrease expenses, reduce errors, increase efficiency, and so on. The employees file some type of work request with the IT organization.

2. Analysts step in to understand the employee needs and translate those needs into a language that the developers can understand. The analysts could be part of the IT organization or part of the user community, as shown in Figures 1-8 and 1-9, respectively. A preliminary list of features is usually written by the analyst.

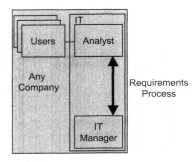

Figure 1-8: IT with Internal Analysts.

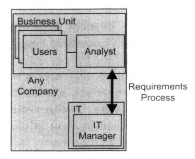

Figure 1-9: IT with External Analysts.

3. Developers respond with an estimate of how long it will take them to complete the requirements. This estimate is usually not within the desired time frame, so requirements triage is often necessary.

4. Eventually, all parties agree on a set of general features, a schedule, and perhaps a budget. Only then is development authorized to write a complete software requirements document.

Requirements Consultants: On occasion, an organization knows that it has a problem that could probably be solved with an information system, but it lacks the expertise to capture its own requirements or evaluate commercially available solutions. In such cases, the organization contracts with a company that has expertise in eliciting and documenting requirements to serve as a consultant (see Figure 1-10).

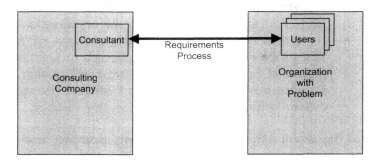

Figure 1-10: Using a Requirements Consultant.

In this situation, the events progress like this:

1. An organization becomes aware of a problem and contacts a company that offers either exclusive requirements analysis assistance or a full range of consulting services, including requirements analysis.
2. The organization negotiates a contract with the consultant.
3. The consultant works with the potential users to understand the organization's needs. A preliminary list of features is usually written by the consultant.
4. Discussions are held between the consultant and the potential users concerning the candidate features and their relative priorities.
5. The consultant delivers to the organization a requirements document or a database of requirements. This is often the end of the contract with the consultant.
6. The organization (with the help of the consultant, if still under contract) performs a search for commercially available systems that meet the requirements. At this point, one of three possibilities will occur:

   - An ideal, commercially available system is found at an acceptable price and is acquired for use by the organization.
   - A variety of commercially available systems are found, each with some advantages and disadvantages (including price, absent features, and so on). A comparative analysis is performed (again, with the help

of the consultant, if still under contract), and the best alternative is acquired for use by the organization.

- No viable commercially available systems are found. The problems are significant enough to warrant the high cost of purchasing a custom-built system. The organization issues an RFP and follows the steps of custom software development described earlier.

In all of the above contexts, we are eliciting, pruning, and documenting requirements in order to increase the probability that the eventual system will solve the intended problem or make good use of the intended opportunity [DAV97].

THE RELATIONSHIP BETWEEN SCHEDULE AND REQUIREMENTS

A few years ago, there was a widespread debate in the industry about whether the waterfall model [ROY70] or the spiral model [BOE86] was an inherently better way of looking at software development. I never considered the two to be particularly different. The waterfall model says to go through a series of phases in producing a product and start over with each new product. The spiral model says to build iteratively. In each iteration, the product goes through a series of phases. Perhaps the only difference is whether you originally planned to do it iteratively or are just doing it iteratively as an afterthought. Interestingly, the authors most often associated with these models, Winston Royce and Barry Boehm, considered their models to be planned iteration.

In any case, I always considered the debate to be about whether you should try to satisfy all of your requirements or only a subset in your next iteration. If that is what people have been arguing about, then the argument can end. Shorter iterations are better than longer iterations. And shorter iterations imply only satisfying a small subset of the requirements. This section explores this as well as a few other issues relating to life cycles, schedules, and requirements.

How Much Time to Spend on Requirements?

The time you should spend performing requirements activities varies greatly from project to project. No magic formula exists that says you should devote a certain percent of the total development budget to requirements. There are many reasons for this variation:

- Fuzzy problems require more time than well-understood problems.
- More time is required when multiple stakeholders have varying needs than when only one stakeholder exists.
- Constantly changing problems require more attention to requirements than static problems.
- Complex problems require more attention to requirements than simpler problems.

Kevin Forsberg and Harold Mooz's study of NASA projects [FOR97] shows that when NASA devoted 5 percent or less of the total development budget to planning activities (including requirements), it typically experienced overall project cost overruns of 40 to 170 percent (see Figure 1-11). When NASA devoted 10 to 20 percent of the total development budget to planning activities (including requirements), it experienced overall project cost overruns below 30 percent.

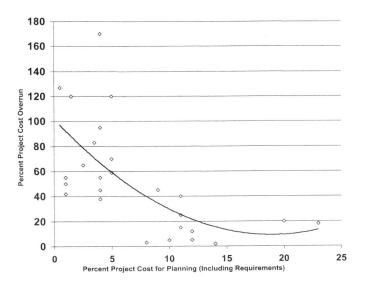

Figure 1-11: Requirements Time versus Cost Overruns (Adapted from [FOR97]).

*Kevin Forsberg and Harold Mooz, "System Engineering Overview," *Software Requirements Engineering*, eds. M. Dorfman and R. Thayer (Los Alamitos, Calif.: IEEE Computer Society Press, 1997), p. 45. © 1997 IEEE. Used by permission.

Use this data to support your case for spending more time on requirements. For example, let's say you have spent only 5 percent of your planned budget on requirements, and you know you only have a little understanding of the requirements. By all means, use this graph to argue for more time and resources. On the other hand, do not use this graph as an excuse to waste time. Let's say you have spent 5 percent of your planned budget on requirements and you have a solid understanding of them—in such a case, do not use this graph as an excuse to twiddle your thumbs for a few months.

Who Should Define the Schedule?

Most organizations think that the development team should create the schedule from the requirements. Obviously, development needs to determine a reasonable schedule within which it can deliver, but customers or marketing should drive the desired schedules just as they should drive the requirements. A desired delivery date is not something the development organization is in a position to define. Customer needs (urgency, criticality, market window, and so on) prescribe the desired schedule.

The right way to plan a project is to find out the desired requirements and the desired schedule; then compare the two and see if they are compatible. If they aren't, massage one or both of them during requirements triage to arrive at a satisfactory balance. When customers define the requirements and development organizations define the schedule, conflict occurs. Instead, let the customers define both. Development's job is to assist the customer in understanding the probabilities of success given the constraints. The customer may have to choose between having the system on time, with fewer requirements satisfied, or having it later, but with all the requirements satisfied. Development should serve as a facilitator to help the customer better understand the trade-offs.

Schedule Should Drive Requirements

Yet another issue is the question of whether requirements should drive schedule or schedule should drive requirements selection. I feel strongly that schedule should drive requirements. Let's say the market window demands that we deliver something in six months. The challenge, then, is to determine the appropriate subset of requirements that can be satisfied within that schedule at an appropriate level of risk. This is quite similar to the "design to cost" philosophy of engineering. The reverse simply does not work. If we start with a long list of requirements, the derived completion date will always be unsatisfactory.

How Much Time Between Releases?

A final issue relating to schedule and requirements is the length of time between releases. The shorter the cycle, the more likely you are to achieve on-time delivery. The longer the cycle, the more likely you are to deliver late. To show how this works, let's look at an example of a company that has already released a product (Release 1.0) and is planning the next release (Release 2.0).

Let us assume that the company's typical development process is one year long, as shown in Figure 1-12, and that intelligent requirements management is being conducted. Thus, at the beginning of the planning stage for Release 2.0, requirements are elicited and triage is conducted to ensure that requirements that can be completed within the one-year time frame are selected. Requirements that cannot be satisfied within one year are deferred either to a subsequent release (say, Release 3.0) or to a date that's even later. The agreed-upon requirements are documented and baselined.

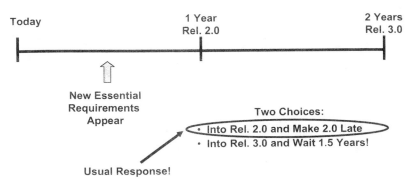

Figure 1-12: A Long Development Cycle.

Regardless of how much attention is given to requirements, they will still change during development. If a new requirement becomes evident midway into the development life cycle, we need to analyze whether we want to add it to the current release's baselined list of requirements or defer it to a later release:

- If we add the new requirement to the current baseline, the current delivery date will be jeopardized. You have two choices here: Either announce a slip of Release 2.0 to accommodate the new requirement, or naïvely march on and develop the product with the new requirement added, only to deliver the product late, anyway.[3] Either way, the product will be delivered late; your only choice is whether to announce it now or later.

- If we defer the new requirement to a later release, we will have to notify the customer that although the requirement is important, we won't satisfy it until Release 3.0—perhaps eighteen months away! It will be difficult to convince the customer that we are being responsive.

Due to the negative ramifications of deferring requirements, accepting the requirement and delivering late is more common. To make matters worse, when Release 2.0 is delivered, say, two months late, the start of development for Release 3.0 will also be delayed two months. So, Release 3.0 becomes two months late even before it starts. And the cycle repeats. Every release is delayed evermore by the constantly changing requirements.

Contrast this scenario with one in which we plan much smaller releases in, say, three-month cycles, as shown in Figure 1-13.

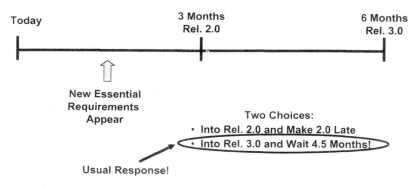

Figure 1-13: A Shorter Development Cycle.

Let's make the same assumptions as before. Namely, that intelligent requirements management is being conducted; that at the beginning of the planning stage for Release 2.0, requirements are

---

[3]See the end of the "Requirements Management" section, presented earlier in this chapter, for other choices.

elicited, triage is conducted to select requirements that can be completed within the three-month time frame, requirements needing more than three months are deferred to a later date, and the agreed-upon requirements are documented and baselined.

As with the one-year cycle above, regardless of how much attention is given to requirements, they will still change during development. If a new requirement becomes evident midway into this shorter development life cycle, we still need to analyze whether we want to add it to the current release's baselined list of requirements or defer it to a later release.

- If we add a new requirement to the current baseline, the delivery date will be jeopardized. As with the longer development cycle, you have two choices: Either announce a slip of Release 2.0 to accommodate the new requirement or naïvely add the new requirement and deliver the product late, anyway. As before, the product will be delivered late; your only choice is whether to announce it now or later.
- If we defer the new requirement to a later release in our shorter development cycle, we will still have to notify the customer that we will try to satisfy the requirement in Release 3.0. Fortunately, that's just four-and-a-half months away! This sounds like we are really being responsive.

Due to the negative ramifications of delaying a release, it is common for such requirements to be deferred when the development cycle is short. While deferring a requirement in the one-year development cycle meant an eighteen-month wait, in this case, the wait is brief. Deferral results in on-time delivery of Release 2.0 and all subsequent releases.

THE COMPONENTS OF REQUIREMENTS MANAGEMENT

As I noted earlier, the primary components of requirements management are requirements elicitation, requirements triage, and requirements specification.

As shown in Figure 1-14, elicitation consists of a two-way interaction between the requirements team and the stakeholders. The requirements team needs to be interdisciplinary. It should include subject-matter experts (SMEs) and experts in requirements techniques. It should include individuals who tend to be left-brained (to demand precision) and those who tend to be right-brained (who can *feel* the problems of the customers).[4] The team should also include individuals who want to see the development organization succeed and people who want to see the customer succeed (these two desires should not be mutually exclusive). For complex problems, the team should have experts in every major discipline covered by the system.

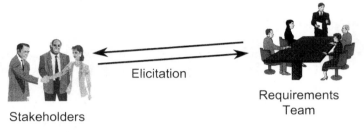

Figure 1-14: Requirements Elicitation.

The titles given to members of the requirements team vary greatly from organization to organization. In IT organizations, where the customers are internal—in a different department of the same organization—the team members are usually called analysts, systems analysts, or business analysts. In ISVs, the team members are usually culled from the marketing organization and are often given titles such as marketing representative, product manager, product marketing manager, or project manager. In companies where software is just a part of a larger system, the team members may have titles like business analyst, systems engineer, marketing representative, software project manager, or system architect. Regardless of their titles, the members of the requirements team are crucial; they are tasked with learning the almost-unlearnable needs of the stakeholders.

As the team discovers parts of the problems experienced by the stakeholders, it is likely to think of pieces of possible solutions. Rather than suppressing these thoughts, use them to gain a better understanding of the needs. For example, if stakeholders say they want a means of communicating commands between geographically dispersed personnel, try drawing a picture of or creating a

---

[4]A left-brained person is outward-looking, logical, and analytical. Inventors, engineers, and scientists tend to be left-brained. A right-brained person is inward-looking, creative, passionate, intuitive, and emotional. Artists and designers tend to be right-brained.

model of a telephone.[5] You will quickly learn whether or not this is what the customer wants. Furthermore, seeing a picture or model will often cause stakeholders to think of additional needs. Some authors of requirements books argue that elicitors should always avoid discussing solutions; in fact, they would argue against drawing a picture of the telephone because it prematurely "pushes" for a specific solution. Their primary motivation is to create *optimal* solutions, and they feel that jumping to a specific solution too early will lessen the likelihood of arriving at an optimal solution. However, with so many of our industry's software systems failing to meet customer needs at all, I'd rather create a solution that works (I'd perhaps optimize it later). Figure 1-15 shows how modeling pieces of the solution can help create feedback elicitation.

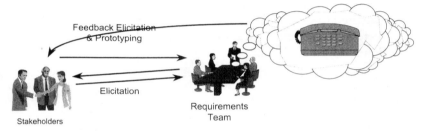

Figure 1-15: Requirements Elicitation with Feedback.

As elicitation continues, discrete candidate requirements will emerge. These should be documented in a list, as shown in Figure 1-16.

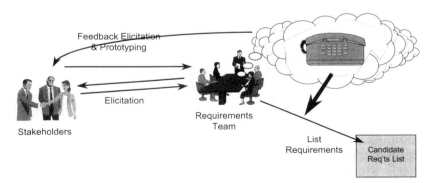

Figure 1-16: Elicitation Results in a List of Candidate Requirements.

---

[5]This might be as simple as an actual drawing on a piece of paper, or as complex as a fully functional prototype.

It is impossible to say what the right level is for these requirements. Ideally, you want to have about 100, although the actual number may vary anywhere from, say, 30 to 200. Requirements stated at this level of abstraction are often termed *features*. The argument for having around 100 requirements is that you will soon be performing triage on this list, and it is difficult to perform intelligent triage on more than 200 or so. The payoff from doing triage on fewer than 30 is questionable. On the other hand, elicitation usually identifies requirements at many levels of detail, some very abstract and some very specific—so don't worry *too* much about the actual count.

When you examine this list of candidate requirements and compare the efforts necessary to satisfy them with the available schedules and resources, you will quickly determine that you cannot satisfy all the requirements. Thus, requirements triage must be performed. As shown in Figure 1-17, triage can be thought of as a sieve that determines which of the candidate requirements will be satisfied and which will not.

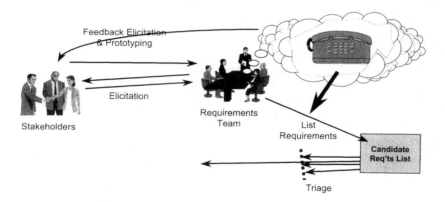

Figure 1-17: Requirements Elicitation and Triage.

Once triage is complete and we know which requirements are to be satisfied, the selected requirements should be refined and expanded, reducing their ambiguity. The expanded list of selected requirements is often called a *software requirements document* or a *software requirements specification* (SRS), as illustrated in Figure 1-18.

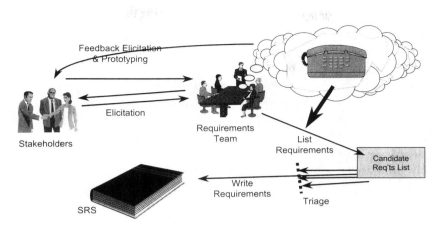

Figure 1-18: Requirements Elicitation, Triage, and Specification.

The previous discussion seems to imply that elicitation, triage, and specification are strictly sequential events. This is not the case.

Let's explore the activities of requirements management as they occur in real time. Rarely do people simply sit down and ask, "Okay, what are the requirements for the new system?" Instead, what generally happens is that one or more (automated or manual) systems already exist, customers are unsatisfied with the service provided, and pressure for change slowly builds. Sometimes, when a business opportunity arises, a company visualizes some features of a system that might leverage the opportunity, and then it decides to expand the preliminary visualized features. In most cases, the sources of requirements are

- customers (people who have an unfulfilled need)
- competition (sources of alternative solutions)
- technology (source of new ideas and capabilities)
- bug reports (reports of defects in the existing system)
- unsatisfied requirements from previous releases (if we are working on the requirements for Release i, then we can assume that we performed a similar exercise when planning Release $i-1$ and at the time consciously decided not to satisfy all the requirements)

Figure 1-19 shows how all these sources are combined to produce a single list of candidate requirements. To emphasize the fact that these requirements are likely to be vague, possibly inconsistent, and at various levels of detail, I call them "candidate features" rather than "candidate requirements." The arrow from "Customers & Competition," labeled "Marketing," is meant to represent marketing in the broadest sense possible—any person or group responsible for keeping track of the needs of the customer or a broader market. Although, in a commercial setting, this function is typically called marketing, in an internal IT organization, the people in this group are typically called analysts. And in some circumstances, they are the customers themselves. Similarly, the arrow labeled "Development" goes from "Technology" to the "List of Candidate Features" because development or research and development (R&D) organizations usually watch trends in technology. The important thing, however, is for *somebody* to be aware of technology trends.

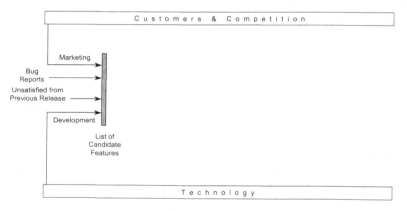

Figure 1-19: The Overall Requirements Process—in the Beginning . . .

You are going to have to analyze these candidate features in a variety of ways. In preparation for this analysis, it is a good idea to annotate them with certain kinds of information. Although many kinds of information may be appropriate for your specific situation, two annotations are applicable in just about any situation: relative priority and estimated cost to satisfy. Figure 1-20 shows the result of this analysis: an annotated list of candidate features.

The figure shows marketing and development working in parallel to arrive at relative priorities and development efforts, respectively. Although they can work in parallel, they cannot work independently, for the following three reasons:

- Development will find that some features are defined so abstractly that it cannot possibly estimate the effort required to address them. In these cases, the best strategy is for development to contact marketing to schedule a meeting at which the features can be jointly refined.

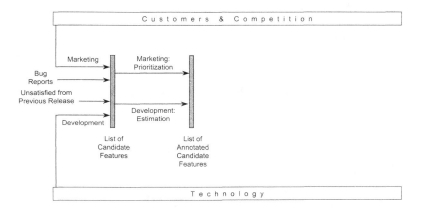

Figure 1-20: Annotating the Requirements.

- Development may need to spend three months investigating alternative ways of satisfying a requirement before it can determine whether it will take one week or six months to solve. In such cases, the best strategy is once again to meet with the marketing people to find out what they are looking for. Of course, development may learn in the meeting that the requirement is low in priority, in which case it isn't necessary to estimate the effort required to satisfy it.
- Marketing may be unable to determine the relative priority of some requirements without knowing the efforts required to address them. Although it is reasonable in theory to demand that marketing look just at the relative importance of requirements, without worrying about their costs, this usually does not work, in practice. For example, marketing might be able to determine that feature i is clearly more important than features j, k, l, and m, but if the satisfaction of feature i consumes all the resources available for the current release, then it makes more sense to include the other features instead. In such cases, the best strategy is for

marketing to contact development to find out what percentage of the total resources available for the current release will be consumed by trying to satisfy feature i.

As the development team attempts to generate estimates of the effort required to satisfy requirements, it is likely to have internal disagreements. Such disagreements are usually symptomatic of requirements that are too abstract. When this occurs, the best idea is to refine the problematic requirements into sub-requirements. For example, if the original requirement is

    A. *The system shall produce an accounts receivable report.*

then we might refine it into the following:

    A. *The system shall produce an accounts receivable report with the following characteristics:*

       A1. *organized into columns corresponding to the number of days outstanding: 0 to 30 days, 31 to 60 days, and over 60 days*

       A2. *organized into rows alphabetically listing the names of customers whose accounts have current balances*

       A3. *within each row, the amounts currently due in each category of days outstanding shall be printed in the appropriate columns*

       A4. *the user may request that the report be printed, displayed on the screen, or stored in a file*

After such refinement, the development team may find it easier to reach a consensus. If not, sub-requirements that are still problematic should be further refined.

    As the marketing team attempts to determine the relative priorities of the requirements, it is also likely to have internal disagreements. There are two likely causes of such disagreements: poor understanding of the requirement as stated, and genuine differences in priorities from disparate customers. In the former case, refinement of the requirements will usually work well. In the latter case, the best idea is to either establish priority attributes for each constituency and record the viewpoints separately or use the consensus-building methods described in Chapter 3, for requirements triage.

Once most of the requirements have been annotated and sufficiently refined, add up the estimated efforts. Compare this to the available budget. The sum of the estimated efforts will always exceed the budget. In fact, the total of the estimated efforts is usually many times larger than the budget. Figure 1-21 shows the triage step as a broad, vertical, dotted line. Triage's job is to determine the subset of the candidate requirements that is "right" for inclusion in the next release, given the (un)availability of resources. Note in this figure how only a subset of the candidate features passes through the triage activity.

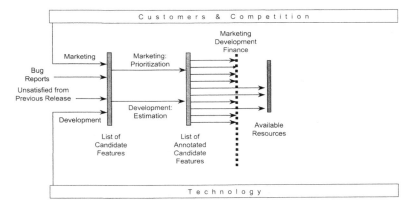

Figure 1-21: Available Resources Are Never Enough.

The three roles shown in the figure—marketing, development, and finance—are generic names for the parties representing the customers, the development organization, and the sources of capital for the development organization, respectively. These three roles do not necessarily have to be three individuals. They could be three teams of people, or all three hats may be worn by just one person—for example, a product manager. The important thing to consider is that the party or parties present in the triage meeting must be able to fairly represent all three constituencies. Any two of these parties can arrive at a resolution extremely easily . . . at the expense of the third, as in the following examples:

- If marketing is absent, development and finance could just agree to remove all the requirements that would be expensive to satisfy (thus ignoring the needs of the customers).

- If development is absent, marketing and finance could just decide to halve all the effort estimates previously supplied by development—and thus be able to agree to satisfy all the requirements within the resources constraints.
- If finance is absent, marketing and development could simply agree to exceed the available budget in order to meet customer needs.

If the politics of your situation demand that you allocate all your resources up front, then, by all means, do so. However, two things are inevitable:

- New requirements are going to appear.
- The effort estimates made by development are going to be proven inaccurate; and when this happens, they are almost always too low.

Because of this inevitability, it is wise for the triage activity to allocate only a percentage of total available resources. The right percentage to aim for is going to vary from organization to organization but is likely to range from 50 to 90 percent, depending on the following:

- How volatile are the requirements likely to be? The more volatile they are, the more room you want to preserve for such expansion (keep the percentage low).
- How underestimated have the development efforts been, traditionally? If development traditionally underestimates the schedule and budget, then maintain more management reserve (keep the percentage low).
- How risk-tolerant are you? The more you thrive on risk, the less reserve you need to maintain (keep the percentage high).
- How flexible are the parties? If customers generally understand that adding new requirements will cause the budget to increase and the schedule to expand, then there is less need to protect development and the customer from disasters (keep the percentage high).

Figure 1-22 shows this, assuming that only 60 percent of the available resources are allocated.

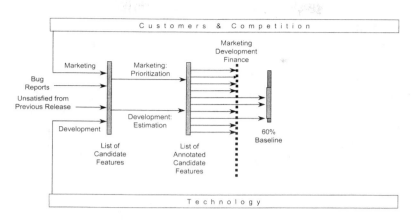

Figure 1-22: Allocating 60 Percent of the Available Resources.

Once this partial baseline (or the entire baseline, if your politics dictate it) is agreed to, development can begin, as illustrated in Figure 1-23. In particular, the development organization can start writing a detailed software requirements document. This has the side effect of enabling the development team to refine its original estimates. The development organization can also start defining and documenting the system's architecture. Most textbooks on software engineering dictate that you should not commence design until all the requirements are agreed to. This is poor advice because (a) you will *never* know all your requirements, anyway, and (b) starting the design early is likely to uncover new requirements.

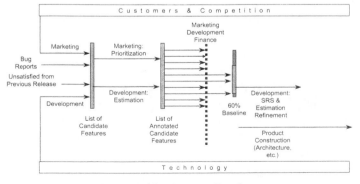

Figure 1-23: Starting Development.

Designers should be allowed to see not only the agreed-to requirements but also the entire set of candidate requirements, including their relative priorities. This way, the designers can build-in appropriate hooks, early.[6]

Obviously, at some point before you complete product development, you will need to agree on the full set of requirements to be satisfied. Thus, there is a need for another triage meeting, as shown in Figure 1-24. Ideally, at this step, all of the requirements previously selected for the 60-percent baseline should be included. Plus, requirements that did not make the earlier cut can be included, as well as new requirements that have appeared since the last agreement.

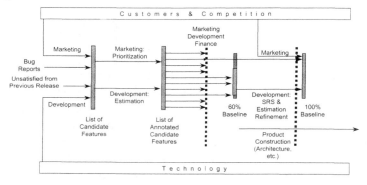

Figure 1-24: Agreeing to 100 Percent of the Requirements.

No matter how carefully these steps are managed, new requirements will still appear. This is a phenomenon called *requirements creep*. When this happens, another triage meeting must be held. This particular triage meeting is often called a change control board, or CCB. The purposes of this meeting are to adjudicate any newly suggested requirements and decide whether they are important enough to be included in the current baseline or can be delayed to later releases. This process is made much simpler by having all the current requirements carefully prioritized and estimated beforehand. As each new requirement is suggested, it is given a relative priority and an estimated effort. These new requirements are then compared with the currently accepted requirements. The subsequent triage meetings are shown in Figure 1-25.

---

[6]When a designer builds a *hook* for some feature, he or she does not expend the effort to implement the feature; instead, he or she designs the software in such a way that minimal effort will be required to later implement the feature.

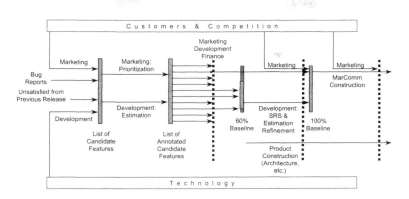

Figure 1-25: The Complete Requirements Process.

The practices of requirements management overlap with many other disciplines. For example,

- *Project management,* on system development projects, is the discipline of ensuring that a product is constructed within budget and on schedule, in a way that meets the needs of the intended customers. Most requirements management activities are performed under the direction of project managers. Often, project managers perform some of the requirements management functions themselves—most commonly, parts of elicitation and triage.
- *Product management* generally refers to complete responsibility for the life of a product, including its conception, development, deployment, implementation, and resulting financial return on investment. Product managers often play a major, if not exclusive, role during requirements triage.
- *Configuration management* is the discipline of managing all changes to a software product during its development and subsequent use. Once the requirements are agreed to, they are placed under the control of configuration management so that any subsequent changes are controlled appropriately. But the most significant overlap between configuration management and requirements management occurs when changes are proposed for inclusion in the requirements baseline. Members of the change control board are drawn from the discipline of configuration management,

representing the group responsible for deciding which proposed requirements changes are to be accepted. In the discipline of requirements management, a CCB is a particular type of triage session. The distinction, however, is not really important. What is important is to insure that the appropriate procedures are followed.

- *Systems engineering* denotes a wide variety of activities, but generally, it refers to the application of proven principles to the efficient creation of effective solutions to real problems, regardless of the material used to create the system. In practice, systems engineers are the individuals who define the overall system architecture that optimizes resource utilization and customer satisfaction. This optimization role has many similarities to requirements triage, which has the responsibility of optimizing the selection of requirements. I see systems engineers as key participants in the requirements triage process.

THE IMPORTANCE OF REQUIREMENTS MANAGEMENT

No lack of studies exist to prove that more time and attention should be devoted to requirements. Perhaps the earliest studies were performed by Barry Boehm, Ed Daly, and Michael Fagan, as reported by Boehm [BOE76]. These studies showed that when errors are found later in the life cycle, they cost significantly more to detect and repair than errors found earlier in the life cycle. Therefore, we should devote considerable effort during the requirements phase to the detection of errors, when they are much less expensive to find and fix.

Subsequent studies have been done, in an attempt to understand what percentage of all errors made in software development can be traced to problems occurring during the requirements phase. One of the earliest studies, performed in 1975 by Albert Endres [END75], discovered that 46 percent of all errors are attributable to poor understanding or communication of the problem (see Figure 1-26). Another study [SHE92] reported that 41 percent of all errors detected during the life cycle of an Air Force systems development project could be traced to requirements (see Figure 1-27). A more recent study performed by Tracy Hall, Sarah Beecham, and Austen Rainer [HAL02], which surveyed 200 people from 12 companies, reported that 48 percent of all problems experienced on software development projects were requirements-related (see Figure 1-28).

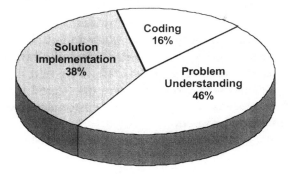

Figure 1-26: Endres's Distribution of Error Types (Based on [END75]).

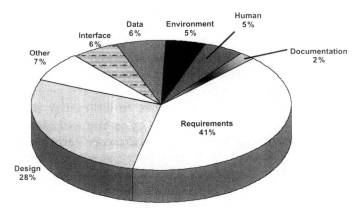

Figure 1-27: Sheldon's Distribution of Error Types (Adapted from [SHE92]).*

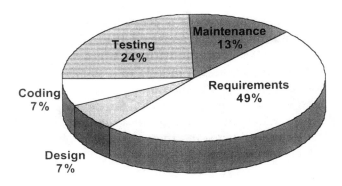

Figure 1-28: Hall's Distribution of Error Types (Based on [HAL02]).

*F. Sheldon et al., "Reliability Measurement: From Theory to Practice," *IEEE Software,* Vol. 9, No. 4 (July 1992), p. 19. © 1992 IEEE. Used by permission.

Unfortunately, it is quite difficult to say anything conclusively about the percentage of errors that are attributable to requirements. For example, imagine we have just delivered a system to a customer, and soon afterward, the customer complains, "But I thought the system was going to do such-and-such." Of course, the customer never mentioned that during elicitation. Do we declare it a requirements error? After all, if we had done a better job of elicitation, perhaps we could have uncovered it. Or, do we declare it an enhancement request? Or a customer misconception? Or a communication problem?

Three general classes of requirements errors exist:

1. *Knowledge errors:* A knowledge error occurs when a requirement is not known. It may be known by the customers but not to the development organization, or it may be unknown by all parties. If a requirement is known by the customers but the development organization fails to learn about it, it clearly was overlooked due to poor elicitation. Some requirements, however, are not known by anybody. In such cases, techniques like prototyping may be helpful because the more functionality the customer sees, the more requirements he or she will identify. Often, however, the best way to uncover requirements that nobody knows yet is to deliver the product incrementally. Each time customers receive a release, they will quickly think up dozens of functions they would also like to have. Some developers find this upsetting; they complain that the customers are never happy. I prefer to think of this as healthy. It is a fact that the number of new requirements that customers will think of is proportional to the number of requirements that are satisfied [BEL76]. This is not unlike Maslow's aforementioned hierarchy of needs [MAS70]; if you provide a bicycle to a starving child, she will not appreciate it. But as soon as you provide her with food, she will then desire a bicycle. So, developers should be pleased when new requirements emerge soon after product delivery. It means they are satisfying real needs with the current system.

2. *Triage errors:* A triage error occurs when a requirement or set of requirements is selected for inclusion in a release, but

the available resources are insufficient. After learning that a requirement needs to be satisfied, one needs to be realistic about the practicality of satisfying it, given the available time, money, and other resources. Repeated late deliveries of products is symptomatic of a process that disregards triage errors.

3. *Specification errors:* A specification error occurs when a requirement that is known and correctly selected for inclusion in a product is documented in a manner that does not ensure a common understanding by all parties. If a requirement is stated in an ambiguous fashion, for example, customers may expect a function to behave in a way that's different from what the developers implemented. Or, two developers may make different assumptions about what the ambiguous requirement means and may waste considerable resources resolving the conflict or, worse, deliver a system that behaves in an unreliable or unpredictable manner.

TWO

Requirements Elicitation

In this chapter, you will learn what requirements elicitation is, why it is so important, what its role is in the overall system development life cycle, and how you can perform it effectively without taking inordinate amounts of time.

DEFINITIONS AND TERMINOLOGY

Requirements elicitation is the art of determining the needs of stakeholders. It usually includes listening to or observing the stakeholders. The people who perform it are given a wide variety of names (systems analyst, problem analyst, interviewer, facilitator, and so on), but for the purposes of this book, they shall be referred to by their most common title, analyst. The purpose of elicitation is to determine as many requirements as possible. I say "determine," to capture the full spirit of what is happening during elicitation. For example, some requirements are discovered: The stakeholders already know the requirement, and the analyst attempts to discover it (I am not implying here that the stakeholder is somehow trying to thwart the discovery). Some requirements are created—perhaps the analyst knows something about the problem being solved or the application, and can synthesize the requirement with little stakeholder involvement. Some requirements are *extracted*, such as when the analyst is following some procedure that extracts the requirement from the stakeholder. And finally, some requirements are just *captured* as they are verbalized by the stakeholder.

Requirements elicitation is known by many other names, including systems analysis [COU73, KEN01], problem analysis [DAV93], inception [ROY98], analysis [MCL01], needs analysis [FLE02], and mission needs assessment [USA97]. Although there are likely subtle differences between the meanings of these terms, they are basically the same concepts.

Although I have defined elicitation as primarily a listening and observing activity, effective elicitation usually entails doing something to make whatever you are listening to or observing more relevant. Thus, elicitation also includes sending appropriate stimuli to the stakeholders, and establishing an appropriate environment.

The process of elicitation usually includes involvement with stakeholders. Stakeholders are people (and perhaps organizations and other systems) who will in some way be affected by the presence of a new system. As shown in Figure 2-1, the following groups are typical stakeholders:

- *Customers* are the people or organizations buying the system. Since they are paying for it, they are fairly important, and you want to keep them happy. There are often multiple levels of customers. For example, if you are defining requirements for a product to be sold in retail stores, your customers include the wholesaler or distributor, the retail channel, and the consumer. If you fail to address the requirements of any of the three customers, you are likely to produce a product that will not sell. If you are in an IT organization of a large corporation, your customers include the entire management hierarchy of the division to which your product is aimed. If you are a government contractor, your customers include the contracting officer (CO), the contracting officer's technical representative (COTR), and the agency that is providing the funds to the CO.
- *Users* are the people or organizations who are actually going to use either the system or the outputs of the system.

Since they are the people who will be using the system to solve a problem, they are also quite important. There are often multiple levels of users, including all classes of operators of the system and all individuals who receive data, information, or reports generated by the system.

```
Customers
Users
Marketing
Development
System Testers
Loser Users
Support Personnel
```

Figure 2-1: Stakeholders.

- When building commercial systems, most companies employ *marketing* personnel who are experts in trends in the market, future needs of the users and customers, feature mixes that make sense, features that are easiest to sell, and so on. This is marketing's job; people in marketing get paid to make the really tough decisions concerning product positioning. When they call the shots correctly, they advance. When they miss a market, they may get fired. Development personnel tend to mistrust them, but if the product misses the market, development rarely suffers; marketing is (rightfully) blamed. Internal IT organizations rarely have a marketing arm. More likely, they will have individuals called analysts who help to coalesce, interpret, and extrapolate the needs of the users.

- *Development* personnel are stakeholders, but as mentioned in the previous paragraph, their role as stakeholders is often subservient to that of marketing. Developers often have a technical perspective that allows them to suggest requirements that are possible with new technology, help filter out unrealistic requirements, and advocate certain requirements that will make future requirements easier to incorporate. Marketing personnel tend to mistrust development because product delivery is so consistently late and development personnel are so consistently negative when new requirements appear. Nonetheless, when a product is delivered late, development is blamed. So, one really can't fault development for trying to protect itself (and the company) from late deliveries.

- *System testers* are responsible for verifying that the system as built meets the requirements as specified. With their extensive experience in this arena, they are able to quickly assess whether specific requirements are testable. Their involvement during requirements activities increases over time, reaching its peak shortly before the requirements are finally baselined in preparation for system building. However, even at the early stages of elicitation, testers can help by alerting everybody to potentially untestable candidate requirements.

- According to Don Gause and Jerry Weinberg [GAU89], a *loser user* is an individual or organization that will lose power as a result of the introduction of a new system. For example, a loser user for an automated robot for an assembly line might be the factory worker. A loser user for a burglar alarm is the burglar. The loser user for an automated filing system is the file clerk. When eliciting with loser users, remain aware of the threat the system poses to them. The information they provide may be valuable or deliberately misleading. Of course, when talking with loser users, never remind them that they are loser users!

- *Support personnel* includes anybody who provides support to the user community—technical writers, trainers, customer support personnel, and so on. Since these people are constantly in touch with users, especially with respect to their problems, they are in a terrific position to provide the elicitation team with insight into the needs of the users.

This heterogeneous set of stakeholders highlights that determining requirements is nontrivial. *Extreme Programming*, one example of agile development, recommends that a customer be present at all times during the development process, to guide development [BEC99, COC02, HIG01]. Unfortunately, one customer cannot speak for all the diverse stakeholders.

One goal of elicitation is to improve our understanding of problems being experienced by the user community. As defined by

Don Gause and Jerry Weinberg [GAU90], a *problem* is the difference between things as perceived and things as desired. When I first saw this definition, I must admit I was shocked. I had always thought that a problem had something to do with reality. It doesn't. It is all about perceptions. For example, suppose George is a customer, and you are in the heating, ventilation, and air-conditioning (HVAC) business. You visit George in his office and he tells you that he is very warm. In other words, he is saying that the temperature he perceives is warmer than the temperature that he desires. Notice that reality (the actual temperature in the room) is irrelevant. You could tell him that you feel cool or show him a thermometer that reports the actual temperature as 60°F, but will that make him feel any less warm? The thermometer reports reality but is totally irrelevant to George's problem. In other words, what the customer perceives is the problem *is* the problem. This fact will no doubt upset the many development organizations that think they somehow understand customers' problems better than the customers!

Elicitation is not just a phase that a project goes through. Elicitation is something that can never stop occurring. After all, when can you ever afford to stop listening to the customer? It is true, however, that in a typical product development effort, elicitation activities accelerate dramatically soon after the parties realize that a demand exists for a new product or a new release of an existing product. The ovals in Figure 2-2 highlight the initial and some of the recurring elicitation activities.

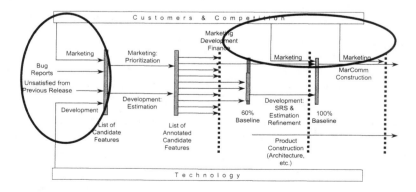

Figure 2-2: Elicitation in the Requirements Process.

WHY DO ELICITATION?

In an attempt to do *just enough* requirements management, you might be tempted to dispense with elicitation. Here are the pro's and con's:

- *Pro's of elicitation:* Not doing elicitation is like saying, "I am not going to find out from my customers what they need." But the reason we build software is to solve real problems. And we can only solve them if we understand those problems. If you do not do elicitation, requirements changes during development are likely to be more insidious and more persistent, and you run the risk of building the wrong system. A wrong system results in unhappy users and unsatisfied customers—not to mention a product that is not used by the intended users, that does not provide an adequate return on investment, and that will not sell. For me, building a wrong system is the ultimate "project failure."
- *Con's of elicitation:* It could take a long time to meet stakeholders and learn their needs. So, doing elicitation may result in a delay to the delivery. If you spend excessive effort doing elicitation, the project inception will be unduly delayed and the product will be delivered late.

The trade-off is one of risk. If you do too much elicitation, your project will be delivered late; if you do too little elicitation, your product will probably not meet customer needs. Look for the right balance on each project you work on.

ELICITATION TECHNIQUES

The trick to performing *just enough* elicitation is to select the *right* techniques and use them intelligently. The right techniques for one project may be the wrong techniques for a different project. Techniques must be selected based on the situational characteristics of each project. Unfortunately, many of the requirements methodologies prescribed today advocate using just *one* elicitation technique in all situations. The rules of good elicitation are not much different from the rules of any process that involves communication:

- *Care:* Of all the emotions, caring is the most difficult to fake. If you do not genuinely care about understanding your stakeholders' problems, find somebody else to do elicitation.

- *Show the other party how smart you think he or she is:* Many analysts spend their time trying to convince stakeholders that they, the analysts, are smart. The goal should be quite the reverse. Case in point: A customer says, "My elevators are too slow." The right response is, "I see. Can you tell me more?" or, "Can you explain how you found out they are too slow?" Note that in both cases, you are implying that you believe the customer. You should not say, "I don't think so. I think you have an elevator throughput problem, not an elevator speed problem." This is an insult to the customer.

- *Be human:* Get off your pedestal. You are just a human trying to help a fellow human. Show it. Admit your weaknesses. Become vulnerable. Show some humor. See [DAV98].

- *Listen:* You are meeting with stakeholders to learn, not to teach. You cannot learn without listening.

- *Prepare for change:* No matter how thoroughly you perform elicitation, requirements are going to change; the problem is going to change; and stakeholders' perceptions of the problem are going to change. And the more that requirements are refined or discussed, the more new requirements stakeholders are going to think of. And that's okay. Just be prepared for it. Don't ever say to the stakeholder, "Okay, so that's your final requirement, right?"

- *Maintain a glossary:* In her book *Requirements by Collaboration,* Ellen Gottesdiener describes how she has found that many disagreements among stakeholders are based on simple misunderstandings of how each party is using a word [GOT00]. Maintaining a glossary is not extremely time-consuming, but it is absolutely essential. Often overlooked, a glossary can be a simple fix to what appears to be a complex problem. Gottesdiener recommends assigning an individual as the "glossary guardian," whose job (not usually full-time) it is to keep the glossary of terms up to date and to constantly watch for individuals using new terms.

Given the above caveats, it is still useful to be aware of basic elicitation techniques and when to apply them. These techniques should be instinctive once you hear about their basics; you should not have to take a week-long course on how to perform them. Selecting the most appropriate technique for your situation, however, is less instinctive, and is a function of a wide variety of situational characteristics [HIC02]. In the following sections, I present the basics of interviewing, facilitated group meetings, computer-supported cooperative work, observation, questionnaires, prototyping, scenarios, and modeling notations.

Interviewing

Interviewing is just what you would expect it to be: asking questions and listening to the answers. The best treatises on how to interview are by Don Gause and Jerry Weinberg [GAU89, GAU90, WEI88]. Here is a summary of how to keep interviewing simple:

- *Listen:* If you are not listening, why are you bothering to interview? The stakeholder can easily tell if you are really listening. Make eye contact and don't let your eyes glaze over.
- *Take notes:* Taking notes tells the stakeholder that not only are you listening, but you consider what is being said very important. Besides, taking notes will enable you to remember what was said.
- *Piggyback:* To piggyback is to ask follow-up questions. For example, instead of just asking, "Can you describe the functions needed by users?" try "You mentioned a few minutes ago that there were three kinds of users. Can you elaborate on how their needs differ?" Not only will this give you more information, but it will also show the stakeholder that you are really listening.
- *Ask open-ended questions:* Ask questions that require thought, not just yes or no responses. You may learn more from how the stakeholder chooses to answer than from the actual answer. Once again, Gause and Weinberg describe this at length (see the discussion of context-free questions in [GAU89]).
- *Ask if you can ask more questions later:* Toward the end of the session, ask the stakeholder if you can ask him or her some

more questions over the next week or so. Here is how I do this: Before entering the stakeholder's office, I look over the list of questions I am going to ask. I don't try to memorize them, and I don't bring them to the meeting with me because I have found I do not sound natural when reading off a list. I conduct the actual interview as if it were just a conversation, asking the questions off the top of my head. At the end of the interview, I say that I will look over the information gathered and I ask if I may follow up if I have any more questions. Stakeholders almost always say yes. Then, when I get back to the office, I review my list of questions. I mark those I forgot to ask and make a note of any additional questions I may have. I then wait a week and call the stakeholder to get more information.

- *Be careful about tacit knowledge:* As Ludwig Wittgenstein said, "The problem is always at the beginning, where we think we know what we do not know" [WIT01]. Tacit knowledge is information that a person knows but cannot express. It can be as simple as, say, tying one's shoelaces—something we are all good at *doing*, but not very good at explaining orally. Or it can be something that even the stakeholders themselves don't realize that they know, such as background sounds they don't hear consciously but that trigger some specific behavior, as in the case of London stock traders who changed how they tracked market activities when trading volume increased—triggered by the rise in ambient noise [GOG94].

Interviewing is the technique of choice when the number of people who know a great deal about what you want to learn is small enough to permit meeting them within the available time. This is common sense. After all, why would you interview somebody who only has a little knowledge? And why would you try to interview more people than you have time for?

Facilitated Group Meetings

A *facilitated group meeting* is the activity of gathering many stakeholders together in one room, posing an issue to them, and having them work together to address that issue. The best treatise on how to conduct such meetings is by Ellen Gottesdiener [GOT00]. One classic type of facilitated group meeting is a brainstorming session. In such a session, participants express their views, ideas, and opinions aloud, and a means is established to record those contributions for later analysis. When brainstorming as part of requirements elicitation, these views, ideas, and opinions generally concern requirements. To keep brainstorming simple, do the following:

- *Distribute markers and sticky notes:* Provide everyone in the room with a pad of 3" by 5" sticky notes and a thick-point black marker. Instruct participants to print their ideas in large writing, horizontally. Do not use regular pens or markers with thin points. That would make it difficult for others to read later, when the notes are posted on the wall.
- *Pose the issue to be discussed:* Once the rules of brainstorming are presented to all the participants, you should pose the issue to be solved. Consider the following examples:

  - "As you know, we are the leading producer of engines for lawn mowers. We are no longer satisfied with lawn mower companies getting all the credit for having great reliability, when it is clearly our engines that make them so. Our corporate goal is to be the manufacturer of the entire lawn mower, not just the engine. Furthermore, we want to be supplying seventy-five percent of the lawn mowers sold in America within five years. What features should our lawn mower exhibit to make this dream into a reality?"
  - "As the IT division of this company, we are depended upon to supply the most accurate and reliable systems possible to the operating divisions. During the past five years, it has become clear that system x has become unreliable and greatly outdated. It now contributes to, rather than prevents, our terrible record of lost sales, lost customers, and incorrect bills. It is time to consider building from scratch the next generation of system x. What features should it exhibit?"
  - "Our competitors are winning more and more of our market share because our system y is no longer state-of-the-art. What features should we consider adding to its

current capability so that we can once again take our position as the leading supplier?"

- *Express no criticism:* Make sure that the participating stakeholders understand the importance of not criticizing ideas in any way. This makes for an environment where everybody feels willing to participate. One way to exemplify this is to say,

> "Suppose John is going to be contributing ten ideas during the brainstorming session. And suppose that the first nine turn out to be really bad ideas, but the tenth one is so insightful and so revolutionary that we all embrace it as the new direction for the company's product lines. Now, if any of us were to criticize any of his first nine ideas, we are likely to have forced John to either stop contributing altogether or spend a great deal more time thinking before saying anything else . . . and as a result we might never have the privilege of hearing his tenth idea."

- *Ask for "outrageous" answers:* I always explicitly encourage outrageous ideas because often these ideas are piggybacked upon. And a series of sequential piggybacks starting with an outrageous idea may actually lead to the best ideas of the entire session.
- *Express ideas aloud:* When participants think of an idea, they should say it aloud so all in the room can hear it.
- *Write the ideas down and post them:* After stating an idea aloud, participants should use their markers to record it on a sticky note. It is your job as the facilitator to collect the stickies on a regular basis during the session and post them on a wall where everybody can read them. Do not take on the participants' responsibility of recording their ideas. When the facilitator records the ideas, there is a reduction in the number of ideas that can be surfaced in a given amount of time and conflict can occur if you edit the comments as they are being recorded.
- *Encourage piggybacking:* Explicitly encourage participants to piggyback on ideas expressed by others. Thus, for example, a participant may say, "I think the lawn mower should put itself away in the garage." This induces another participant to add, ". . . and fold itself up in the corner."

Sometimes, the best ideas are those that are piggybacked off of an earlier idea. Some call this "hitchhiking."

- *Fill in when lulls occur:* A lull occurs when ideas stop being generated for a minute or two. When this happens, do one of four things:

    - *Reconnoiter:* Take a few minutes to summarize the progress made so far. Highlight the primary results. Describe the general categories of ideas thus far generated.[1]

    - *Contribute another (perhaps outrageous) idea:* Generally, you are busy posting ideas on the wall and are trying to be as objective as possible. However, if you happen to have an idea to contribute, by all means, state it (as if you were a participant), but don't risk doing this during non-lull times—you don't want to risk cutting off anybody else.

    - *Ask another question:* You might notice that some of the posted ideas were quite fertile, but there was never an opportunity to piggyback on them. In such cases, you might say something like, "Around ten minutes ago, somebody suggested that the lawn mower might turn itself off immediately upon sensing the proximity of a toe. That was a great safety idea. Can you think of any other safety features that would be important for us to consider?"

    - *Quit:* Eventually, the session will need to end. If you have gathered a wealth of ideas and the allotted time is close to an end, a lull is a perfect time to call an end to the session.

Many variations of facilitated group meetings have been developed over the years to optimize various aspects of the sessions and to accommodate unique situational characteristics. These include joint application development (JAD) [COH95, WOO95], requirements workshops [LEF00], group sessions, collaborative sessions, focus groups [KRU00], and computer-supported cooperative work (which is discussed in the next section), to name but a few.

Facilitated group meetings are the technique of choice when you have between, say, five and twenty-five people who each

---

[1]"Reconnoiter" was first used in this context by J.D. Berdon, Melinda Mello, and Ann Zweig.

know a little about what you want to learn. The theory is that if you gather twenty people in one room (or a virtual room, in the case of a distributed session) and each person understands only 5 percent of a situation but the group understands 30 percent as a collective (due to overlap), the group may walk out of the room after the session understanding 75 percent of the situation. This makes sense because the parties will fill holes in each other's knowledge, so the collective thinking results in a great deal of new knowledge. Meanwhile, if a few of the people you are considering inviting to a session already know 75 percent of the situation, you are better off just interviewing them. Otherwise, they are likely to dominate the session, giving others little opportunity to contribute.

Computer-Supported Cooperative Work

Computer-supported cooperative work (CSCW) is a generic term used to describe any use of computers to facilitate same-time/different-place communications among individuals in a group of people. It is also called distributed support systems (DSS) [SPR82], group decision support systems (GDSS) [HUB84], and electronic meeting systems [NUN91]. Most CSCW systems provide at least two windows on the screens of the participants: one for a scratch pad (similar to the pad of sticky notes in conventional brainstorming), and one for the posting of all the ideas entered by the stakeholders (similar to the wall covered with notes in conventional brain-storming).

There are a variety of reasons why one would want to conduct a group session using CSCW:

- *To allow for anonymity:* In some situations, participants in a session may like to contribute their ideas anonymously, perhaps out of intimidation by a peer or superior.
- *To allow for distributed participants:* In non-CSCW sessions, the parties need to be in the same location. Not so for CSCW, where the only requirement is for the parties to be able to communicate via a network.
- *To allow for non-oral communication:* Some people communicate better orally, and some communicate better through writing. Obviously, CSCW uses written communication, while face-to-face sessions generally use oral communication.

- *To facilitate electronic capture:* In same-place sessions, the ideas are captured on sticky notes or a similar medium, which have to be manually transcribed into electronic media for future reference and annotation. With CSCW, the ideas are all captured immediately, electronically.
- *To facilitate organization and voting:* Soon after ideas are gathered, they need to be organized and eventually voted upon. In traditional sessions, the notes on the wall are grouped, arranged, and rearranged. This is much easier to do when the ideas are in a spreadsheet or database. When using CSCW, the ideas are already captured electronically, and can be organized and voted upon immediately.
- *To overcome shyness:* Some individuals may be reluctant to speak aloud in a group. CSCW overcomes this by providing a written, relatively anonymous medium.
- *To look modern:* Although this really should not be a major driver, I have seen numerous companies adopt CSCW just so they can *look* like they are at the forefront of technology.

CSCW is the technique of choice when all the conditions for brainstorming are present, and (a) it is infeasible to gather the stakeholders together in one place, (b) anonymity is important, or (c) you want to eliminate the tedious step of entering ideas one at a time into a database after manually recording them.

On the other hand, CSCW does introduce some problems not present in face-to-face brainstorming. For example, studies by Mark Knapp and Judith Hall [KNA97] have shown that over half of the communication that occurs during face-to-face meetings is the result of nonverbal communication such as body language, facial expressions, and so on. By using CSCW, the bandwidth of the communication mechanism is reduced.

Observation

Observation is the passive study of stakeholders while they perform their duties. It often reveals requirements that other techniques fail to uncover. This is because other techniques rely on the verbalization of requirements, and stakeholders' knowledge of the requirements is often tacit. As I mentioned earlier, tacit knowledge is knowledge somebody possesses but is unable to express; in this case, stakeholders may not know exactly what is happening or why or how they do something.

For example, let's say an analyst wants to understand the requirements for an automated system to assist a stock trader. One way to do this is for the analyst to fully immerse him- or herself in the world of stock trades. This could be done by actually becoming a stock trader or by spending time with stock traders, carefully observing their business. Perhaps the analyst could videotape the stock traders at work and then carefully examine the resultant videos. Joseph Goguen and Marina Jirotka [GOG94] provide the best collection of essays and case studies about the use of observation and other ethnomethodological techniques for requirements capture.

Observation is the technique of choice when failing to uncover a requirement could be life-critical or when the process you want to automate or improve is currently performed by highly skilled professionals.

Questionnaires

Questionnaires are sets of questions distributed to a large group of stakeholders for completion. The answers are then tallied and conclusions are reached based on the results. Perhaps the biggest difference between questionnaires and all the other forms of elicitation is their presupposition that you can formulate relevant questions prior to collecting data from stakeholders. Although questionnaires seem straightforward, they are fraught with danger. The way the questions are worded greatly affects their outcome. The way the answer options are stated greatly affects the outcome. The sample population used greatly affects the outcome. Many books exist that discuss these issues and provide guidance on how to select questions, word the answer choices, select a suitable sample, and tally the results; for example, see *Survey Research Methods* [FOW93]. Of all the elicitation techniques described in this book, this is the most difficult to get right in a *just enough* fashion.

Questionnaires are the technique of choice when you need answers to a very specific set of questions. For example, one very effective way to use questionnaires is in facilitated group meetings or interviews, for gathering most of your requirements. You can then use questionnaires to validate whether a larger population agrees with the thoughts generated by the smaller groups involved in the sessions and interviews.

Prototyping

Prototyping is the process of presenting to the stakeholders a partial implementation of a software system, with the explicit purpose of discovering aspects of the approach that they like and dislike, as well as new requirements [DAV95a]. In a typical situation, we may have defined a list of tentative requirements. We are not too sure we have a common understanding of those requirements, so we construct a quick prototype and show it to the stakeholders. They play with it awhile and provide us with feedback, saying, perhaps, that features x, y, and z are precisely what they had in mind, but that features u, v, and w are not even close. As you can see, the prototype was able to surface the problems with u, v, and w long before an investment has been made in the quality product, thus averting customer disappointment. Furthermore, while stakeholders are playing with the features of the prototype, they may conceive additional features r, s, and t, which they would like to have in the final system. These are all recorded as candidate features.

Make sure that you construct a prototype quickly. Use whatever is available: the forms designer of your favorite database package, the library of user-interface components available with any modern object-oriented language, a user-interface building tool, and so on. The idea is to create it fast, so you can get quick feedback from customers and other stakeholders. Do not attempt to build quality into the prototype; all you will be doing is wasting time and resources.

Do not plan to adapt the prototype after receiving feedback so that it will evolve into the final system. This will give you opposing goals during construction. After all, the goals "build it quickly" and "build it to be a quality product" are just not compatible. There will always be hackers who will claim they can do it; after all, they *are* the greatest programmers in the world, with the greatest tools in the world. I can assure you, however, that speed and quality are *not* compatible.

Incidentally, there is nothing wrong with iteratively refining the prototype a few times before throwing it away. Just don't expect it to ever become the actual production system.

Scenarios, Use Cases, Stories, and Storyboarding

A *scenario* is a sample interaction between a user (or any other external system) and the proposed system. Scenarios have been in widespread use since the dawn of computers, in the 1960's. Their first documented use was by Walt Disney in the 1930's, when he was frustrated by seeing feature-length cartoons for the first time only after hundreds of hours of work by his artists. He started to demand to see the story line (his equivalent of requirements) before any cels (implementation) were drawn. He called these story lines *storyboards*. Later, in the 1970's, the terms "scenario" and "service" [TAY80] became popular, and the use of scenarios to define requirements for real-time systems came into widespread use [CAR00]. See Figure 2-3 for an example.

```
 1.  Pilot detects enemy target visually.
 2.  Pilot asks system to confirm it is an enemy.
 3.  System sends confirmation to pilot.
 4.  Pilot asks system to lock on target.
 5.  System locks on target.
 6.  System confirms "lock on."
 7.  Pilot asks system to ready missile.
 8.  System readies missile.
 9.  System confirms "ready."
10.  Pilot asks system to load target info onto missile.
11.  System loads target info onto missile.
12.  Missile ACK's to system receipt of info.
13.  System ACK's to pilot that missile is ready.
14.  Pilot asks system to launch missile.
15.  System launches missile.
16.  Missile strikes target.
```

Figure 2-3: Example of a Scenario.

By the late 1980's and early 1990's, object-oriented development (OOD) became popular. OOD lacked the idea of a "story" that had made many earlier methods useful during the requirements phase, so Ivar Jacobson [JAC92] introduced the term *use case.* The sequence diagram of a use case documents a scenario. The object-oriented community (with use cases) and the agile methods community (with *stories)* have created a resurgence in popularity of scenarios [ARM01, COC01, KUL00]. See Figure 2-4 for an example of how the scenario of Figure 2-3 can be documented using the sequence diagram of UML. The three tiers of use case specifications (environment, structure, and event), as defined by Björn Regnell, Kristopher Kimbler, and Anders Weslén [REG98], also provide sufficient details to warrant being called a scenario.

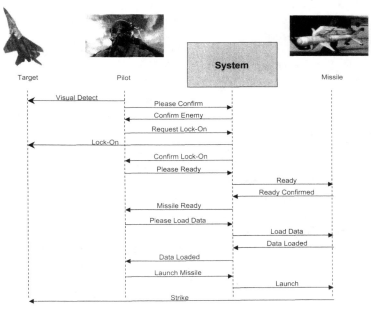

Figure 2-4: Sequence Diagram.

The previous sections on elicitation describe general *methods* of doing elicitation, while use cases, stories, scenarios, and storyboards are primarily modeling *notations.* As with any popular notation, myriad methods have been proposed that make use of the notation. The fact is that use cases or scenarios are terrific adjuncts to facilitated group meetings and interviews. For example, during a brainstorming session, the facilitator may start elicitation by posing the following question: "What are the features you would like to see this system exhibit?" For a feature-rich application, the items on the resulting list become candidates for the names of use cases, and further discussion may lead to an elaboration of the steps within each use case. Similarly, during an interview, the interviewer may ask, "Could you list the steps you follow when such-and-such occurs?" In this case, the interviewer is using scenarios as a means to understand the requirements. Note the similarity of this approach to the bottom-up approach of defining data flow diagrams in essential systems analysis [MCM84].

Scenarios or use cases are applicable to any application that is rich in interactive features. Since many systems built today have some sort of interactivity, scenarios can play some role in most system development.

Modeling Notations

As pointed out so well by Laszlo Belady and Manny Lehman [BEL76], the more that you show a customer, the more the customer will want. Thus, any notation that expresses system functionality or behavior can be used as a part of elicitation. For example, let's say a customer has just been interviewed for a half-hour, and some requirements have emerged. The interviewer could then capture what he or she learned from the customer using some notation (such as a statechart [HAR87], modechart [JAH94], data flow diagram [DEM79], context diagram [DEM79], object model, or scenario) and then show the resulting model to the customer. If the notation used was easily understood by the customer, he or she would see that the interviewer understood the needs and would also likely think of additional requirements.

Literally hundreds of notations are used, or have been used, to document requirements as they appear during elicitation [DAV93, KOW92, RAM78, WIE96]. Be careful, however; many of these "formal" notations can be instant turn-offs for stakeholders. Remember, the customers have a problem they want to solve; they do not wish to be given another problem—in this case, learning some new language—regardless of how easy *you* think it is. One trick I have used effectively for many years is to use the appropriate notation at the appropriate time, but to never use the name of the notation or act as if you are teaching the stakeholder some new notation [DAV03a]. Let's say I am interviewing the owner of a unique commercial building, where, due to the special needs of the tenants, the elevators must operate in some unique fashion. As I learn more and more about these unique needs, I draw a picture. I draw the picture while the stakeholder is talking, so I can obtain instant verification that what I understand is exactly what the stakeholder is trying to convey. Although I happen to be drawing a finite state machine, I don't use the terms normally associated with one. Instead, I speak in layman's terms so that the stakeholder will understand. Thus, I say, "So, when the elevator doors are closing and the tenant presses the down button on the outside wall, you want the elevator doors to open regardless of whether the elevator is going up or down?" I do *not* say, "So, as I see it, the elevator can be in any one of six different states. Let's call these states S1 through S6. If the elevator is in state S3 and the down button is pressed, the elevator should enter state S5."

Models are also useful in organizing the disparate information gathered during elicitation. For example, constructing an object model or a data flow diagram can aid considerably in illustrating where more information must be gathered.

THE RESULT OF ELICITATION

The result of elicitation is a list of candidate requirements, as shown in Figure 2-5. This particular figure shows the outcome of elicitation for a system that controls two traffic lights on either end of a one-lane bridge.

It is quite likely that some (or perhaps many) requirements appear in hierarchies. These hierarchies are the natural by-products of investigating the meanings of candidate requirements. They may be built top-down, bottom-up, or peer-to-peer. For a top-down example, consider this: When an interviewer or brainstorm facilitator asks the question, "What do you mean when you say the system must have a friendly user interface?" the answers offered can be documented as sub-requirements of the requirement,

The system shall exhibit a friendly user interface.

A bottom-up example might be when an interviewer or brainstorm facilitator asks the question, "What do you mean when you say the lawn mower should know where it is relative to the lawn boundaries?" and the stakeholder answers,

The lawn mower should always know where it is on the lawn.

The original requirement would then inherit the latter requirement as a parent. And finally, a peer-to-peer example. A stakeholder states,

The lawn mower should not cut off toes.

Here, the interviewer or facilitator could ask, "Can you think of any other safety requirements?" In this case, the original toe-related requirement and all of its peer requirements will be documented as parts of the safety requirements.

---

programmable for default green direction

programmable for maximum green duration

programmable for minimum green duration

programmable for duration of the amber light

safe and fair access to one-lane bridge

two sets of traffic lights

"East" traffic lights located at the east end and "West" traffic lights located at the west end

when one light is "green," other light shall be "red"

allow all cars to exit before changing light direction

vehicle sensors detect waiting vehicles

vehicle counters count vehicles

weighs bridge to find vehicles

Figure 2-5: The Result of Elicitation—a List of Candidate Requirements.

Figure 2-6 shows the same example as Figure 2-5 after the refinement of some requirements and the institution of a hierarchical structure. As you will see, I'll add more requirements, increase the detail, remove ambiguity, and add more hierarchies as this example progresses through the book, which is what happens while progressing through requirements activities in the real world.

Reqt. No.	Requirement Text
1	The system shall be programmable by the operator.
1.1	The system shall be programmable by the operator to set the default for the green direction to be "East" or "West."
1.2	The system shall be programmable by the operator to set the maximum duration for the light to remain green in the non-default direction.
1.3	The system shall be programmable by the operator to set the minimum duration for the light to remain green in the default direction.
1.4	The system shall be programmable by the operator to set the duration of the amber light prior to it changing to red.
2	The system shall provide safe access to a one-lane east-west bridge via green/amber/red traffic lights.
2.1	Two sets of traffic lights shall be controlled by the system.
2.2	When either set of lights is "green," the other set of lights shall be set to "red."
2.3	When the system determines that it is time to switch the direction of traffic, it shall do so in a safe manner.
2.3.1	When the system determines that it is time to switch the direction of traffic, it shall change the green light to amber, and then to red.
2.3.2	After the green light has been turned to red, the other direction shall remain red until the same number of vehicles have egressed as have ingressed.
6	The system shall interface to vehicle counters capable of counting vehicles as they pass through each of the two entrances.
6.1	Two counters shall be provided, one at the east and one at the west entrances/exits for the bridge.
6.2	The vehicle counters can be reset to zero by the system.
6.3	The system can inquire from a vehicle counter the number of vehicles that have passed that counter since last reset.
7	The system shall sense the weight of vehicles on the road and not allow either light to turn to green while a vehicle remains on the bridge.

Figure 2-6: The Result of Elicitation with Hierarchy and More Detail.[2]

THE SECRETS OF *JUST ENOUGH* ELICITATION

If you perform too little elicitation, you run the risk of building the wrong system. If you perform too much elicitation, you may spend so much time worrying about the problem you want to

---

[2]Notice that I have omitted requirements 3, 4, and 5 from this example. I did this because although those requirements fit more logically between requirements 2 and 6, they have not yet been discussed in the text. Obviously, in the real world, I would not know where any future requirements would fit, so I would number the current requirements 1 through 4 and would add the later requirements as 5, 6, and 7 when I discovered them.

solve that you risk not having enough time left to solve it. The secrets of performing *just enough* elicitation are as follows:

- Never lose sight of your goal: to understand enough of the problem to proceed with minimal risk of building the wrong system.
- Never think you understand the problem better than the customer. It is no coincidence that only those with limited experience think this! It is only after you have been burned enough times taking this obviously bad path that you realize just how stupid it is. The fact that more than half the systems we build fail to meet stakeholders' needs is *not* going to improve unless we try to understand their needs. If you believe that you know the requirements better than the customer, you are part of the problem, not the solution.
- Never assume that one stakeholder can speak for all stakeholders.
- Maintain a glossary of terms.
- Realize that avoiding elicitation altogether will significantly lengthen the overall development time, not reduce it.
- Prepare for change. The more the stakeholders discuss, the more they will want. Don't solve this "problem" by cutting off the stakeholder. An involved stakeholder is a happy stakeholder.
- Accept that stakeholders have the right to change their mind. You may not like this, but it is a fact. The trick is to look at every suggested change as an opportunity, not a threat. Involve the stakeholders in creating new requirements. Involve them in the decision process to include or exclude new requirements in the next release.
- Prepare for active, explicit, and overt triage.

THREE

Requirements

Triage

As you discovered in the previous chapter, poorly executed requirements elicitation can hamper development. In this chapter, you will learn more about the second major area of requirements management: requirements triage.

DEFINITIONS AND TERMINOLOGY

After eliciting and creating a list of requirements, you will likely want to establish (or learn about) the desired schedule and the available budget. No matter how ample either of these appears to be, one of them, if not both, will be insufficient to address all the requirements. To solve this problem, you will need to find some way to balance the desired requirements, your available budget, and the desired schedule. *Requirements triage* is the art of selecting the right requirements to include in the next release of your product [DAV03]. Although many people with many diverse titles are assigned the task of performing elicitation, very few ever acknowledge this responsibility.

In most organizations, triage is not performed explicitly. Instead, it is performed by some combination of intimidation, inertia, osmosis, and incompetence. Here are some typical scenarios:

- *The "You're Not a Team Player" Approach:* Development and marketing cannot agree on a set of requirements and a schedule. Specifically, marketing "demands" that all the requirements must be included by a particular date "or the product might as well not be built." Development knows that the date is totally unreasonable, given the set of requirements, and fights back. Notice that both parties are trying to represent the best interests of the company. Frustrated, marketing approaches executive management, explains how important it is to have all the requirements satisfied by the date, and then informs the boss of development's "obstructionist attitude." Development is then seen as "not a team player," and executive management demands that it conform. The manager of development agrees to the date even though he knows it is impossible to meet. The project is not delivered on schedule. Notice that the development organization is able to be late and still say, "I told you so."

- *The "You Don't Understand Technology" Approach:* Development and marketing cannot agree on a set of requirements and a schedule. Specifically, marketing "demands" that all the requirements must be included by a particular date "or the product might as well not be built." Development knows that the date is totally unreasonable, given the set of requirements, and fights back. Frustrated, development approaches executive management, explains how important it is for the company to be successful, and then informs the boss of marketing's "death wish." Marketing is seen as trying to set up the company to fail by insisting that it try to accomplish the impossible. The manager of marketing agrees to either reduce requirements or delay the product release, even though she knows that the product will no longer be competitive. When marketing fails to meet revenue goals, it has the perfect scapegoat: development.

- *The "Over-Estimate" Approach:* Development knows from past experience that it is going to be forced to accept a ridiculously tight schedule. Therefore, developers overestimate the effort needed to address each requirement. They hope that by doing so, they will have enough slack built into the schedule for them to actually succeed. This scenario may result in a successful product delivery. Unfortunately, the games being played make it impossible to ever repeat the process in a predictable manner. None of the players learn anything about why it worked or how to improve it. Executive management may walk away from the project feeling that it was successful, but for all the wrong reasons.

- *The "Over-Demand" Approach:* Marketing knows from past experience that development is going to deliver late regardless of what is needed. Therefore, it gives development an earlier deadline for product delivery, hoping that when the product is delivered, although late relative to the deadline, it will still be early enough to meet the real market window. This scenario may result in a successful product delivery. Unfortunately, the deceit involved makes it impossible to ever repeat the process in a predictable manner. No one involved learns anything about why it worked or how to improve it. But the worst part of this scenario is that development gets an undeserved "bad rap."

Synonyms for requirements triage include release planning [CAR02], requirements prioritization [WIE03], optimal attainment of requirements [FEA02], requirements negotiation [IN01], requirements selection [KAR96, RUH03], and requirements allocation.[1] I prefer the term "triage" because the analogy to triage in medicine is so fitting. As I described in [DAV03], after a medical disaster, medical personnel "systematically categorize victims into three groups: those who will die whether treated or not, those who will resume normal lives whether treated or not, and those for whom medical treatment may make a significant difference. Each group requires a different strategy. The first group receives palliative care, the second group waits for treatment, and the third requires some ranking in light of available resources. As new victims appear, personnel must repeat the categorization."* Notice how similar this is to the software world. Some requirements are no-brainers—we

---

[1] "Requirements allocation" more commonly connotes the assignment of requirements to specific software components or sub-systems rather than to specific releases.

*Alan Davis, "The Art of Requirements Triage," *IEEE Computer,* Vol. 36, No. 3 (March 2003), p. 42. © 2003 IEEE. Used by permission.

absolutely must address them or the product won't do its job. Other requirements are a different kind of no-brainer—just dreams that should remain unfulfilled until the appropriate resources are available. The third set requires ranking in light of available resources. As new requirements emerge or resources change, new rankings must be performed.

Triage is the most interdisciplinary of the three areas of requirements management. Successful triage requires close interplay between those responsible for understanding customer needs and the timing of those needs,[2] those responsible for expending resources to satisfy requirements,[3] those responsible for the allocation of money to the project,[4] and those responsible for overall project success.[5] Successful triage requires knowledge of the following:

- *The needs of the customers:* What problems does the customer have, and what is the relationship of various product requirements to the solution of those problems?
- *The relative importance of requirements to the customers:* Which requirements have the most (and least) value to the customer? If you simply ask this question directly, in most cases the answer will be, "They are all critical." Later in this chapter, I discuss better ways to determine relative importance.
- *Timing:* What is the market window? By when does the customer need each requirement addressed? If you simply ask this question directly, in most cases the answer will be, "I need them all today."[6] Later in this chapter, I discuss better ways to determine relative timing.

---

[2]In an organization planning to sell the product being specified to a commercial market, these individuals are typically called *marketing personnel.* In an organization planning to build a product for internal use, they are typically called *analysts.* In an organization planning to build a custom product for an individual customer, they are typically the *customers* themselves.

[3]When building software for internal business use, these individuals are typically called the *IT department.* Otherwise, they are called the *R&D organization,* the *software development organization,* or *software engineering.*

[4]These are the individuals responsible for funding the software development organization, and will vary based on whether the funding is allocated via corporate line management, by the customer directly, or by a project organization.

[5]Typically called a *product manager, project manager,* or *program manager.*

[6]Or worse, "yesterday."

- *Relationships among requirements:* Which requirements make sense only when other requirements are already present? For example, it makes little sense to include a requirement to bill for a particular service if the service itself is not being provided by another requirement. Are some requirements easier to implement after other requirements have already been implemented? Which ones? Which requirements are no longer needed when other requirements are met? Which requirements are incompatible with which other requirements?
- *Sensible subsetting* [PAR76]: Which sets of requirements make business sense only when all members are present?
- *Cost to satisfy each requirement:* How many resources (measured in terms of currency, effort, or elapsed time) will need to be expended in order to satisfy each requirement?

Triage should be performed for every planned release of a product, as indicated by the left-most oval in Figure 3-1. It is during this time that most requirements are assigned critical attributes and major decisions are made concerning which requirements will be addressed in the next release. As shown by the center and right-most ovals in Figure 3-1, triage activities are repeated each time new requirements arise or new resources become available.

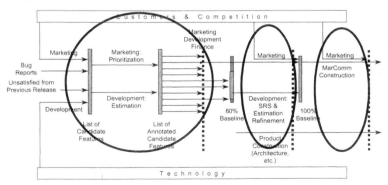

Figure 3-1: Triage in the Requirements Process.

Why Do Triage?

In an attempt to do *just enough* requirements management, you may be tempted to dispense with triage. After all, most organizations don't do it, anyway. And it is difficult to do. Furthermore, in most companies, development, finance, and marketing rarely get along with each other. So why bother? The answer lies in the fact that most systems built today do not meet customer expectations. Perhaps the lack of triage is the very reason for this. Not doing triage guarantees that your organization is taking huge risks: the risk of satisfying the wrong requirements, the risk of promising to meet a schedule only to miss it significantly, the risk of agreeing to satisfy requirements for a given budget only to exceed it significantly, and so on.

Performing triage is the most effective way to achieve *just enough* requirements management. It is triage that enables the rest of system development to proceed on schedule while still providing a quality product. Not performing triage is not an option. If you do not do it explicitly, it will occur implicitly. And if performed implicitly, you are leaving the success of your project to pure chance.

BASIC TRIAGE TECHNIQUES

This section of the book differentiates between *basic* and *advanced* triage. Basic triage is the art of achieving a balance between requirements, development cost, development schedule, and risk. It is the minimal amount of triage that should be performed when trying to accomplish software development in a *just enough* manner. Basic triage can be thought of as performing a balancing act upon a three-person seesaw, as shown in Figure 3-2. If the requirements are too "heavy" for the seesaw, then the schedule and cost arms rise, indicating excessive risk of failing to meet schedule and cost. If the desired schedule or cost is too "light" for the seesaw, then the requirements arm falls, indicating excessive risk of failing to meet all the requirements.

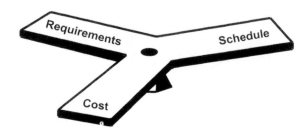

Figure 3-2: Basic Triage Represented as a Three-Person Seesaw.

Performance of basic triage necessitates that you know something about the requirements being considered for inclusion. At a minimum, this knowledge should include the relative importance of the requirements (from the customer perspective) and the cost of satisfying each requirement. There are many other attributes, but these are the two that you cannot afford to omit.

Prioritizing Candidate Requirements by Importance and Cost

Numerous techniques exist to determine the relative importance of requirements. Ironically, one technique that does *not* work is to simply ask individual customers to prioritize the requirements. If you do this, most customers will tell you that all the requirements are of equal importance and they are all critical. Instead, gather stakeholders together in a room, show them the list of candidate requirements, and ask them to apply the hundred-dollar test, the yes-no vote, or the five-way priority scheme.

To apply the hundred-dollar test [LEF00], explain to the stakeholders that they each have one hundred (imaginary) dollars that they must distribute among the candidate requirements—in this case, let's say we have 100—in such a way that if requirement i is x times more important than requirement j, then they should give it x times more money. Also, explain to them that it would be pointless to give $1.00 to each requirement because when we sum all the votes, their vote would have no effect on the outcome, so this is equivalent to not voting at all. If the group is small enough, simply point to each candidate requirement, conduct a short discussion to make sure that everybody understands the requirement sufficiently, and then go around the room asking each stakeholder for his or her points. Add as you go, and write the sum of the votes next to the requirement. Repeat this for every candidate requirement. Sort the requirements from most to least points, and—voilà!—you have your prioritization.

If the group is too large to count the votes in real time, you may do the counting one of two ways. First, if the candidate requirements are already in an electronic medium, have all the stakeholders record their votes using a computer. If the candidate requirements are written down (on cards, as a result of brainstorming, for example), simply give the stakeholders a marker and ask them to record their votes on the cards. The biggest advantage of the hundred-dollar test is that stakeholders can vote how they really believe, so if they believe one requirement is ten times more important than another, they can give it ten times more votes.

The biggest disadvantage is that the hundred-dollar test can easily be "gamed." Let me tell you about a situation that occurred a few years ago, an excellent example of gaming: We had gathered seven or eight stakeholders together in a room to discuss the next release's features. We started with a two-hour discussion of all the requirements. During this time, one stakeholder expressed his view that only four of the requirements were of high importance to him. It also became evident that everybody else in the room shared his assessment of three of the four, but only he cared about the fourth one. When it came to a vote, he realized he would be wasting his vote on the first three, since the other stakeholders would vote for them. So, he put all one hundred dollars on the fourth requirement. After tallying the votes, we discovered that the fourth requirement received the highest number of total votes, even though only one stakeholder cared about it.

Collusion is another game that stakeholders sometimes play. This also happened to me a few years ago: I had gathered together six stakeholders for a hundred-dollar test. I had warned them up-front of the futility of giving every requirement the same number of points. I pointed to the first requirement and added up the votes: $6.00. I pointed to the second requirement and added up the points: $6.00 again. After this happened eight more times, I realized that they must have colluded before entering the room. I could imagine them saying, "Davis is going to try to get us to agree that some of the requirements are less important than others! We all know that they are all of equal importance, so let's not let him get away with it." When this became evident to me, I suggested a short recess. During the recess, I cornered one of the developers and asked him to join us for the rest of the voting. Upon reconvening, I announced, "I have asked Quinn to join us for the remainder of the voting. As you all know, I strongly believe that developers' opinions on the importance of requirements are not as important as customers' opinions. For that reason, I am giving Quinn just $1.00 to distribute in one-cent increments among the one hundred candidate requirements. Nobody should feel intimidated by Quinn's presence. After all, no matter how he chooses to vote, any one of you can easily out-vote him with just one of your hundred dollars." And so we continued the voting process. The first requirement Quinn voted on earned $6.10, the next earned $6.01, and so on. Within a few minutes, it became clear to the stakeholders that if they continued with their collusion game, Quinn would be making all the prioritization decisions. Finally, one of the original stakeholders asked if we could start over again. During this second run, the stakeholders voted more accurately. Some would say I tricked the stakeholders into voting in a differentiated manner, but Quinn's presence would not have had any effect on their votes if their votes actually reflected how they felt about the relative priorities of the requirements.

To address the inherent weaknesses of the hundred-dollar test, some organizations use a much simpler voting system: the yes-no vote. In this system, simply point to each requirement and ask stakeholders to indicate their interest-level in the requirement by raising their hands. There is no reason to establish limits on the hand-raises. If stakeholders choose to raise their hands to all or none of the requirements, they should feel free to do so. No matter how many people are in the room, it is pretty easy to tally the number of raised hands. Record these numbers next to the requirements and sort them from highest to lowest to find the relative prioritization of your candidate requirements. The yes-no vote is very easy to administer, but has two major problems:

- What does it mean for a stakeholder to not raise a hand for a requirement? Does it mean that he or she does not care if the requirement is satisfied in this release? Or does it mean that he or she believes that including the requirement in the current release would actually detract from its usefulness?
- How should a stakeholder vote if he or she really believes that one requirement is twice as important as another requirement, but that both should be included in the next release?

To overcome the weaknesses of the yes-no vote while maintaining simplicity, try using the five-way priority scheme, which is the system I use most. Conduct the voting the same way that the yes-no vote demands, but give the stakeholders five options. They can vote +1 if they are for the requirement's inclusion in the next release, 0 if they don't care, and -1 if they are against its inclusion.

They can also vote +2 if they feel the requirement is extraordinarily important, and -2 if they feel its inclusion is extraordinarily destructive to the release. To make the tallying process easy, ask the stakeholders to vote with their fingers, as shown in Figure 3-3. When I am facilitating a triage session with ten or fewer stakeholders, I usually record all their votes rather than just the sum, as shown in Figure 3-4. My reason for doing this is simple: Let us say that two requirements each score 0 points, but one is the result of every stakeholder voting 0 and the other is the result of five stakeholders voting +2 and five stakeholders voting -2. In the former case, the requirement should be excluded from the baseline. But the votes for the latter requirement indicate that we may need to consider two versions of the product.

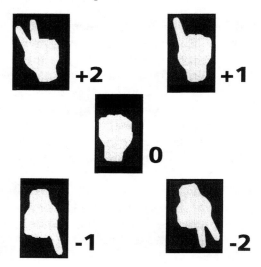

Figure 3-3: Five-Way Priority Scheme.

The above prioritization schemes work as stated when the stakeholders are all equally important. If some stakeholders are more important than others, you may want to modify the data collection method somewhat. First of all, if the politics of the situation are such that all parties understand which stakeholders are most important, then simply weight those individuals' votes accordingly. For example, if everybody knows that stakeholder x is twice as important as anybody else, just count his or her votes twice. If the politics dictate that the relative importance of stakeholders remain clandestine, then it is best to collect all the votes electronically (or secretly) and do the tallying remotely.

Reqt. No.	Requirement Text	Priority by Stakeholder									
		A	B	C	D	E	F	G	H	I	J
1	The system shall be programmable by the operator.	+2	+2	0	-1	+2	+1	+2	+2	0	0
1.1	The system shall be programmable by the operator to set the default for the green direction to be "East" or "West."	+2	+2	0	0	+1	+1	+2	0	0	0
1.2	The system shall be programmable by the operator to set the maximum duration for the light to remain green in the non-default direction.	+2	+2	0	0	+2	+2	+2	+2	0	0
1.3	The system shall be programmable by the operator to set the minimum duration for the light to remain green in the default direction.	+2	+2	0	0	+2	+2	+2	+2	0	0
1.4	The system shall be programmable by the operator to set the duration of the amber light prior to it changing to red.	+2	+2	0	-2	+2	+1	+2	0	0	0
2	The system shall provide safe access to a one-lane east-west bridge via green/amber/red traffic lights.	+2	+2	+2	+2	+2	+2	+2	+2	+2	+2
2.1	Two sets of traffic lights shall be controlled by the system.	+1	+1	0	+2	+2	0	+2	+1	0	+2
2.2	When either set of lights is "green," the other set of lights shall be set to "red."	+2	+2	+2	+2	+2	+2	+2	+2	+2	+2
2.3	When the system determines that it is time to switch the direction of traffic, it shall do so in a safe manner.	+2	+2	+2	+2	+2	+2	+2	+2	+2	+2
3	The system shall control eastbound traffic coming from northwest and southwest converging roads.	+2	+2	+2	-2	-2	-2	+2	+2	+2	+2
4	The system shall control westbound traffic coming from northeast and southeast converging roads.	+2	+2	+2	-2	-2	-2	+2	+2	+2	+2
5	The system shall interface to vehicle sensors capable of determining if there is a vehicle waiting at either of the two entrances.	+2	+2	+2	+1	+1	-1	+1	+1	+1	0
6	The system shall interface to vehicle counters capable of counting vehicles as they pass through each of the two entrances.	+2	+1	+1	+2	+2	+2	+2	+2	0	+1
7	The system shall sense the weight of vehicles on the road and not allow either light to turn to green while a vehicle remains on the bridge.	-2	0	-1	+2	-1	+1	+2	+2	-1	+1

Figure 3-4: A List of Prioritized Candidate Requirements.[7]

---

[7]Sometimes, prioritization is only applied down to a certain level of refinement; in this case, it's to the second level only. That is why I have omitted requirements 2.3.1 and 2.3.2 from this figure.

During the triage discussion, one stakeholder decided that he needed a more complex system: one that controlled four roads (as opposed to two) converging on the one-lane bridge. I have therefore added new requirements 3 and 4. Note that the votes indicate quite a bit of controversy surrounding these new requirements.

Another stakeholder, during the triage session, realized that we had inadvertently omitted an important requirement—interfacing to sensors that detect arriving traffic. This is why requirement 5 was added. Look at the votes for this one. Here, one stakeholder voted "-1" because she felt it was "obvious."

If you are looking for a technique that incorporates multiple stake-holders, each with differing levels of importance, and a way of propagating such data to the decision process, take a look at quality function deployment (QFD) [MIZ94]. In QFD, a table is created with each stakeholder name and its relative importance atop each column, and each individual requirement labeling the rows. In each column, record that stakeholder's votes for the requirements. After completing the data entry, do a weighted sum of the rows,[8] and record that sum in a new column to the right. This becomes your relative priority of requirements.

Estimating Effort for Candidate Requirements

There are many books that can assist organizations in determining the quantity of resources required to build software to solve a problem (for example, see [BOE00, JON98]). When distilled, though, all of them will tell you basically the same thing:

- Estimate the size of the problem that needs to be solved or the solution that needs to be built.[9]
- Tweak the size based on some attributes of the problem to be solved, the people working on the project, or the type of solution.
- Use historic data to see how many resources were required in the past to tackle such an endeavor.

The effort estimation should be done on a per-requirement basis. In other words, you should estimate the effort required to satisfy each requirement. The units of effort can be anything you like: feature points, function points, lines of code, person-years, person-months, person-weeks, person-hours, dollars, and so on. Figure 3-5 shows the example of Figure 3-4 with the individual stakeholder priorities summed and with the estimate efforts, in person-hours.

---

[8]If the table entry at the intersection of row (requirement) i and column (stakeholder) j is termed v_{ij}, and the relative importance of stakeholder j is r_j, then the relative priority p_i of each requirement i is the weighted sum, that is,

$$p_i = \frac{\Sigma\ (r_j \times v_{ij})}{j}$$

[9]Although arguments exist for just about any method of measuring the size of the endeavor, I will not cover them—the methods or the arguments—here.

Reqt. No.	Requirement Text	Priority	Person-Hours
1	The system shall be programmable by the operator.	10	120
1.1	The system shall be programmable by the operator to set the default for the green direction to be "East" or "West."	8	20
1.2	The system shall be programmable by the operator to set the maximum duration for the light to remain green in the non-default direction.	12	20
1.3	The system shall be programmable by the operator to set the minimum duration for the light to remain green in the default direction.	12	20
1.4	The system shall be programmable by the operator to set the duration of the amber light prior to it changing to red.	7	15
2	The system shall provide safe access to a one-lane east-west bridge via green/amber/red traffic lights.	20	200
2.1	Two sets of traffic lights shall be controlled by the system.	11	incl
2.2	When either set of lights is "green," the other set of lights shall be set to "red."	20	incl
2.3	When the system determines that it is time to switch the direction of traffic, it shall do so in a safe manner.	20	incl
3	The system shall control eastbound traffic coming from northwest and southwest converging roads.	8	150
4	The system shall control westbound traffic coming from northeast and southeast converging roads.	8	150
5	The system shall interface to vehicle sensors capable of determining if there is a vehicle waiting at either of the two entrances.	12	40
6	The system shall interface to vehicle counters capable of counting vehicles as they pass through each of the two entrances.	15	120
7	The system shall sense the weight of vehicles on the road and not allow either light to turn to green while a vehicle remains on the bridge.	3	200

Figure 3-5: A List of Candidate Requirements with Effort Estimates.[10]

Disagreements Concerning Relative Priority of Requirements

Let's say that two members of the marketing team have seriously differing opinions about the relative priority of the following requirement:

A. The system shall provide service x to the customers.

---

[10]As indicated by "incl" in the Person-Hours column, it is sometimes impossible to divide the effort of a requirement into its sub-requirements. If this is so, don't worry about it; just record that you have made that decision.

There could be a variety of reasons for this disagreement. One possibility is that the two marketing people represent two disparate groups of customers with different needs, based on the jobs that they do. In that case, the best route is to record multiple attributes for each requirement, one for each of the priorities, for each of the groups, as shown in Figure 3-4. Averaging or combining the priorities is unlikely to be of much value. For example, if a requirement is essential to meet the needs of one class of customer but unimportant to another, nothing worthwhile results from recording an average priority of "important." The fact is that if the requirement is met, the first group of customers will have its needs met. And if the requirement is not met, that group's needs will not be met. The satisfaction of the second group of customers is completely unrelated to this requirement.

Another possible basis of the disagreement is that the two marketing people have different interpretations of the candidate requirement. In this case, the correct route is to refine the requirement. By refining it, you will improve your understanding of the requirement and discover the basis of the disagreement. So, in the above example, we could refine the requirement into, say, three sub-requirements:

A1. The system shall provide service $x1$ to the customers.

A2. The system shall provide service $x2$ to the customers.

A3. The system shall provide service $x3$ to the customers.

This is what was done to create some of the hierarchies of requirements shown in Figure 3-4.

Once this is done, it often becomes clear that the person who rated requirement A highly did so because service $x3$ is of critical importance (and perhaps $x1$ and $x2$ were actually of little value). And the person who gave a low rating to requirement A did so because he or she thought that x referred only to $x2$, rather than $x1$, $x2$, and $x3$. With the refined requirements, however, the parties realize that they actually agreed with the priorities—requirement *A1* is low-priority, requirement *A2* is low-priority, and requirement *A3* is high-priority. But, equally important is the side effect this refinement has of reducing the ambiguity of requirement A.

Disagreements Concerning Effort to Satisfy a Requirement

Let's say that two members of the development organization have seriously differing opinions about the effort required to address the aforementioned requirement A.

There could be a variety of reasons for the disagreement. One possibility is that the two developers have different assumptions concerning the development resources that are to be applied. For example, Sally may be assuming that she will be assigned to the development effort, and she knows she is highly skilled in this type of work. Knowing this, she has provided a relatively low estimate of effort. Meanwhile, John may be assuming that he will be assigned the development effort, but really does not like doing this type of work. Feeling this way, he has provided a relatively high estimate of effort. These are but two of the many games developers play when making estimates.[11] If such is the case, the best route is to find out from Sally and John "where their heads are at." That is, try to ascertain what games they are playing, so you can make the right decisions. Then select either Sally's or John's estimate, and be sure to record the assumptions that you are making. Whatever you do, do *not* average the two estimates.

An equally likely reason for the disagreement is that the two developers have different interpretations of the candidate requirement. In this case, you should take the same action as in the case of a disagreement among marketing personnel—refine the requirement:

A1. The system shall provide service x1 to the customers.

A2. The system shall provide service x2 to the customers.

A3. The system shall provide service x3 to the customers.

Once this is done (as we did above, to clarify relative priority), it often becomes clear that the person who estimated that it would require a lot of effort to satisfy requirement A did so because service $x3$ is very difficult to provide (and perhaps $x1$ and $x2$ are easy to provide). And the person who estimated that it would require little effort to satisfy requirement A did so because he or she thought that x meant $x2$ only, rather than $x1$, $x2$, and $x3$. After

---

[11]For a more complete description of these games, read [DAV04].

refinement, however, the parties realize that they actually agree with the estimates. Equally important is that the ambiguity of requirement *A* has been reduced.

Establishing Requirements Relationships

The preceding subsections assumed that requirements are independent. In reality, this is rarely the case. The following sections describe just some of the relationships that may exist between requirements.

Necessity Dependency

In this relationship, it makes sense to satisfy requirement *A* only if we are also satisfying requirement *B*. For example, consider this dependency:

> *Requirement A: The stop button shall be red.*

> *Requirement B: The system shall provide a stop button.*

Sometimes, such a dependency is bidirectional, as in this case:

> *Requirement A: The system shall provide the Fiends and Famine capability for our customers.*

> *Requirement B: The system shall bill customers $3 per minute when they use the Fiends and Famine feature.*

If such dependencies exist between requirements, you should record the relationships, as shown in Figure 3-6 and Figure 3-7. The record of this relationship will be used during requirements triage. As we try to select an optimal subset of the requirements to implement, we will want to avoid subsets that include a requirement without including all requirements on which it depends. Pär Carlshamre *et al.* [CAR01] differentiate between two types of necessity dependence: AND (which indicates bidirectional necessity dependence between two requirements) and REQUIRES (which indicates a unidirectional necessity relationship between one requirement and another).

ID	Requirement Text	Necessity Dependency
A	The stop button shall be red.	
B	The system shall provide a stop button.	

Figure 3-6: Unidirectional Necessity Dependency.

ID	Requirement Text	Necessity Dependency
A	The system shall provide the Fiends and Famine capability for our customers.	
B	The system shall bill customers $3 per minute when they use the Fiends and Famine feature.	

Figure 3-7: Bidirectional Necessity Dependency.

Effort Dependency

In this relationship, requirement A will be easier to satisfy if we are also satisfying requirement B. For example, such a dependency may exist between the following:

Requirement A: The system shall provide reports of accounts receivable older than 60 days.

Requirement B: The system shall provide a general-purpose report-generation utility.

If such a dependency exists between requirements, you should record that relationship, as shown in Figure 3-8. Unlike necessity dependency, effort dependency is not used to select compatible requirements. Instead, it is used to determine the actual implementation cost for selected subsets. So, in the case of Figure 3-8, the cost of satisfying requirement A is four person-months and the cost of satisfying requirement B is five person-months, but the cost of satisfying both requirements A and B is seven person-months, because satisfying requirement B reduces the effort required to satisfy requirement A by two person-months.

ID	Requirement Text	Effort Estimate	Effort Dependency
A	The system shall provide reports of accounts receivable older than 60 days.	4	-2
B	The system shall provide a general-purpose report-generation utility.	5	

Figure 3-8: Effort Dependency.

Pär Carlshamre *et al.* [CAR01] separate this relationship into two subtly different characteristics: TEMPORAL dependencies, to capture the fact that one requirement should be implemented before another, and ICOST dependencies, to capture the incremental cost reduction gained by implementing one requirement before another.

Subset Dependency

If requirement A is satisfied, then requirement B will be satisfied. That is, requirement B is part of requirement A.

If such a dependency exists between requirements, you should record that relationship. Notice from the list of requirements shown in Figure 3-9 that we have refined the parent requirement into three child requirements. In this case, the three children do not represent the entirety of the parent's functionality. The intent is for them to exemplify or capture the *spirit* of the parent. Notice in this case that developers must satisfy the full essence of the parent requirement—in doing so, they'll satisfy the three children requirements, but that is not sufficient. Note also that during the actual triage process, when selecting an optimal subset of the requirements to satisfy, you may select all, some, or none of the children. And if you select all the children, then you may also select the parent if you wish. However, if you select the parent, you *must* select all its children. You will notice that there is no need to define effort dependencies between parent and children requirements. If we select A for satisfaction, we will automatically select B, C, and D, and the total effort will be 27 person-months. If we select only a subset of B, C, and D, then the effort will be only the sum of the efforts of the selected requirements.

ID	Requirement Text	Effort Estimate	Subset Dependency
A	The system shall enable the user to specify the order of the displayed list in a wide variety of ways.	5	
B	The system shall enable the user to specify that the list be displayed in alphabetic order.	7	
C	The system shall enable the user to specify that the list be displayed in chronological age order.	2	
D	The system shall enable the user to specify that the list be displayed in employment seniority order.	13	

Figure 3-9: Subset Dependency.

An alternate way to represent subset dependency is by numbering the requirements accordingly, so that if a parent is numbered 3, then its children are numbered 3.1, 3.2, 3.3, and so on. This is precisely what is being represented in Figure 3-4. That figure has also indented the requirements texts for children so they can be even more easily identified. In such cases, there is no need to use a separate column to show the dependency. Juha Kuusela and Juha Savolainen [KUU00] call this an AND dependency because child requirements 3.1 *and* 3.2 *and* 3.3 represent the parent requirement 3.

Cover Dependency

This is a special case of subset dependency in which the union of the children's functionality *is* the parent's functionality. If requirements *B*, *C*, and *D* are satisfied, then requirement *A* will be satisfied; and if requirement *A* is satisfied, then requirements *B*, *C*, and *D* will be satisfied. That is, requirements *B*, *C*, and *D* represent a refinement of requirement *A*.

If such a dependency exists between requirements, you should record that relationship. You will notice from the list of requirements shown in Figure 3-10 that we have refined the parent requirement *A* into three child requirements—*B*, *C*, and *D*—and we *do* wish to imply that the sum of the three children completely captures the parent. Note that during the actual triage process, when selecting an optimal subset of the requirements to satisfy, you may select all, some, or none of the children. And if you select all the children, then you have indeed selected the parent by inference. If you select the parent, you have selected all children requirements by inference. Notice that once again there is no need to include effort dependency.

ID	Requirement Text	Effort Estimate	Cover Dependency
A	The system shall enable the user to specify the order of the displayed list in three ways.	5	
B	The system shall enable the user to specify that the list be displayed in alphabetic order.	7	
C	The system shall enable the user to specify that the list be displayed in chronological age order.	2	
D	The system shall enable the user to specify that the list be displayed in employment seniority order.	13	

Figure 3-10: Cover Dependency.

Value Dependency

If satisfying one requirement lowers (or raises) the need for another requirement, then a value dependency exists between them [CAR01].

If such a dependency exists between requirements, you should record that relationship as you would other types of dependencies. When a value dependency exists, triage will become a bit more complex: The relative priority of requirement *B* will change as a result of including requirement *A* in the next release. If the dependency has not been recorded, the triage participants are likely to include requirement *B* even though it is no longer that important.

Pär Carlshamre *et al.* [CAR01] also describe a requirements relationship they call an OR dependency. When two requirements possess an OR relationship, then one of the requirements should be satisfied, but not both. I believe that this is just a special case of a bidirectional value dependency. In particular, if requirement *A* is selected for inclusion, the priority of requirement *B* becomes negative, and if requirement *B* is selected for inclusion, then the priority of requirement *A* becomes negative.

Documenting the Dependencies

In all of the above cases, I have shown the relationships as arrows in the figures. There are a variety of ways of maintaining these relationships on an actual project:

- *Manual:* If you want requirement 1 to refer to requirement 2, simply type "requirement 2" in the appropriate attribute field of requirement 1. This requires almost no effort at all to do initially, but maintenance is extremely painful [ANT01, DÖM98, RAM98]. Every time a requirement changes, you must manually check to see if other requirements are impacted.
- *Hyperlink:* Much better than manual maintenance, this requires you to enter a hyperlink [HAY96] called "requirement 2" in the appropriate attribute field of requirement 1. The biggest advantage of this is you can quickly move from one requirement to all the related requirements. This makes maintenance somewhat easier.

- *Requirements Tools:* Ideally, when you change requirement 1, you want to immediately see a list of all requirements related to it on a first- and second-order basis (what relates to requirement 1 and what relates to what relates to requirement 1, respectively), and so on. The easiest way to do this is to use a requirements management tool,[12] which makes maintenance a lot easier. But with the benefit comes the extra overhead of having to learn how to use (and having to pay for) the tool.

Performing Triage on Multiple Releases

The essence of the triage decision is to decide whether or not each candidate requirement will be included in the next release, given the available time and resources. As described earlier, this is always the result of a cooperative process among multiple stakeholders. I highly recommend that you always plan at least two releases at a time. If you plan just one release—say, Release 3.0—every requirement necessitates a binary (yes or no) decision. There is no compromise position. If you plan two releases at a time, a compromise position is available. So, let's say one stakeholder insists a requirement be included in Release 3.0 and another stakeholder insists that it be excluded from Release 3.0. It might be possible to formulate a middle-of-the-road position by agreeing that it will be satisfied in the following release, Release 4.0. To make this even more palatable, you might consider numbering the following Release 3.1, or even 3.01 (rather than 4.0), to make it sound even more imminent and thus even more of an acceptable compromise (see Figure 3-11).

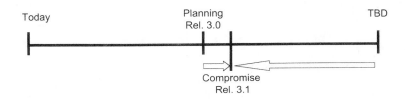

Figure 3-11: A Compromise Release.

---

[12]See www.incose.org for a list of available requirements management tools.

Making the Triage Decision

Now that you have a relative ranking of requirements as created by your stakeholders, you need to determine which ones to include, based on the available resources. Because of the complex relationships that exist among and between requirements, the decision is not as simple as just selecting the most desirable requirements for inclusion. Also, you can't just include all the requirements, as you have a limited amount of resources. Three general approaches exist for doing triage: optimistic, pessimistic, and realistic.[13] In the optimistic approach, you place the available budget and desired schedule on their respective arms of the seesaw shown earlier, in Figure 3-2, and then you place *all* the candidate requirements on the third arm. Remove requirements one at a time from the requirements arm until it balances. This is by far the most common way of performing triage, but not necessarily the most efficient. In the pessimistic approach, you place the available budget and desired schedule on their respective seesaw arms, and then you place requirements onto the requirements arm one at a time until it balances. In the realistic approach, you place the available budget and desired schedule on their respective seesaw arms, and a reasonable amount of candidate requirements on the requirements arm. Then you refine your requirements selection by adding and removing requirements.

Think of this process as manipulating a radio dial, one associated with each requirement.[14] The values for the positions of the dials include one position for each release being considered, one for "done" (already satisfied), and one for "TBD" (to be determined). Figure 3-12 shows what such a radio button would look like for considering Releases 2.0, 2.1, 2.2, and 3.0, while Figure 3-13 shows what the list of requirements from Figure 3-5 look like after they have been allocated to different releases. (Of course, if your tool doesn't support radio dials, you can replace them in Figure 3-13 with the appropriate version/release number.)

---

[13]Martin Feather and Tim Menzies [FEA02] use a tool to iterate through random choices toward an optimal solution.

[14]When the radio dial for a requirement is turned to a planned release, it is added to that release. When the radio dial is used for a requirement with a necessity, subset, or cover dependency on other requirements, those other requirements are also added. When the radio dial for a requirement is one of a set of requirements for which another requirement has a cover dependency, and all other members of the set are already included in the release, then the parent requirement is also added.

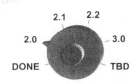

Figure 3-12: Requirement Selection Dial.

Reqt. No.	Requirement Text	Priority	Person-Hours	Release
1	The system shall be programmable by the operator.	10	120	
1.1	The system shall be programmable by the operator to set the default for the green direction to be "East" or "West."	8	20	
1.2	The system shall be programmable by the operator to set the maximum duration for the light to remain green in the non-default direction.	12	20	
1.3	The system shall be programmable by the operator to set the minimum duration for the light to remain green in the default direction.	12	20	
1.4	The system shall be programmable by the operator to set the duration of the amber light prior to it changing to red.	7	15	
2	The system shall provide safe access to a one-lane east-west bridge via green/amber/red traffic lights.	20	200	
2.1	Two sets of traffic lights shall be controlled by the system.	11	incl	
2.2	When either set of lights is "green," the other set of lights shall be set to "red."	20	incl	
2.3	When the system determines that it is time to switch the direction of traffic, it shall do so in a safe manner.	20	incl	
3	The system shall control eastbound traffic coming from northwest and southwest converging roads.	8	150	
3.1	During the period while the eastbound traffic light is authorized to be green, the system shall provide equal time for the traffic coming from the southwest and the northwest.	8	incl	

Figure 3-13: Candidate Requirements Showing Which Will Be Satisfied in Next Release.

Reqt. No.	Requirement Text	Priority	Person-Hours	Release
4	The system shall control westbound traffic coming from northeast and southeast converging roads.	8	150	2.1 2.2 / 2.0 3.0 / DONE TBD
4.1	During the period while the westbound traffic light is authorized to be green, the system shall provide equal time for the traffic coming from the southeast and the northeast.	8	incl	2.1 2.2 / 2.0 3.0 / DONE TBD
5	The system shall interface to vehicle sensors capable of determining if there is a vehicle waiting at either of the two entrances.	12	40	2.1 2.2 / 2.0 3.0 / DONE TBD
6	The system shall interface to vehicle counters capable of counting vehicles as they pass through each of the two entrances.	15	120	2.1 2.2 / 2.0 3.0 / DONE TBD
7	The system shall sense the weight of vehicles on the road and not allow either light to turn to green while a vehicle remains on the bridge.	3	200	2.1 2.2 / 2.0 3.0 / DONE TBD
8	If a vehicle is disabled on the bridge, the system shall automatically notify a tow truck.	1	Unknown	2.1 2.2 / 2.0 3.0 / DONE TBD

Figure 3-13, continued: Candidate Requirements Showing Which Will Be Satisfied in Next Release.[15]

The only way I know to determine that the seesaw is in balance is to compare the desired schedule and available budget against the original schedule (*not* actual) and original budget (*not* actual cost) of previously completed projects that required approximately the same amount of work.

Most effort estimation techniques (examples include COCOMO [BOE00], KnowledgePLAN® [JON98], and SLIM [PUT78]) generate estimates based on the *actual* schedules and budgets of previously completed projects. The problem with this is that most organizations create their systems within a unique, unchanging culture. Thus, the rate at which requirements change (usually called "requirements creep") is similar on every project; the amount of inaccuracy of development effort estimations is similar on every

---

[15]During the triage process, one stakeholder expressed confusion about the meaning of requirements 3 and 4. A discussion ensued, and the agreed-upon clarifications were added as requirements 3.1 and 4.1, respectively.

Another stakeholder, during the triage discussion, thought of a new dream requirement. It was added as requirement 8. The team voted quickly on its priority, and all agreed to postpone the decision of which release it should be included in, so its release was given the value "TBD" (to be determined).

project;[16] and the politics that force under- or over-estimation are similarly unchanged [DAV04].

Although most cost and schedule estimation textbooks and methods show the distribution of similar, previously completed projects in a probabilistic distribution, such as in Figure 3-14, I have found that a cumulative probability curve, as shown in Figure 3-15, is more useful when performing triage.

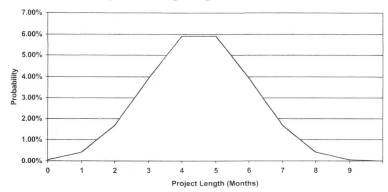

Figure 3-14: Typical Historic Project Distribution (Adapted from [DAV04]).

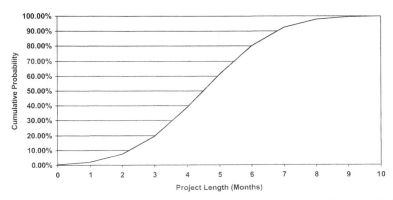

Figure 3-15: Cumulative Probability Historic Project Distribution (Adapted from [DAV04]).

---

[16]At one company I worked for, we discovered that the effort estimates given by the development team were consistently 25 percent lower than the actuals. So we decided on the next project to escalate all the development team's estimates by 25 percent as soon as we received them. Lo and behold, the actuals were *still* 25 percent too low. It seems that *this* corporate culture always induced the work to expand to fill 25 percent of whatever was originally estimated. This phenomenon may be true at all companies. The solution is to recognize that the up-front estimates will be 25 percent low—not to "fix" them!

In Figure 3-14, the y-axis shows the "likelihood of the project completing exactly as estimated," but in Figure 3-15, it expresses the "likelihood of the project completing at or better than the estimate," which is precisely what you want to know—the probability of success. Since the graph is a function of the weight or size of the currently selected candidate requirements, it suffices to superimpose a vertical bar on the graph (representing the desired budget, as shown in Figure 3-16, or the desired delivery date, as shown in Figure 3-17) to assess the current degree of balance in the seesaw. It is not difficult to create graphs like these for your own organization; see the Sidebar on the following page.

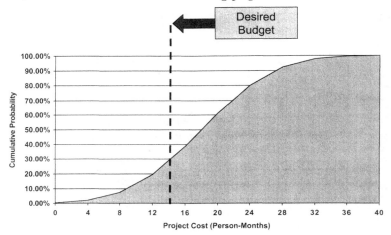

Figure 3-16: Historic Project Distribution (Cost) with Current Budget (Adapted from [DAV04]).

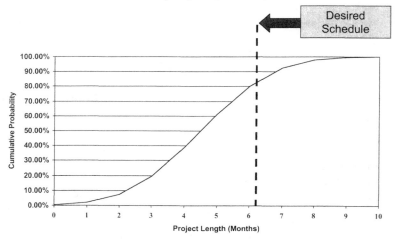

Figure 3-17: Historic Project Distribution (Schedule) with Current Desired Delivery Date (Adapted from [DAV04]).

SIDEBAR

To create a graph like Figure 3-17 for your own organization, simply examine a series of past projects and collect just two pieces of information about each: the original estimate of size (in any standard units—in this case, I've used person-months), and the actual elapsed time spent on the project. Let's say that data for twenty projects look like this:

Project Number	Range of Original Estimate of Size (person-months)	Actual Project Duration (months)	Project Number	Range of Original Estimate of Size (person-months)	Actual Project Duration (months)
1	10-19	2	11	30-39	4
2	10-19	2	12	60-69	9
3	1-9	2	13	40-49	7
4	40-49	6	14	20-29	6
5	30-39	3	15	1-9	1
6	80-89	8	16	40-49	6
7	20-29	4	17	110-119	8
8	20-29	5	18	10-19	5
9	1-9	3	19	30-39	5
10	40-49	6	20	20-29	4

Now, let's say that you have a new product and you are considering the inclusion of requirements estimated to be 27 person-months in the next baseline. You can see from the above table that in the past, when you have tackled projects in the range of 20 to 29 person-months, you have never succeeded in completing them in less than four months; you completed them in four months 50 percent of the time; you managed to complete them in five or fewer months 75 percent of the time; and you succeeded in completing them in six or fewer months 100 percent of the time. So, your graph looks like this (just smooth out the lines and you're all set):

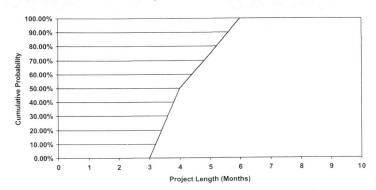

Is this extremely accurate? No, but it is good enough for making the triage decision.

Whether or not the seesaw is balanced has a lot to do with the degree of risk the organization can tolerate. For example, the graph shown in Figure 3-16 might be acceptable to an organization that thrives on risk, but the same graph might be totally unacceptable to a development organization that was recently burned severely and is looking to take a more conservative approach to product development until it regains its credibility.

Triage can be performed in a relatively orderly manner, as shown in Figure 3-18. Start with your optimistic, pessimistic, or realistic subset of candidate requirements and follow these guidelines:

1. Select the higher-priority requirements before the lower-priority ones.
2. If you include a requirement that has a necessity dependency upon another requirement, include that requirement as well.
3. Stay cognizant of which groups of requirements make sense as a commercially viable and useful product.
4. Initially, exclude any requirement that raises considerable controversy (the subsequent iterative refinement process will resolve this).

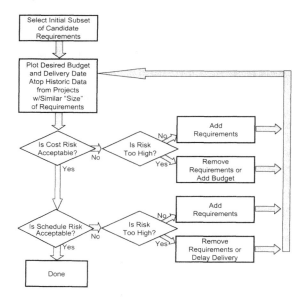

Figure 3-18: A Basic Requirements Triage Process.

Next, add up the "effort estimations" for all the selected require-ments,[17] and then plot graphs (like those in Figure 3-16 and Figure 3-17) showing how previously completed projects have fared when attempting the same amount of requirements. Then, atop these two graphs, draw vertical bars representing your desired budget and schedule.

Next, examine the cost-risk graph. If the graph looks like Figure 3-16, your project has a 30-percent likelihood of completing these requirements with the desired budget. Is this an acceptable level of risk for your project? Most organizations will accept a like-lihood of 80 percent or more as tolerable. Anything below that number, however, and you must decide on your level of risk adver-sity and, more importantly, the effect that exceeding the budget will have on the organization:

- Will additional funds be available?
- Will the project be cancelled?
- What will happen to the careers of the project members?
- What financial impact will this have on the company?
- If we are talking about human resources (which is likely for software development projects), will you be permitted to do additional hiring?

If the total picture is positive (or at least acceptable), then proceed to the next step. Otherwise, you have only two alternatives: Remove requirements or find additional resources. It is that simple.

When removing requirements, be sure to remain cognizant of the four considerations you used when selecting the initial set of candidate requirements (as described above). When adding resources, you need to know how many you need. To figure this out, just look at the graph in Figure 3-16; look at the horizontal distance between the current position of the vertical bar (the current budget) and the desired position of the vertical bar (the budget at which the risk is acceptable). To raise the likelihood of success in Figure 3-16 from the current 30 percent to a more accept-able 70 percent, just shift the vertical bar to the right until it inter-sects the graph at the horizontal 70-percent line. If you do that, you will have the graph shown in Figure 3-19, and you will need ten more person-months in the budget.

---

[17]Adding the estimations is not as simple as plain addition. You must consider the effects of any selected requirements with subset dependency and effort dependencies, discussed earlier.

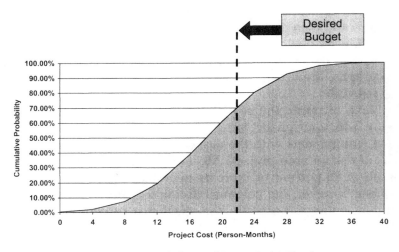

Figure 3-19: Imbalance of Figure 3-16 Fixed.

Next, examine the schedule-risk graph. If the graph looks like that in Figure 3-17, your project has an 83-percent likelihood of completing these requirements by the desired delivery date. Just as we asked of the cost-risk graph earlier, ask, Is this an acceptable level of risk for your project? Again, if the likelihood is 80 percent or more, most organizations will accept it. Below that number, you must decide on your level of risk adversity and, even more impor-tantly, the effect that delivering the project late will have on the organization:

- Will the product still be useful?
- What are the financial implications (revenues if the product is to be sold, excessive expenses if the product is designed to reduce costs, and so on)?
- Will the project be cancelled?
- What will happen to the careers of the project members?

As before, with cost risk, if the total picture for schedule risk is positive (or at least acceptable), then you are done with triage. If the total picture is negative, you have only two alternatives: Remove requirements or extend the delivery date. It is that simple.

When removing requirements, be sure to remain cognizant of the four considerations described above. When extending the date, you will need to know how far to extend it. To decide this, just look at the graph in Figure 3-17. Look at the horizontal distance between the current position of the vertical bar (the current desired delivery date) and the desired position of the vertical bar (that date where the risk is acceptable). You can see that in order to raise the likelihood of success from the current 83 percent to, say, 97 percent, you will need to extend the delivery date by around one month, as shown in Figure 3-20.

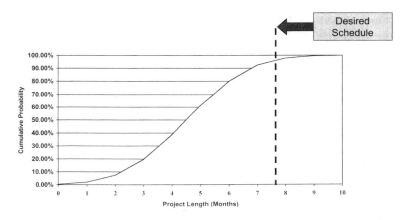

Figure 3-20: Imbalance of Figure 3-17 Fixed.

In practice, triage is rarely practiced as a sequential series of adaptations that slowly converge toward an optimal solution. Instead, progress toward an optimal solution is made in spurts.

In October 2000, I was consulting for a large manufacturer of mass storage devices. The product manager had called me in to resolve a problem the company was experiencing: Mark, the marketing manager (not his real name), was demanding that the next release of the product, Version 3.0, be delivered to the customers in nine months. Meanwhile, Dev, the software development manager (also not his real name), was insisting that such a date was impossible to achieve. They had reached an impasse when I was called in. I asked each party to describe his position. Here is what I heard:

Mark: "Look, the window of opportunity starts in nine months. We know that the competition is planning to release similar products ten to twelve months from now. Since their products and our 3.0 release are so similar, the only way we are going to be successful is if we are the first to market."

Dev: "I understand what you are saying. But I also know what is realistic. Just wishing for something is not going to make it happen. Read my lips: My team cannot produce all the features you want in Release 3.0 in nine months. It simply cannot be done."

Mark decided to try appealing to Dev's corporate allegiance: "Don't you realize that you'll be letting down the entire company if you don't build it when it's needed?"

I saw where this was headed, and it was not good.

Dev counterattacked: "Look, Mark, remember a year ago when we were planning the 2.4 release? You demanded that I deliver it in just five months. I told you then that we had two choices: Build it in five months without an architecture that could support any additional features, or build it 'right' and deliver it in eight months, in which case the architecture would be able to handle additional requirements. *You* chose the first option. So, it is *your* fault that we are in this mess now! The current architecture simply cannot support the 3.0 features. I need a full year in order to revamp the architecture and then add the new features."

Ouch! The debate continued for about an hour and they made little progress toward a mutually agreeable solution. During that time, I presented the schedule-probability graph (as shown in Figure 3-21) to the team. It was clear that Dev was not lying; the graph reported a meager 37-percent chance of success.

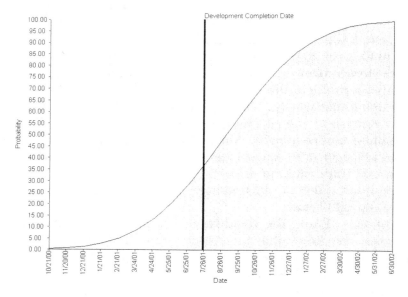

Figure 3-21: Case Study—Schedule-Probability Graph.

We took a short break, during which I took Dev aside and asked him to imagine that he owned a majority of the company's stock, and that the project's success or failure in the marketplace was key to his personal financial success. Clearly, promising to deliver something in nine months when it would actually take twelve is not productive. Nor is delivering it in a year to a stale market. I asked Dev what he would do with the project. He answered, "Interesting situation—here's what I would do. I'd increase my headcount so I could afford to staff two parallel development teams. One team would work on incorporating as many of the 3.0 features as possible into the old architecture. We could release it seven-to-eight months from now. We could call it Release 2.5. The other team would start revamping the architecture and be ready to deliver the full 3.0 capability in a year."

I told Dev I liked his suggestion and wanted him to present it to the assembled team after the break. He said, "Okay, but there's no way Mark is going to find it acceptable."

After we reconvened, Dev made his suggestion. Mark's response? "Wow! Would you really do that for me?" We had finally reached a tentative agreement in principle. We worked a few more hours to see if it was realistic. First, we checked to see if the twelve-month schedule was really reasonable for the 3.0 release. All we did was move the vertical line shown in Figure 3-21 to the right by three months, which resulted in Figure 3-22.

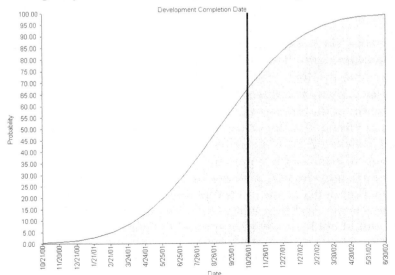

Figure 3-22: Case Study—Schedule-Probability Graph for Proposed 3.0 Release.

As you can see, the likelihood of success moved from 37 percent to 67 percent. But the real test came next. Was Release 2.5 possible? We allowed the development team to select the subset of requirements it was able to include with the old architecture. Figure 3-23 was the result. Once again, the graph indicated an acceptable level of risk, an 82-percent chance of success.

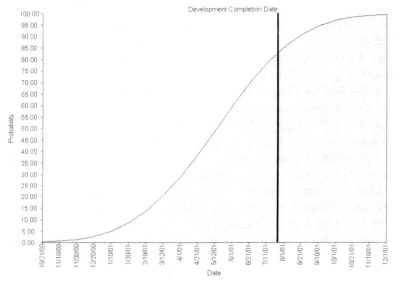

Figure 3-23: Case Study—Schedule-Probability Graph for Proposed 2.5 Release.

After this, Mark was reluctant to sign up for the proposed strategy; the requirements that Dev had suggested did not make a very impressive product. Then Mark had a great idea: The proposed Release 2.5 was not as good as the products the competitors were to release in the ten-to-twelve-month time frame, but it was better than anything else currently on the market. Mark's plan was to offer Release 2.5 to customers at a very low price—not even enough to recover the company's R&D and manufacturing costs. This early introduction at such a low price could seriously dampen the market demand for the competing products coming out a few months later. And then when 3.0 came out, the competitors' products would not have already captured the market.

So, as you can see, this project did not add or remove single requirements or tweak the schedule repeatedly until it converged upon a viable solution. Instead, it was the result of out-of-the-box thinking to envision two releases, followed by equally innovative thinking concerning how the product could be marketed and priced relative to the competition. This is often the case.

Delivery Date: Talking Apples and Apples

When parties agree to a delivery date, make sure they are talking about the same thing. For example, development organizations often think of "delivery" as the date they are no longer responsible for the product. In some companies, this could mean releasing the product to the independent testing team within the company. But in most companies, marketing thinks of delivery date as the date that the company can ship the product to the first buyer. Here is a list of some of the events that various people think of as "delivery":

- release to test
- release to quality assurance
- release to manufacturing
- release to (tactical) marketing
- release to sales
- release to beta customer
- release to revenue customer

Depending on the complexity of the product, these dates could be many months apart. It really does not matter which delivery date the parties are talking and negotiating about, as long as they are all talking about the same date.

ADVANCED TRIAGE TECHNIQUES

The triage process described in the previous section balances delivery date and development budget against desired requirements. However, in a real business environment, other factors need to be considered. This section describes how to perform triage when considering the many other factors that can influence the packaging of requirements into releases. These factors include

- risks inherent in addressing specific requirements
- market size
- market window

- market penetration
- price
- costs
- revenue
- return on investment

Advanced triage can be thought of as balancing a multi-person seesaw. Obviously, manipulating any of the variables could have dramatic effects on the other variables. For example, adding a few extremely unique requirements might allow us to sell the product at a much higher price and accept a smaller market penetration, and still achieve desired revenue and profitability goals. We will now discuss each of the above factors and describe how it affects the requirements triage process.

Considering Risks Inherent in Addressing Specific Requirements

Even though the size estimates for two requirements may be identical—say, ten person-weeks—one requirement may have some inherent risks that the other does not. For example, we may already have the right skills on board for one, but the other may require us to hire some people. Or, in one case, satisfaction of one requirement may depend heavily on a subcontractor delivering a subcomponent on time, but the other does not.

To capture such differences, annotate individual requirements with the inherent risk associated with their successful satisfaction. This can be captured most easily as a percentage representing the likelihood that the situation will go awry. A requirement having an associated risk of 25 percent means that there is a 25-percent chance that we will fail to satisfy the requirement, even after expending the specified number of resources, as illustrated in Figure 3-24.

Although not shown in Figure 3-24, a comment describing the source of risk is a good addition. Requirements triage demands that not only must the probabilities of completion on schedule and within budget (as shown previously in Figure 3-19 and Figure 3-20) be acceptable, but also that the requirements being considered for inclusion must exhibit acceptable levels of inherent risk.

Reqt. No.	Requirement Text	Risk
1	The system shall be programmable by the operator.	10%
1.1	The system shall be programmable by the operator to set the default for the green direction to be "East" or "West."	10%
1.2	The system shall be programmable by the operator to set the maximum duration for the light to remain green in the non-default direction.	10%
1.3	The system shall be programmable by the operator to set the minimum duration for the light to remain green in the default direction.	10%
1.4	The system shall be programmable by the operator to set the duration of the amber light prior to it changing to red.	10%
2	The system shall provide safe access to a one-lane east-west bridge via green/amber/red traffic lights.	30%
2.1	Two sets of traffic lights shall be controlled by the system.	10%
2.2	When either set of lights is "green," the other set of lights shall be set to "red."	10%
2.3	When the system determines that it is time to switch the direction of traffic, it shall do so in a safe manner.	30%
3	The system shall control eastbound traffic coming from northwest and southwest converging roads.	40%
3.1	During the period while the eastbound traffic light is authorized to be green, the system shall provide equal time for the traffic coming from the southwest and the northwest.	15%
4	The system shall control westbound traffic coming from northeast and southeast converging roads.	40%
4.1	During the period while the westbound traffic light is authorized to be green, the system shall provide equal time for the traffic coming from the southeast and the northeast.	15%
5	The system shall interface to vehicle sensors capable of determining if there is a vehicle waiting at either of the two entrances.	10%
6	The system shall interface to vehicle counters capable of counting vehicles as they pass through each of the two entrances.	60%
7	The system shall sense the weight of vehicles on the road and not allow either light to turn to green while a vehicle remains on the bridge.	75%
8	If a vehicle is disabled on the bridge, the system shall automatically contact a tow truck.	80%

Figure 3-24: A List of Candidate Requirements Annotated by Inherent Risk.

The easiest way to visualize the inherent risk associated with a proposed release is to examine a histogram showing the distribution of the requirements currently being considered for inclusion, as shown in Figure 3-25.

In this case, 59 percent of the requirements being considered for inclusion (10 out of 17) have a 19 percent or lower risk; 18 percent (3 out of 17) have a 60 percent or greater risk, and the rest lie in between. The shape of an acceptable risk histogram varies widely from project to project and company to company for two reasons: First, some companies or projects thrive on risk, while others are risk-averse; second, members of different projects are likely to calibrate risks associated with requirements in different ways.

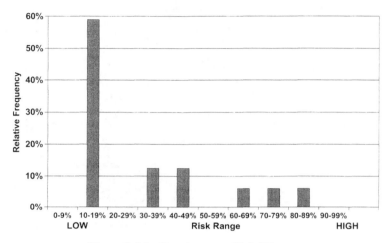

Figure 3-25: Requirements Risk Histogram.

While you're performing triage, if you find that the risk histogram indicates unacceptably high levels of risk, consider one or more of the following actions:

- Move some of the riskier requirements out of the baseline and defer them to a later release.
- Consider removing a high-risk requirement while adding one or more lower-risk requirements.
- Examine the requirements that represent unacceptable levels of risk. I have seen many cases in which the development group labeled a requirement high-risk because of some aspect of that requirement that the customer didn't even care about. To uncover this situation, refine high-risk requirements into sets of simpler requirements (as described in Chapter 1). Now, reanalyze the relative priorities and risks of the children requirements. You may discover that you can include high-priority, low-risk children requirements and exclude other lower-priority, high-risk children requirements.

Discuss the high-risk requirement within your group. Focus on what makes it high risk. Explore alternative solutions to satisfying a requirement.

Considering Market and Market Size

A *market* is a group of people with an unresolved need and sufficient resources to apply to the satisfaction of that need. For a company that sells its software externally, the market is the set of all potential customers. For an internal IT organization whose mission is to address the information-processing needs of its revenue-producing sibling organizations, the market is the set of individuals within the company who will eventually use the IT system in order to improve its ability to produce revenue, reduce overhead, increase profits, and so on.

An organization that is trying to define its market has a great deal of flexibility. For example, let us say we manufacture cherry soda. We could define the market as all humans on earth. Our justification would be that every human, in theory, could buy our soda. If we defined our market thusly, we would discover that the market size is huge, but that we could only succeed in selling to a minuscule fraction of our market. On the other hand, if we defined our market as only those people who have ever purchased a cherry soda, we would have a relatively small market size but would experience a much better record of selling to that market.

If there were a "right" approach, it would be to narrow your market definition to the subset of the population that you and your competitors are seriously trying to capture. Thus, as a cherry soda manufacturer, we should probably define our market as the people who purchase any type of sweet, carbonated beverage.

Your market may change as you add or remove features. For example, if you manufacture laser printers and you need to decide to include color printing in your next product (or not to), your market (and its size) will change.

Do not try to define the changes to the market size as a function of the addition or removal of individual requirements. It is more productive to understand and record major market changes as they relate to the addition or removal of large subsets of requirements. A simple example will suffice: Let's say you are in the United States and are building your first software product. You are wrestling with a long set of potential features (requirements). Twenty of them relate to various aspects of the internationalization of the product, and ten of these relate in particular to the software's ability to handle multi-byte characters. By omitting all twenty features, the market is limited to just the United States; by including the ten requirements that do not relate to multi-byte characters, the market is expanded to include roughly half of the world; and by including all twenty of the internationalization requirements, the market expands to include most of the world.

As you perform requirements triage, you need to remain cognizant of how adding or deleting requirements affects your market size. Otherwise, you may delete some requirements in order to make the market window, only to discover that you now have no market. As a general rule, the more features you add to the product, the larger the market, as shown in Figure 3-26. Of course, there are many exceptions to this usual pattern. For example, in some markets, the simplest and most basic product may have the largest market. Furthermore, as software products become more and more overloaded with functionality, they often become cumbersome and fewer people want to buy them.

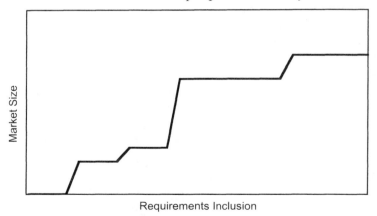

Figure 3-26: Usual Relationship Between Requirements Inclusion and Market Size.

Considering the Market Window

The *market window* is the period of time during which customers will buy a product. Extending this concept to an organization that builds a software system for internal use, the market window is the period of time during which the company can best utilize the software system. For the current discussion, we will assume that the earlier in the market window you introduce a product, the more successful the product sales will be.

However, the reader should be aware that this is not always the case. In a landmark study at Iowa State [IOW57], researchers found that as a market window progresses, different types of buyers become active (see Figure 3-27). Buyers in the early phases (innovators and early adopters) are more likely to be impulse buyers and to buy something just because it is new. On the other hand, buyers in the later phases (early majority and late majority) are more likely to make careful buying decisions. And those in even later phases (laggards) will not buy until the product is well proven and extremely mature. In addition, Donald Reinertsen [REI97] points out that in some types of markets, it may be better to be late than early because you spend less money educating the market about the product. For systems designed for internal use, though, this is rarely, if ever, the case.

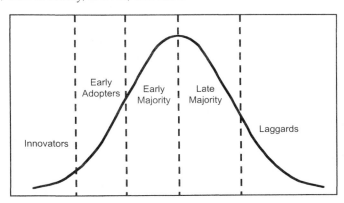

Figure 3-27: Market Window (Adapted from [IOW57]).

Marketing departments are acutely aware of market windows, and often work hard to target a product's delivery to the right place in that window. However, as features are added to a product, the following may occur:

- The delivery date is generally delayed, so the product enters the window at a later stage.

*The Diffusion Process, Agriculture Extension Service, Iowa State University, Special Report No. 18 (Ames, Iowa: 1957). Used by permission.

- The inclusion of those features may change the market window (in other words, the market window for one set of features is different than for another), shifting it either forward or backward. For example, adding a specific feature may make sense only to innovators or early adopters, so adding that feature but delaying its introduction to the market makes no business sense. Or, adding a specific feature may make sense only to early and late majorities, so delaying delivery to add that feature may make business sense.

As features are removed from a product, the following may occur:

- The delivery date is generally contracted, and the product enters the window at an earlier stage. Even though the product may be feature-poor, it may be attractive to innovators and early adopters because it is so early (assuming it does have the right kinds of features for these buyers).
- The removal of features may change the market window (again, the market window for one set of features is different than for another), shifting it either forward or backward.

Considering Market Penetration

It is one thing to hit a market window at the desired time, but it is another to successfully capture that market. *Market penetration* is the percentage of the market that you have sold to. The amount of market penetration your product achieves depends on the features selected for inclusion, your pricing, the softness of the market, the features of your competitors' products, and your competitors' pricing. For internal IT projects, market penetration is the percentage of relevant company transactions that the company executes using the new system.

Market penetration will be a function of time. Figure 3-28 shows a simplified model of how you could specify the percentage of the market that you expect to successfully sell your product to, given a specific set of features.

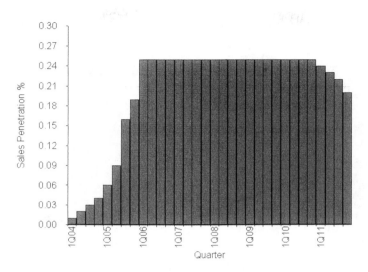

Figure 3-28: Market Penetration Graph.

Considering Price

Price is the amount a customer is charged for one or more copies of the product. Pricing strategies often include multiple tiers, quantity discounts, different pricing for different kinds of customers, partner-agreement-based pricing, and so on. There is no real equivalent of price for internal IT organizations, unless you want to consider it the effort expended by the internal customers.

Often, the marketing organization conceives of a particular feature mix in the next product release based on a long list of assumptions, many of which are not documented. In fact, many may be tacit and may have never even been expressed. One such assumption may be the price of the product. When marketing makes a statement such as, "The customer absolutely needs to have requirement *x* satisfied," it is actually saying, "The customer absolutely needs to have requirement *x* satisfied *if* we are going to charge *this* price." A company desiring to produce the best possible achievable product needs to consider the trade-off between feature mix, price, and timing. Furthermore, the "perfect" product—one that has all the right features and is released on budget and within schedule—is an utter failure if it cannot be sold at the desired price.

When selecting the price for software products, many factors need to be considered:

- How many units will you sell at a given price? As a general rule, the higher the price, the smaller the volume, as shown in Figure 3-29.

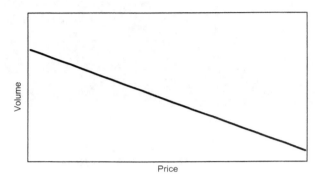

Figure 3-29: Price and Units Sold.

- The higher the price, the higher your revenues per unit will be. As a general rule, a curve like that shown in Figure 3-30 is applicable. That is, if you charge zero dollars for your product, you will have no revenues, but as you increase your price, revenues increase. This continues until your price becomes too high, at which point sales decrease significantly enough that your total revenues decrease.

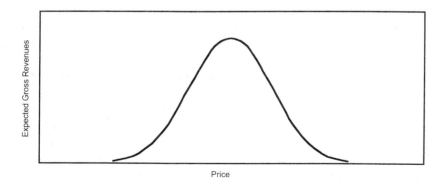

Figure 3-30: Price Modeling View.

- Unlike the pricing of manufactured products, the pricing of software is not related to the cost of raw materials or manufacturing. In software, these are both close to zero.
- To some degree, users may perceive the quality of a higher-priced product to be greater than a similar but lower-priced product.
- The higher the price, the higher your margins (profit per unit sold) will be.
- You may want to maximize market penetration and not revenue, in which case you might offer your products earlier and at a lower price than the optimal point shown at the peak of the curve in Figure 3-30.

Here are some questions to ask yourself regarding pricing:

- For each market segment, what is the expected average price that customers will pay per unit? Or, for each market segment, what is the expected average order size (in currency and number of units)?
- What special discounts will apply? For volume orders? For special customers? For promotions?
- Will you offer elasticity from advertised prices? For example, I know two companies in a particular marketplace. One advertises a price twice as high as the other, but they both experience the same gross revenues per unit sold. The reason is that one company allows its sales force to offer "special" discounts to every customer. Both have a unique strategy, and both work. The company that offers discounts makes every customer feel special by offering them those steep discounts, while the other gets its foot in more doors by advertising a lower price.
- How will you discount the product for resellers?
- Will you sell the software at a relatively low price, and offer customization services, which will become your major source of revenue? Or will you sell the software at a higher price, and allow third parties to do the customization?
- Will you offer the software to customers on a per-use basis rather than a per-site or per-copy basis? The most common way to do this is to offer it as an application service provider (ASP): Users pay for access to the software over the Web.

For software products destined for internal use, rather than external sale, there is no real price, per se, as I mentioned above. Instead, "benefit" should be analyzed as part of triage. Software for internal use is typically developed to assist other parts of the company in performing some business function. Typical motivations are to reduce the cost of doing business, reduce errors, or collect additional revenue. The questions to ask when analyzing the benefit of the software are as follows:

- What will the average cost savings per transaction be?
- What percentage of errors is expected to be eliminated?
- What is the average cost to the company of each error?
- What additional revenues are expected as a result of introducing the product?

In summary, during the triage process, price must be considered. Adding extra features may enable you to increase the price and compensate for a slightly later delivery. Removing some features may enable you to deliver early enough that you can afford to charge less and perhaps capture the market before the competition.

Considering Costs

Labor costs incurred by a company in creating a new software system are usually nontrivial. According to generally accepted accounting principles (GAAP), *costs* are usually expensed in the year they are incurred and thus have a direct and immediate impact on both cash and profitability.[18]

When considering the construction of a new software system, the impact on the company's cash and profitability must of course be considered, but it is also useful to examine the effect of costs on whether it makes sense to build the product at all. For example, when a company spends x dollars developing a product, it takes some time to recover those costs through sales (for companies that sell the products) or through use (for companies that deploy the product internally).

Recovery is usually measured in units sold (or elapsed time or transactions processed). Let's assume that recovery is measured in terms of y units sold. Each time a unit is sold, we are, in effect,

---

[18]In some cases, these costs may be capitalized, in which case they have an immediate negative effect on the company's cash flow but no immediate effect on profit. The costs are then depreciated over the software's useful life.

recapturing x/y of the original outlay of cash. And after selling y units, we have recovered all the original x dollars (ignoring, of course, the time value of money—see the net present value discussion later in this chapter).

As more and more features are added to a product,

a. Development costs increase.
b. Because of the increased costs, we will need to sell more units to recover the costs.
c. Because we need to sell more units, the time required for recovery will increase.
d. Product delivery may be delayed.
e. Due to the delay, once again, the time required for recovery will increase.

On the other hand,

f. Adding features may increase the rate at which units are sold.
g. This would lead to a decrease in the time required for recovery.

When features are removed from a product,[19]

a. Development costs generally decrease.
b. Because of the decreased costs, we will need to sell fewer units to recover the costs.
c. Because we don't need to sell as many units, the time required for recovery will decrease.
d. Product delivery may be accelerated.
e. Due to earlier delivery, the time required for recovery will decrease.

On the other hand,

f. Removing features may decrease the rate at which units are sold.
g. Due to the slower rate of sale, the time required for recovery would increase.

---

[19]Although items *a* and *d* seem logical, once development begins, the removal of a feature could actually increase costs and delay delivery because of the extra effort to undo something that has already been done!

As you can see, c and e are opposing forces to g in both cases. Finding an optimal set of features is nontrivial.

Although most companies will not compute all these items precisely, it is important to understand the general effect of adding features to a product or removing them. The bottom line is that adding features to a proposed product will definitely increase development cost, but it may increase or decrease the time for recovery. On the other hand, removing features from a proposed product will generally decrease development cost, but it may increase or decrease the time for recovery. Finally, in software development, there are very few recurring costs (such as the cost of manufacturing or of goods sold, as in the case of material goods).

Considering Revenues

The *revenue* associated with a product is the sum of all the gross receipts related to the sale of the product. Given the earlier definitions of market size, market penetration, and price, we could also define revenue (at least conceptually) as

$$revenue \approx market\ size \times market\ penetration \times price.$$

That is, as market size, market penetration, and price increase, so does revenue. However, as pointed out in previous sections, the three variables on the right side of the above equation are not independent. Changing the market so that market size increases will lower penetration, and changing the price can have dramatic effects on market penetration.

Given the following, we should be able to predict expected revenue as a function of time: a fixed market segment (as discussed earlier, in the subsection entitled "Considering Market and Market Size"), a set of features (as shown in Figure 3-13), and our expected market penetration (as shown in Figure 3-28).

Considering the Effect of Investment

Each of the above factors should be considered carefully when deciding to include or exclude a requirement from a software product. However, the ultimate indicator of whether a feature should be included or excluded is how it contributes to return on investment (ROI). In general, *return on investment* is defined as a measure of how effectively the company is using its capital to generate profits. There are many ways to calculate a return on investment:

- *Accounting definition:* The official definition of ROI is the annual income (profit) divided by the sum of shareholder's equity and long-term debt.
- *Annualized percentage rate (APR):* If you invest, say, $100 this year, and in five years it has increased in value to $128, you have received an overall rate of return of 28 percent. But to be able to compare two different potential investments, you want to look at the annualized rate of return. In this case, the annualized rate of return is 5 percent ($100 × 1.05^5). That is, if you invest $100, and every year thereafter you earn 5 percent on your money, at the end of five years, you will have $128. Now, let's say you have the choice between the following two potential ways to invest $100:
  - $100 today will become $128 in 5 years.
  - $100 today will become $115 in 1 year.

  If you want to know which is the better option, just compare their APRs. In the first case, the APR is 5 percent. In the second case, the APR is 15 percent. The second is a better investment even though it has a smaller total gain.
- *Internal rate of return (IRR):* IRR is quite similar to APR, but is expressed as a multiple, rather than a percentage. So, a 5-percent APR is expressed as a 1.05 IRR, a 15-percent APR is expressed as a 1.15 IRR. If you invest $100 today and it becomes $1,600 in four years, that represents an IRR of 2; in other words, you have effectively doubled your money every year for four years. Spreadsheets take away the difficulty of computing IRR by providing built-in formulae for this.
- *Break-even:* At the break-even point, your cumulative revenues and your cumulative costs are equal. In a typical software development effort, you incur significant up-front costs of product development, as well as the ongoing costs of maintenance and upgrades to the software (see Figure 3-31 for a graph of these cumulative costs).

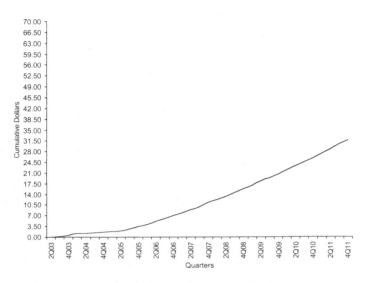

Figure 3-31: Cumulative Costs.

Meanwhile, if you are selling the software externally, you are receiving revenue from your customers for both initial purchases and annual maintenance contracts. Or, if you are using the software internally, you are reaping some reward—some combination of increased revenues, decreased costs, or increased efficiency (see Figure 3-32).

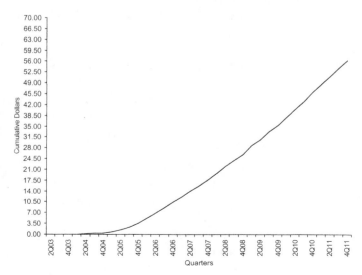

Figure 3-32: Cumulative Benefits (Revenues or Savings).

Considering that revenues and other benefits generally do not start until well after the software development stage, it should be no surprise that the curve of Figure 3-31 shows non-zero amounts (by the third quarter of 2003) earlier than they are shown in Figure 3-32 (by the third quarter of 2004). The break-even point is found by overlaying the two graphs, as shown in Figure 3-33.

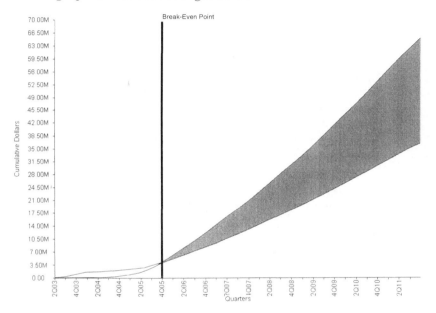

Figure 3-33: Break-Even Graph.

The shaded areas between the two graphs represent where the benefits exceed the expenses. However, be aware that on *real* software projects, there is a point of diminishing returns, when the cumulative expenses (being fed by escalating maintenance costs) once again exceed the cumulative benefits, as shown in Figure 3-34. You will note in this figure how the area turns from "in the red" (unshaded) initially, to being shaded, and then the lines cross again and the area is unshaded ("in the red") once again.

• *Net present value (NPV):* Net present value is used to compare the return on investment of a candidate product (with selected features) with other potential investments or alternative feature sets. It is the net financial result of a multi-year investment expressed using the current dollar valuation.

Let's look at a few parts of this definition. "Net" means that we are looking at the final effect of all outflows (the investments made in R&D for building the software product, as well as the ongoing maintenance) and all inflows (all types of revenues resulting from sales of the product and maintenance contracts). "Financial result" indicates that NPV will be expressed in monetary units. "Current dollar valuation" indicates that NPV considers the time-value of money (for example, $1.00 today is worth more than $1.00 will be worth next year). The formula for computing NPV factors in the interest you would have earned (called the discount rate) if you did not make the investment currently under consideration. Like IRR, every spreadsheet today provides a built-in formula for NPV; just plug in the discount rate, inflows, and outflows for each year, and the spreadsheet will compute it for you. If the NPV for your new product is higher than some other alternative you are considering, then you might consider building it. If NPV is less, it is probably not wise to make the investment.

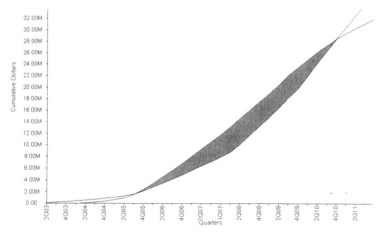

Figure 3-34: A More Realistic Break-Even Graph.

Putting It All Together

The balancing act that is triage is nontrivial, but quite doable. Figure 3-35 shows how each of the factors influence each other, all driven by the decision to add or subtract features from the next release. This figure highlights the conflicting facts. For example,

- As you add features, costs increase, which delays break-even.
- As you add features, the price may increase, resulting in higher revenues, which accelerates break-even.

Or consider these facts:

- As you add features, delivery is delayed, decreasing volume and delaying break-even.
- As you add features, market size may increase, increasing volume and accelerating break-even.

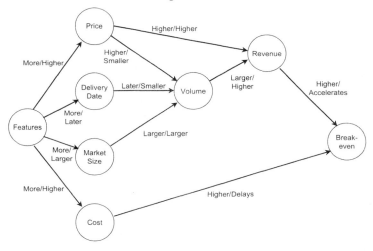

Figure 3-35: Complexity of Advanced Triage Factors.

THE RESULT OF TRIAGE

Triage is completed when the organization has determined which subset of requirements will be satisfied in the next release of the product. If we're conducting basic triage, then we know everything shown in Figure 3-36. If we're conducting advanced triage, we know everything shown in Figure 3-37. In both of these figures, the first item in each column is usually documented in a preliminary version of the requirements document, to be expanded in the subsequent requirements specification phase. All other items are likely to be documented in a business case document [REI03], preliminary project plan [IEE98a], or preliminary marketing plan [BER01].

For Products to Be Sold	For Products for Internal Use
• *which* requirements we will strive to satisfy	• *which* requirements we will strive to satisfy
• *when* the product will be delivered, and with what likelihood	• *when* the product will be delivered, and with what likelihood
• *how much* development is expected to cost, and with what likelihood	• *how much* development is expected to cost, and with what likelihood

Figure 3-36: What We Know at the End of Triage (Basic).

THE SECRETS OF *JUST ENOUGH* TRIAGE

If you pay too little attention to triage, you run the risk of trying to build a system that cannot be built within your time and resource constraints. If you spend too much time on triage, priorities will change before you even start doing requirements specification, resulting in a never-ending delay to project initiation. The secrets of accomplishing *just enough* requirements triage are as follows:

- Learn to accept that there is no such thing as a perfect solution to the triage dilemma. Compromise is necessary.
- Always annotate your candidate requirements with a relative priority and an estimated cost.
- Record interdependencies between requirements.
- Plan more than one release at a time [DAV03].
- Plan to replan before each new release [DAV03].
- If the voices (usually from marketing) crying "Add more functionality!" are allowed to overcome the voices of moderation, late delivery is guaranteed.
- If the voices (usually from development) crying "We can't implement that much functionality!" are allowed to overcome the voices of moderation, a weak product is guaranteed.
- Never lose sight of your goal: to select a subset of the full set of desired requirements so that the product can be delivered on time and within budget.

For Products to Be Sold	For Products for Internal Use
• *which* requirements we will strive to satisfy	• *which* requirements we will strive to satisfy
• *when* the product will be delivered, and with what likelihood	• *when* the product will be delivered, and with what likelihood
• *how much* development is expected to cost, and with what likelihood	• *how much* development is expected to cost, and with what likelihood
• *who* the customers are	• *who* the internal customers are
• *how much* the customer is expected to pay for the product	• *how much* savings or additional revenues the company will incur
• *how much* it will cost to market and sell	• *how much* it will cost to implement
• *how many* units are expected to be sold within the next *x* years	• *how many* transactions are expected to be performed by time period over the next *x* years
• *when* the product is expected to be replaced (the product's expected life span)	• *when* the product is expected to be replaced (the product's expected life span)
• *when* the company will recover its costs (the break-even)	• *when* the company will recover its costs (the break-even)
• *what* the internal rate of return is	• *what* the internal rate of return is

Figure 3-37: What We Know at the End of Triage (Advanced).[20]

- Triage participants must see themselves as a team trying to solve a business problem, not as separate camps trying to get their own way.
- Development should avoid making absolute statements such as, "We cannot build the system by the delivery date if you add that requirement." Instead, make statements such as, "By adding that requirement, our likelihood of delivering on time reduces from 73 percent to 27 percent." This helps create an environment of teamwork since *nobody* on the team wants to deliver the product late.

---

[20]I use the term "implement" in the right-hand column, in the information systems sense, which means, "making it happen in the organization" and includes such costs as training, deployment, purchasing equipment, changing business processes, and so on. I am not using it in the computer-science sense, meaning "code the software."

- Marketing (and customers) should avoid making absolute statements, such as, "We cannot sell (or use) the system if that requirement is excluded." Instead, make statements such as, "By removing that requirement, our expected revenues will be reduced from $20M to $11M." This helps create an environment of teamwork since *nobody* on the team wants to hurt the company's revenue.
- Agreeing to a set of requirements that are impossible to satisfy in the given time guarantees failure. Why would anybody send a company down such a path?
- Avoiding explicit triage altogether means that triage issues will be addressed through intimidation and politics, which will doom the project to failure.
- Stakeholders have the right to change their mind. A requirement that is not important today may become critical tomorrow, and vice versa. Be flexible.

JERM

FOUR

Requirements Specification

As you discovered in the previous chapter, failing to perform requirements triage almost guarantees that you will deliver your product late. In this chapter, you will learn about the third major area of requirements management: requirements specification.

Definitions and Terminology

After elicitation and triage, it would be nice to just start building the product. Unfortunately, great risks remain. In particular, requirements are still quite ambiguous and open-ended. If not improved, the requirements will necessitate that developers make decisions concerning the external behavior of the system. If development personnel immediately start product construction, problems are likely to arise: Developers will make different assumptions than customers had in mind, resulting in a system that is likely to disappoint customers. They are also likely to make different assumptions than other developers, resulting in an inconsistent and perhaps nonfunctional system. The deliberate documentation of requirements to a degree of detail that will make the associated risks tolerable is called requirements specification. Since *specification* means "documentation," then *requirements specification* is simply "the documentation of the desired external behavior of the system." I will use the term "requirements document" for the actual document produced as a result of performing requirements specification.[1]

Requirements specification is that activity associated with creating the final documentation of a system's requirements, as shown in Figure 4-1. However, requirements specification is actually conducted throughout requirements activities. As candidate requirements are suggested during elicitation, they are documented somehow, and this documentation is the specification of requirements. During elicitation and triage, disagreements concerning the meaning of various requirements arise, and these are resolved by providing more detail about existing requirements (this, too, is specification of requirements). In general, the requirements are transformed from the beginning of elicitation to the end of requirements specification in a wide variety of ways, including

- *Agreement:* During elicitation, the requirements are just suggestions. By the time requirements specification is complete, the requirements are fully agreed to by all parties [POH94].
- *Completeness:* Throughout the entire requirements process, we are adding more and more requirements because the more we think *about,* the more we will think *of.* Klaus Pohl calls this the degree of specification [POH94].
- *Detail:* During elicitation, requirements are often stated relatively abstractly. As we approach the end of requirements specification, we add more and more detail to most requirements.
- *Precision:* During elicitation and triage, some degree of ambiguity is tolerable. By the time we get to the end of

---

[1]Terminology is not consistent across the industry. Some use the term "specification" by itself to mean "design specification," a description of the internal workings of the system, including algorithms, data structures, and so on. Others use the term "specification" by itself to mean "documentation of the desired external behavior of the system." Still others use the term "external design" for what I call requirements specification [WAS86]. In my opinion, "external design" is an excellent term, but not common enough to warrant use in this book. Also, the word "specification" is overloaded; it often refers to the process of documenting the requirements as well as the document itself. To facilitate communication in this book, I use the expression "requirements specification" to denote the process, and "requirements document" to denote the resultant document.

requirements specification, much of the ambiguity has been removed. Pohl calls this the degree of representation [POH94].

- *Augmented:* During elicitation, most of the requirements are just sentences. As we move closer and closer to the end of requirements specification, many of these have been augmented with models and pictures, annotated, cross-referenced, and so on.

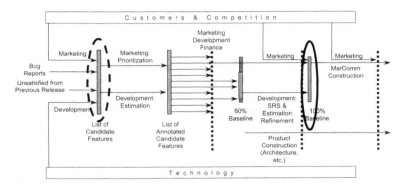

Figure 4-1: Requirements Specification in the Requirements Process.

Of the three primary aspects of requirements management, requirements specification has received the most attention. Many corporate and organizational standards even suggest that documentation of the system's desired external behavior should be the *first* activity performed. Dozens of standards exist to control how individual requirements should be organized into a polished document [DOR90]. More recently, the Robertsons introduced the Volere specification template [ROB99]. This is the first de facto standard that provides a reasonable checklist to help requirements writers decide what belongs in the document and what does not.

After many years of consulting for organizations adhering to these standards, I have become convinced that such organizations spend an inordinate amount of time polishing requirements documents with relatively little gain. If you are following one of these standards, the most important advice I can offer you is to keep your goals in mind. Remember, the goal is not a perfect requirements *document*. The goal is an ideal *product*, and the requirements document is just a means to that end. This chapter presents useful guidance concerning how much polishing is necessary and sufficient. If you spend an insufficient amount of time on the specification, you run a high risk of building an inappropriate system. If you spend too much time on it, you will end up delivering the product late.

CLASSIC REQUIREMENTS DOCUMENTATION STYLES

Here are six classic ways of handling the specification of requirements:

- *No requirements documentation:* This school of thought is based on one of the following assertions:

    "Why waste time documenting requirements? They'll change anyway." True, they'll change, but ironically enough, without documented requirements, change cannot be measured, let alone controlled. Thus, by not documenting requirements, considerably more change will occur. Furthermore, the argument that you should not document something just because it will change is fallacious; one could apply the same argument to code: "Why bother writing code? It will just change anyway!" We write code (even though it will change) because without code, the system won't work. We document requirements (even though they will change) because without requirements, the system won't do what it is supposed to do.

    "We don't have time to document requirements." If that is the case, then we don't have time to build the system, either. The argument is like saying we have time for one more ski run down the mountain, but we don't have time to take the ride up the ski lift.

    "Customers are certainly not going to document requirements; we, the developers, will. Therefore, why bother spending the time? Why don't we just implement requirements the way we think they should be implemented?" The problem with this argument is that although customers will not write requirements, they will certainly review and approve (or not approve) them.

    "Our *methodologist du jour* says we don't need to write requirements." If that is the case, find out how many successful development projects your methodologist has worked on. I suspect the answer is zero—if not, the projects were either very simple or very, very lucky. And luck is *not* a strategy.

- *Large standards-adhering documentation:* In this world, so much time is spent polishing, organizing, and reorganizing the requirements that it is no wonder such projects are almost always late and over budget. In an effort to squeeze out all technical risk, these projects introduce tremendous schedule and budgetary risks.

- *Formal specification:* These projects want to remove any possibility of requirements being misunderstood. This is certainly a worthy goal, but in an effort to accomplish this, developers tend to forget that the customers need to fully understand the requirements, too. As we move away from natural language and toward formal representations of logic, we alienate our customers.

- *Bulleted lists:* Developers who maintain requirements in lists are working in the right direction. They realize they should spend their time verifying that all stakeholders have a common understanding of each requirement, and when they find a problem, they should enhance the quality of that requirement. Thus, all polishing is done to the individual requirement, with relatively little effect on the overall document. If you select this as your preferred approach, make sure you use a reasonable checklist for completion, such as the one outlined by the Robertsons [ROB99].

- *Modeling diagrams:* Models are terrific aids toward understanding a problem and its solution and are thus irreplaceable during elicitation. When used carefully, they can also aid in the description of a system's external behavior. The trick is to use notations that customers understand and to use the right notation for the right purpose. No single notation will be sufficient to describe all types of requirements, and if somebody were to invent such a notation, it would by its very nature be impossible for customers to understand. Some models serve as excellent adjuncts to requirements; for example, pictures of the environment, as shown in Figures 4-2 and 4-3 (which refer to Figure 3-13), or decision trees, which I discuss later. And some models actually provide quite natural specifications of certain requirements. If models are used, make sure they are cross-referenced to textual requirements.

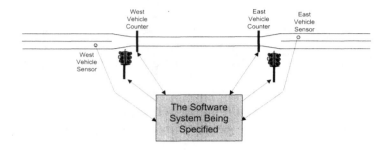

Figure 4-2: Diagram to Support a One-Lane Bridge System.

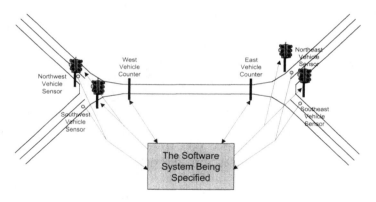

Figure 4-3: Diagram to Support an Extended One-Lane Bridge System.

• *Legacy software maintenance:* When enhancing an existing system, we often have to work without an up-to-date requirements document. This can occur for any of three reasons:

  1. The system was built many years ago, when standards for documenting requirements were immature.
  2. The system was built more recently, but by people who did not care (especially about the future).

3. The system was built in a responsible manner with a then-current requirements document, but over the years, as more and more requirements changed, the original requirements document was abandoned.

Unfortunately, as new requirements are added to the existing system, the requirements document is not updated. However, some companies create and maintain a rudimentary list of new requirements. Very rarely does a company attempt to reconstruct a complete requirements document from the working system (and I would question whether that would be a wise investment).

THE CONTENT OF A REQUIREMENTS DOCUMENT

A requirements document contains all those things that describe the external behavior of a system. Thus, it includes the following:

- *Inputs:* Every input that is accepted by the system must appear someplace in the requirements document. The inputs may all be explicitly defined in one place or they may be defined only by reference. In the former case, requirements would look like this:

  The system shall accept passengers' names.

  The system shall accept passengers' home addresses.

In the latter case, requirements would look like this:

  The system shall ask the operator for the passenger name.

  The system shall check that each passenger name entered is on the current manifest for the current flight.

- *Outputs:* Every output that is produced by the system must appear in the requirements document. These outputs include displays, reports, requests for information, and error messages. Requirements with outputs would look like this:

The system shall request names of passengers.

The system shall display an error message when the passenger name entered is not currently on the manifest.

- *Functions:* The requirements document must include the system's functions (the mappings from all inputs to outputs). Such requirements would look like this:

  When the user clicks on the "report" button, the system shall display a screen with report options as shown in figure.[2]

  When the user rolls the mouse over any passenger name, the corresponding balance due shall be displayed in a rollover window, as shown in figure.[3]

- *Environment:* Software never stands alone. It lives in an environment consisting of people, hardware, and other software. Without this environment, the software would cease to operate. The requirements document should list every aspect of the environment that affects the software. For example, requirements should address such issues as hardware platform, hardware configuration, operating systems, database systems, run-time environments, libraries, other applications, and so on.
- *Performance:* What are acceptable response times for the software? Under what conditions? In what situations? At what rate can inputs arrive without exceeding the system's tolerances? When inputs exceed these rates, how will the system degrade? How many simultaneous users, customers, flights, passengers, and clerks may access or be stored by the system?

---

[2]Where "figure" is a hyperlink to a copy of the actual report.

[3]Where "figure" is a hyperlink to a sample of what a rollover window would look like in context.

In all cases, make sure the requirements describe these aspects from a perspective that's external to the system.

THE ROLE OF A REQUIREMENTS DOCUMENT

A requirements document plays a variety of important roles [DAV93]. It serves as a means for communication among customers, marketing, development, sales, finance, testing, and management. Each stakeholder has his or her own job to do, and for the most part, the stakeholders' tasks can be performed fairly independently. However, the success of their collective actions is only ensured if they are all working toward the same goal: the same system. Documenting requirements ensures that the system being built by the developers is the same system

- that customers are expecting
- that marketing has analyzed for market potential
- that marketing is promoting in its marketing campaign
- that the sales force is studying as it develops sales strategies
- that finance is budgeting
- that management has planned, budgeted, defined tasks for, and scheduled with intermediate and final delivery milestones

None of these parties can do its job without a common understanding of the system's intended external behavior.

Requirements serve as the primary driver of the design team. When two designers ask what they should optimize, they get their answer from the requirements document. When two designers ask what the system should do when the user enters an incorrect value, they get their answer from the requirements document. When two designers have conflicting views about where a particular value should be displayed on a screen or report, they get their answer from the requirements document. Note that all such decisions should be driven by the needs of customers, not by the desires of developers.

Requirements serve as the primary driver of the system test team. Without a requirements document, how can testers possibly know what the system is supposed to do? A few years ago, I was consulting for a large telecommunications company and learned that system testers were not allowed to see the requirements document. When I asked the project manager why he had established such a strange rule, he responded, "I do not want to prejudice testers the same way that the requirements have already prejudiced designers." The right answer of course is to fix the requirements! And then let everybody see them.

Requirements serve as a reference for project managers. Project managers are similar to orchestra conductors. The requirements document, plus the project plan derived from those requirements, is their sheet music. The requirements help them allocate the right resources at the right time, know when people are doing the right thing, and above all, know that everybody on the team has the same sheet music.

The requirements document serves as the basis for controlling the evolution of the system. When Release 1.0 of the system development is complete, it should satisfy all the requirements defined in the 1.0 release of the requirements document. When triage is performed for the 2.0 release, the requirements document is updated to reflect the new requirements, and then the system is built to satisfy those requirements. Thus, at any time during the life of a system, the latest version of the requirements document always defines the current system being built, and the previous version of the requirements document always defines the most recent release.

QUALITIES OF A REQUIREMENTS DOCUMENT

Earlier in the chapter, we looked at six classic ways to document requirements. Of these, the first one, not documenting requirements, is clearly unsatisfactory for all but the most trivial applications and situations. Your customer may demand the second, a large standards-adhering document; however, I hope that this practice disappears over the next few years. The time it takes to polish such a document does not have any extra benefit, other than to make it easier for some bean-counter to check the document's table of contents for conformity to a standard. The third approach, that of a formal specification document, is only practiced in parts of rare, extremely critical applications and is not applicable to 99 percent of applications. The fourth, the bulleted list of requirements, is by far the most cost-effective and beneficial approach. It is simple to create; it is simple to read, regardless of background; and, when stored in a spreadsheet, database, or requirements management tool and augmented with annotations, it has incredible benefits to project management. The last approach, of using modeling diagrams to augment specific subsets of requirements, removes the ambiguity inherent in natural language and—when it's used selectively—makes the bulleted-list approach even more powerful.

The days of large word-processed requirements documents are over. These days, there are too many questions that a manager needs answered quickly—quicker than a word-processed document can manage. For example, a manager needs to know the following:

- How many requirements are there?
- How many high-priority requirements have been delayed to a release after Release 2.0?
- What percent of the requirements for Release 2.0 are low priority?
- Which requirements in Release 2.0 are high priority, are being built for Customer X, and are the responsibility of Sally?

The need for quick answers to questions like these convinces me that the *only* way to record requirements when pressed for time is as a *list* of discrete requirements, each annotated with multiple attributes.

In a 1993 article, my coauthors and I put forth a long list of attributes that a well-written set of requirements should exhibit [DAV93a]. For my part, I must have been feeling obsessive-compulsive at the time. Although it was an interesting academic discourse, the article left one wondering what a practitioner could possibly do with such an enormous list. After much analysis and experience, I now have to admit that only eight attributes are truly important, and of these, some are not even possible to achieve. Here is the list of attributes that I think are important for today's *just enough* world (in decreasing order of importance):

- *Correct: A requirement is correct if it helps to satisfy a stakeholder need.* This is by far the most important attribute because it gets right to the essence of why we are documenting requirements: to help satisfy stakeholder needs. In Figure 4-4, the circular region represents all stakeholder needs. If a requirement helps to support these needs, it is correct; otherwise, it is incorrect. For example, consider the following requirement:

> *The system shall provide a red button labeled stop.*

This is correct if one or more stakeholders need such a button. If no stakeholder has this need, it is incorrect. Didar Zowghi and Vincenzo Gervasi [ZOW02] use the term *redundant* when a requirement fails to help meet a stakeholder need but does not conflict with any stakeholder need. They [ZOW04] use the term *correctness* differently than I do; they use it to indicate the presence of consistency and completeness. Yet only the stakeholders can determine the correctness of a requirement. A project cannot hire a consultant to come in and find correctness errors unless that consultant is intimately familiar with the application and the needs of every stakeholder.

The reason this attribute is so important is simple. If a requirement is incorrect, the product will *fail* to meet stakeholder expectations.

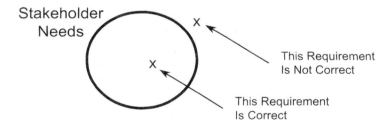

Figure 4-4: Diagram Showing Correctness.

- *Consistent: A requirement is consistent if its satisfaction does not conflict with the satisfaction of another requirement, a set of requirements, or some other previously approved document* [DAV93]. A developer choosing to satisfy requirement *A* in a manner that is inconsistent with another requirement does not make requirement *A* inconsistent. Instead, inconsistency is only an inherent attribute of a requirement in relation to other requirements. If there is some way to satisfy requirement *A* that does not conflict with other requirements, then it is the developer's responsibility to discover and use that approach.

The reason this attribute is rated so highly is simple. If a requirement is inconsistent with other expectations, development will find it impossible to satisfy without failing to satisfy other stakeholder needs.

- *Achievable: A set of requirements is achievable if it is possible to construct some system that satisfies all requirements in that set.* Obviously, if a requirement is inconsistent, then any set of requirements containing that requirement is not achievable. Achievability is meaningful only within a context defined by the capabilities of team members, the state of technology, the amount of available resources, and the desired delivery date.

   This attribute is very important because a lack of achievability makes it impossible to satisfy stakeholder needs.

- *Annotated: A requirement is annotated if it is easy for us to find characteristics of the requirement, including its relationships with other requirements.* Earlier, we discussed annotating requirements by their relative priority (to facilitate triage); estimated cost (to facilitate both triage and project management); and necessity, effort, subset, and cover dependency (to further facilitate triage and project management). Here, we discuss a few more annotations: origin, advocate, responsible party, primary customer, details, and tasks.

   The *origin* (also called a *backward trace* or *upstream trace*) of a requirement is a pointer to or notation concerning *why* it exists. For example, if the requirement is derived from an earlier system-level requirement, this should be a pointer to the specific system requirement. If the requirement is being satisfied because the customer said, "Read my lips—I want the system to be green," then the origin is a notation to that effect. The primary benefit of recording the origin is that it provides the team with a place of referral whenever somebody suggests changing the requirement at a later date. Since between 20 percent [JON96] and 53 percent [STA95] of all requirements change during development, this origin annotation could be extremely valuable. Gotel and Finkelstein [GOT94] report that the inability to find the origin of a requirement was the top complaint cited by 100 practitioners in a survey about their biggest traceability problem.

In some companies, each requirement is assigned to an individual who is ultimately responsible for making sure that it is satisfied. That person is often called the *advocate*.

In some companies, an individual in the development organization is assigned the responsibility for making the requisite changes to the system to satisfy the requirement. This person is often called the *responsible party*.

When there are multiple customers, it is often a good idea to record the *primary customer* next to each requirement. That way, if any questions arise about the requirement's meaning, you know whom to ask.

For many requirements, a sentence is sufficient to convey what is desired. If a requirement needs refinement to be better understood, it is best to refine it into sub-requirements, each in its own new record in the requirements database. If a sentence isn't enough to make a requirement's meaning clear, add more detail or explanation. This should be recorded in a new field called something like *details*. Often, such requirements become better understood with the help of a more formal model. When this is the case, the "details" entries for all related requirements should reference the model. For example, in an elevator control system, there will be many requirements concerning the safe operation of the elevator doors. Although these should all be written in natural language, they should all reference a common model of door operation, perhaps recorded as a finite state machine, decision tree, or statechart.

When the requirements database, list, or spreadsheet is not fully integrated into the project management system, it might be helpful to cross-reference each requirement with the *tasks* in the work breakdown structure being conducted in support of the satisfaction of this requirement.

• *Traceable:* During the system development process that occurs after requirements specification, many intermediate products are created and managed. These include designs, coded components, test plans, test results, user manuals, and so on. Many of these undergo repeated changes, and when they do, it is extremely helpful to understand *why* they exist. In other words, which requirements do they relate to? Also, requirements themselves will change continuously while system development is under way. As this occurs, it is extremely helpful to know what downstream items (completed or under development) will be affected. To facilitate this, maintain *traces* (also called *forward traces* or *downstream traces)* between requirements and all downstream intermediate products of development. Although the creation of such traces is not part of requirements activities, it is important to give every requirement a unique identifier so that later tracing is possible. *A requirement is traceable if it has a unique identifier.* If you are storing requirements in a database, the unique identifier is the primary key. Otherwise, create a column in the requirements list called "ID" to store the unique number or name. Do not use the automatic numbering feature contained in many word processors and spreadsheets, however, because if you decide to delete requirement 17 at any point, what *was* requirement 18 will be renumbered and become 17! Instead, once a requirement is deleted, its identifier should be forever retired. To do otherwise will play havoc with cross-reference reports that you have produced to date.

- *Unambiguous: A requirement is unambiguous if it has only one possible interpretation* [IEE98]. If you attempt to squeeze out all remnants of ambiguity, you will be forced to use formal methods, your costs will skyrocket, and you will run the risk of alienating customers. The alternative is to remain in natural language and accept some degree of ambiguity. I made a good living for many years reviewing and critiquing requirements documents. In a typical assignment, I would find hundreds of ambiguities, and after they were repaired, I could still find hundreds more. The truth is, this process could have continued indefinitely had it not been for my conscience. The legal profession solved this problem many years ago. Although not written, one can assume that every clause of a contract ends with the statement "as interpreted by reasonable and prudent people." I would argue the same for requirements. Yes, you should endeavor to remove glaring ambiguities. No, you should not accept an ambiguous requirement that resulted from a compromise among multiple parties who clearly do not agree. But no, do not go on a crazy ambiguity-hunt just so you can say you did.

- *Complete:* In my 1993 book [DAV93], I write, "a requirement specification is complete if everything the software is supposed to do is included in the [requirements document]." Since the publication of that book, I have seen numerous definitions of requirement completeness in the literature, and most of them are as useless as mine. Of what value is a discussion of the completeness of a requirements document when we all know it is impossible to achieve? The needs of the customer are in constant flux. Even if we could somehow declare a requirements document complete today, it would no longer be complete tomorrow. Time changes needs. Reading a requirements document will trigger the reader to think of more requirements. Using a system will trigger the user to conceive of more requirements. So, I guess one could declare completeness to be an attribute that exists only for an instant. That makes the definition valid—but still useless. To make matters even worse, a requirements document is typically written after triage is performed—and triage deliberately reduces the completeness of the document! So, the best definition of completeness I can come up with is this: *"A requirements document is complete if it includes all the requirements that the stakeholders expect to have satisfied in the corresponding release."*

- *Verifiable:* A requirement is verifiable if there is a finite, cost-effective method to check that the system, as built, meets the requirement as stated [IEE98]. The U.S. Department of Defense demands that every requirement for its procured systems must be verifiable. Unfortunately, this creates a dilemma. If the requirement is ambiguous (see discussion above), then by its very nature, it cannot be verified, for it possesses multiple interpretations. One could argue that the verification method (a test, for example) removes the ambiguity; however, I would counter that the test is therefore the requirement! For example, if we have a requirement R and a test T that verifies the presence of R, and all the system builders need to do is build a system that satisfies T (and not R), then isn't T the actual requirement? The best way to define a verifiable requirement, then, is to state that *"A requirement is verifiable if there exists some finite, cost-effective method to check that the system as built meets the requirement as stated, to a degree sufficient to convince all relevant parties."*

- *Other attributes:* As mentioned above, my 1993 paper included many other attributes. The attribute "understandable by customers" is still important, but I have combined its essence into the discussion of unambiguous requirements. It is of course important for a requirements document to be "modifiable"; however, I'm no longer sure what a non-modifiable requirements document would look like. It is still important for requirements to be "traced" to their origins and "organized," but I now treat those concepts as annotations. The concept of "design independent" is important as well, but once we have agreed that a requirement is only a requirement if it maintains an external perspective and that every requirement by its nature limits design alternatives, it seems unnecessary to insist that a requirement should be design independent. As far as "conciseness" goes, yes, it would be nice if the requirements document was concise, but if it isn't, then what? I would not waste any time trying to make a requirements document any smaller than it is.

No matter how hard you try, you will not be able to squeeze out every last drop of requirements defect. You should strive to make sure that the document is correct, consistent, achievable, and at least annotated by effort and relative priority. The remaining attributes are nice to have, but in attempting to achieve them, be careful not to lose your ability to do requirements in a *just enough* manner.

SPECIFICATION TECHNIQUES

An annotated list of requirements, stored in a spreadsheet, database, or requirements management tool, provides most of what is needed to enable designers to start their job with the assurance that all stakeholders possess a relatively common understanding of the requirements. However, for some applications, further assurance can be achieved by augmenting the requirements with models, as mentioned earlier. Models vary as widely as the types of applications under development. The trick is to select the right model for the right application. More specifically, the trick is to select the right model for the right aspect of the right application.[4]

In the following sections, I describe some aspects of software applications and provide guidance concerning the types of models that might be appropriate. A couple of warnings are in order, first:

- Every application will include some piece of every one of the aspects I discuss below. The goal is not to use as many as possible, but as few as possible. The larger the number of modeling notations used, the more difficult it will be for customers to understand. Select just one or perhaps a couple of modeling notations for the most critical parts of the application. There is no need to model every aspect of every problem.
- Some self-proclaimed modeling gurus try to make us believe that *their* notation is ideal for every aspect of every application. However, when they find some aspect that their notation cannot model, they simply extend their notation.

Feature Intensity

One common way for software to behave is to offer users a multitude of features, each performed by a series of interactions between the user, the system being specified, and perhaps other systems and people. A natural way to specify such applications exists and has been used extensively since the dawn of computers. It has several names, as we saw in Chapter 2: scenario, use case [JAC92], storyboard (in use at the Disney Studios in Hollywood as early as 1928), stimulus-response sequence [DAV79], sample dialog, and others. In essence, each feature of the system is described in time-

---

[4]For a complete description of how to use models for requirements, see [DAV93, KOT98].

sequenced interactions between various parties. Scenarios seem natural in that many users think of their systems as providers of features that are composed of a sequence of steps, and they think of requirements as a set of features composed of a sequence of steps.

Figure 4-5 and Figure 4-6 show examples of simple scenarios (extracted from requirements documents for an airline reservation system and a traffic control system, respectively). Notice that everything in these examples would be easily understandable by their respective customers. Some argue that because such scenarios are so easy for customers to read, they should be used as *the* means of requirements documentation. The advantages of doing so are many, but there are two important disadvantages:

- Not all systems lend themselves to such documentation.
- Even for systems that lend themselves to such documentation, the entire set of requirements cannot be specified this way [ANT01].

In nontrivial systems, scenarios become a lot more complex. For example, in the scenario captured in Figure 4-5, what if the user enters an incorrect flight number? What happens if the user drags the passenger off the plane, rather than to another seat? What if the user drags the passenger to a seat that is already occupied? Similarly, in Figure 4-6, for traffic control, What if a vehicle is broken down on the bridge? What if more vehicles have entered than exited in the opposite direction? All of these can obviously be addressed, but as each extension is made, the documentation becomes more difficult to understand.

Step 1.   The user selects the "change seat assignment" option.
Step 2.   The system asks the user for a flight number and date.
Step 3.   The user enters a valid flight number and date.
Step 4.   The system displays a seating chart for the aircraft, showing the name of any passenger assigned to a seat.
Step 5.   The user clicks on the name of the passenger to be relocated and drags the passenger to the new seat.
Step 6.   The system acknowledges to the user that the seating assignment has been changed successfully.

Figure 4-5: A Sample Scenario for an Airline Reservation System.

Step 1. Vehicle arrives from the east.
Step 2. If the light is green for westbound traffic, vehicle proceeds over the bridge.
Step 3. If the light is red for westbound traffic, then
Step 3a. Vehicle stops.
Step 3b. After minimum-duration-for-default-green expires, light for westbound traffic turns green.
Step 3c. Vehicle proceeds over the bridge.

Figure 4-6: A Sample Scenario for a Traffic Control System.[5]

We want a list of requirements so we can manage them, but specifying requirements as scenarios results in much redundancy. For example, look at the redundancy between Figure 4-5 and Figure 4-7, and between Figure 4-6 and Figure 4-8. Clearly, developers and managers need to see each requirement just once. The solution to this dilemma is to maintain your requirements in a simple annotated list, cross-referenced to models such as these scenarios.

Step 1. The user selects the "make a reservation" option.
Step 2. The system asks the user for a flight number and date.
Step 3. The user enters a valid flight number and date.
Step 4. The system asks for a passenger name.
Step 5. The system acknowledges to the user that a reservation has been made for the passenger.

Figure 4-7: Another Sample Scenario for an Airline Reservation System.

Step 1. Vehicle arrives from the west.
Step 2. If the light is green for eastbound traffic, vehicle proceeds over the bridge.
Step 3. If the light is red for eastbound traffic, then
Step 3a. Vehicle stops.
Step 3b. After maximum-duration-for-non-default-green expires, light for eastbound traffic turns green.
Step 3c. Vehicle proceeds over the bridge.

Figure 4-8: Another Sample Scenario for a Traffic Control System.

---

[5]For Figures 4-6 and 4-8, let us assume that the operator has programmed west to be the default direction.

Figure 4-9 shows the example used in Figure 3-24, with cross-references to Figure 4-2, Figure 4-3, Figure 4-6, and Figure 4-8. Obviously, when complete, many more cross-references would be included. Similar cross-references could be used for any modeling notation, including finite state machines, decision tables, and so on.

Reqt. No.	Requirement Text	Cross-Ref. to Model
1	The system shall be programmable by the operator.	
1.1	The system shall be programmable by the operator to set the default for the green direction to be "East" or "West."	
1.2	The system shall be programmable by the operator to set the maximum duration for the light to remain green in the non-default direction.	
1.3	The system shall be programmable by the operator to set the minimum duration for the light to remain green in the default direction.	
1.4	The system shall be programmable by the operator to set the duration of the amber light prior to it changing to red.	
2	The system shall provide safe access to a one-lane east-west bridge via green/amber/red traffic lights.	Figure 4-2
2.1	Two sets of traffic lights shall be controlled by the system.	Figure 4-2
2.2	When either set of lights is "green," the other set of lights shall be set to "red."	Figure 4-6, Figure 4-8
2.3	When the system determines that it is time to switch the direction of traffic, it shall do so in a safe manner.	Figure 4-6, Figure 4-8
3	The system shall control eastbound traffic coming from northwest and southwest converging roads.	Figure 4-3
3.1	During the period while the eastbound traffic light is authorized to be green, the system shall provide equal time for the traffic coming from the southwest and the northwest.	
4	The system shall control westbound traffic coming from northeast and southeast converging roads.	Figure 4-3
4.1	During the period while the westbound traffic light is authorized to be green, the system shall provide equal time for the traffic coming from the southeast and the northeast.	
5	The system shall interface to vehicle sensors capable of determining if there is a vehicle waiting at either of the two entrances.	Figure 4-2, Figure 4-3
6	The system shall interface to vehicle counters capable of counting vehicles as they pass through each of the two entrances.	Figure 4-2, Figure 4-3
7	The system shall sense the weight of vehicles on the road and not allow either light to turn to green while a vehicle remains on the bridge.	
8	If a vehicle is disabled on the bridge, the system shall automatically contact a tow truck.	

Figure 4-9: Candidate Requirements Cross-Referenced to Models.

State–Based Problems

When one person calls another person on the telephone, what happens after the number is dialed? The next step is either a ring-back tone to the calling party and a ringing tone to the called party, a busy tone to the calling party, or a "call cannot be completed as dialed" message to the calling party. Notice that the next step is not a function of something somebody does, but a function of a *state* of something (or somebody) in the system. If this were the only state-consideration, it could easily be captured in a scenario. But when there are hundreds or even thousands of states in a system, and any of them can drastically affect the system's behavior, we must turn to another modeling notation.

The first notation to consider in such a situation is a state transition diagram. In its most basic form, a state transition diagram uses a circle to denote a state and an arrow to show the possibility of a transition between two states. The arrow is labeled with the name of the event or action that causes the transition. For example, Figure 4-10 shows a system with two states, *Displaying Logon Screen* and *Displaying Welcome Screen*, where a transition will occur from the former to the latter if event *User Enters Valid userID* occurs. Figure 4-11 shows the identical requirement in natural language. For organizations that are reluctant to use models, I suggest using only natural language. For other companies, I recommend using natural language annotated with a cross-reference to a state transition diagram like the model shown in Figure 4-10.

Figure 4-10: A Trivial State Transition Diagram for Logging On.

When the system is displaying the log-on screen and the user enters a valid userID, then system shall display the welcome screen.

Figure 4-11: The Requirement Equivalent to Figure 4-10.

Two classic methods exist for capturing system outputs using state transition diagrams. The first (called a "Mealy model") is to augment the transition label with a slash ("/"), followed by the name of the desired output of the transition, as shown in Figure 4-12. The second (called a "Moore model") is to augment the name of the state with a slash, followed by the name of the output that is always created whenever the system is in that state, as shown in Figure 4-13. For most requirements problems, the latter is preferable because it tends to force requirements writers into the discipline of using only those states that can be perceived by viewpoints external to the system.

Figure 4-12: State Transition Diagram:
Output (R) Associated with a State Transition.

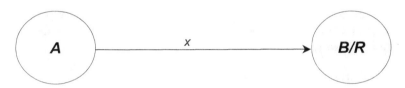

Figure 4-13: State Transition Diagram:
Output (R) Associated with a State.

For cases as simple as these, little benefit accrues from augmenting natural language with the model. However, for nontrivial applications, the reduction in ambiguity and miscommunication is considerable. For example, take a look at the requirements in Figure 4-9. In that case, the model of Figure 4-14 helps increase understandability considerably.

In 1987, David Harel made a variety of additions to state transition diagrams that made them far more useful and thus far more popular among requirements writers. The additions include notations to represent transitions based on time, coordination, and cooperation between multiple, state transition diagrams and techniques to aggregate state transition diagrams into super state transition diagrams.[6]

---

[6]Readers interested in more details concerning these statecharts are referred to either [HAR87] or Section 4.2.2.2 of [DAV93].

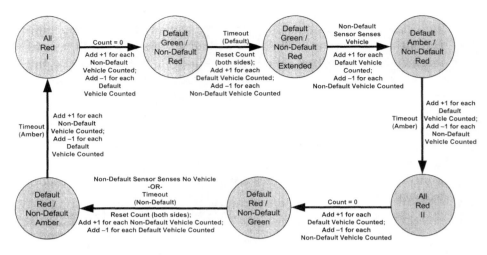

Figure 4-14: A State Transition Diagram Model for Figure 4-9.

Do not attempt to write the entire requirements document using state transition diagrams. True, you can contort such machines to do anything you desire, but as you add more and more, you make the model more difficult for the layperson to comprehend. Use this technique for only those subsets of requirements that deal exclusively with states.

Decision-Based Problems

Many applications are expected to make decisions based on multiple conditions. For example, any type of control system is expected to monitor the state of various sensors and decide whether to send commands to motors or other devices. A nuclear reactor's control system monitors reactor temperature and, when appropriate, inserts or withdraws control rods. Meanwhile, automated aircraft-landing systems monitor the state of the weather, runways, taxiways, and approaching aircraft and decide whether to grant permission to land or to demand that the pilot abort the landing.

In the above cases, the primary function of the systems is to make the appropriate decision. In many applications, decision-making is simply a small part of the overall mission. For example, an operating system must decide what to do when a user tries to print a document when no printer is currently available. Whether a decision concerns a major or minor task of a system, the correct decision-making process must be included in the requirements document. After all, the substance of any decision is clearly about satisfying a user need. However, the decision-making process is not something that designers or programmers should determine, since their expertise is not usually in the application domain. When the decisions we want the system to make have been recorded in the requirements document, they should look like what's shown in Figure 4-15, for a control system for elevator doors.

- When the elevator is between floors or is not stopped, the elevator doors shall remain closed.

- While the doors are blocked, the elevator doors shall remain open.

- While the open-door button is pressed and the doors are not already fully closed, the elevator doors shall open and remain open.

- Ten seconds after the elevator arrives and stops at a floor, or when the close-door button is pressed, the doors shall close—unless the open-door button is pressed or the doors are blocked.

Figure 4-15: The Kinds of Requirements That Necessitate Decision Models.

Although the four sentences in Figure 4-15 (a) provide us with a basic understanding of the expected behavior of the doors, (b) provide us with the ability to annotate and enumerate requirements, and (c) are easily read and understood by customers and users, we have little assurance that they are complete or unambiguous. To address this problem, construct a model of the elevator doors' behavior and cross-reference the textual requirements to the model.

The most commonly used models for recording such decisions are decision tables and decision trees. A typical decision table contains a row for each condition that could exist, and a column for each possible case, where each case represents a combination of conditions, as shown in Figure 4-16. Below each column is an entry for the correct decision, in this case, an "action." Figure 4-16 contains a column for every possible combination of three conditions (C1, C2, and C3), but in practice, "don't care's" are often used to reduce the number of columns.

Figure 4-17 captures part of the control necessary for the doors of an elevator. With seven conditions, the decision table would normally have 128 columns, but by utilizing don't cares, the table ends up having just ten.

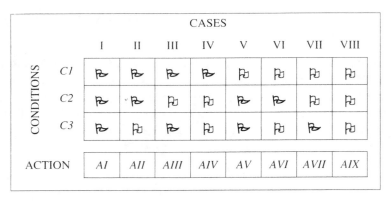

Figure 4-16: The Structure of a Decision Table (Adapted from [DAV93]).*

		CASES							
		I	II	III	IV	V	VI	VII	VIII
CONDITIONS	C1	True	True	True	True	False	False	False	False
	C2	True	True	False	False	True	True	False	False
	C3	True	False	True	False	True	False	True	False
ACTION		AI	AII	AIII	AIV	AV	AVI	AVII	AIX

Legend:
True
False

		CASES									
		I	II	III	IV	V	VI	VII	VIII	IX	X
CONDITIONS	Open Door Button Pushed	True	dc	dc	False	False	True	dc	dc	False	False
	Close Door Button Pushed	dc	dc	dc	True	dc	dc	dc	dc	True	dc
	10 secs. Elapsed Since Arrival at Floor	dc	dc	dc	dc	True	dc	dc	dc	dc	True
	Doors Fully Open	False	dc	False	dc	dc	True	dc	True	dc	dc
	Doors Fully Closed	dc	False	dc	False	False	dc	True	dc	True	True
	At Floor	True	False	True	True	True	True	False	True	True	True
	Door Blocked	dc	dc	True	False	False	dc	dc	True	False	False
ACTION		Open Door	Close Door	Open Door	Close Door	Close Door	No Action	No Action	No Action	No Action	No Action

Legend:
True
False
dc Don't Care

Figure 4-17: A Decision Table for Elevator Doors (Adapted from [DAV93]).*

*DAVIS, ALAN M., SOFTWARE REQUIREMENTS: OBJECTS, FUNCTIONS AND STATES (REVISED EDITION), 2nd Edition, © 1993. Reprinted by permission of Pearson Education, Inc., Upper Saddle River, NJ.

Decision trees capture the same kind of decision-making requirement but are pictorial rather than tabular. For example, Figure 4-18 shows a decision tree that is equivalent to the decision table shown in Figure 4-17.

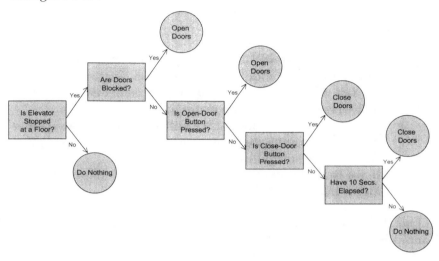

Figure 4-18: A Decision Tree for Elevator Doors.

Decision tables and trees should be included in a requirements document for a variety of reasons:

- The conditions being specified in the models are externally observable. Note: If you create a table or tree and conditions are not externally observable, then you are probably not writing requirements.
- The actions being specified by the models are externally observable. Note: If you create a table or tree and actions are not externally observable, then you are probably not writing requirements.
- The decisions captured by the table or tree are all about the application and how it will behave when viewed by the user. Therefore, the decisions should be captured by requirements writers, not programmers or designers.
- Tables and trees may be easier to read and understand than text for some people. Decision trees, especially, are easily understood by users and customers not versed in computer technology.

To guarantee maximum communication, include textual requirements, such as those in Figure 4-15, cross-referenced to models,
such as those in Figure 4-17 and Figure 4-18.

There are also reasons why decision tables and trees should be
used in conjunction with, not instead of, natural language specifications in a requirements document:

- The document will be read by and needs to be easily
  understood by a wide variety of people. There is no way to
  predict who will find textual requirements easier to read
  and who will find models easier to read.
- If we include just models, we will have no way to answer
  such basic management questions as "How many requirements are we including in the next release?"
- If we include just models, how can we perform requirements triage?

Once I isolate a part of a system that lends itself to decision
analysis, I tend to start by creating either a decision tree or a textual
description. If I find that the problem is more complex than I had
expected,[7] I revert to a decision table, which forces me to analyze
all possible cases. After I complete the table, I can often create a
much simpler decision tree (and make my text somewhat simpler),
which I include in the final requirements document.

Nonbehavioral Requirements

The nonbehavioral requirements do not deal directly with functions of the system (they are also known as nonfunctional requirements, but I find that term somewhat objectionable because it
sounds like they contribute to a nonfunctioning system). The line
between behavioral and nonbehavioral is fuzzy at best. Some
requirements are clearly behavioral:

When the user presses the button, the system shall ring the buzzer.

And some requirements are clearly nonbehavioral:

*The system shall exhibit a mean time between failures of no less
than 6 months.*

---

[7]Just about all the time!

But then there are some requirements that do not fit neatly into either category:

When the user presses the button, the system shall ring the buzzer within 2 seconds.

I am less concerned about drawing the fine line between the two categories than I am interested in helping organizations document all of the requirements that are important to their product development. So, here is a checklist of typical nonbehavioral requirements:

- response time
- capacity
- degradation
- maintainability and adaptability
- reliability
- tailorability
- portability

For any project that you undertake, you should decide which of these are critical to product success. For those that are critical, make sure you specify them somehow, somewhere. It doesn't really matter whether you choose to embed them inside otherwise behavioral requirements or specify them as independent requirements.

Following are some ideas on specifying each of the above categories:

Response time: Response time requirements are requirements for the system to *respond* to its environment within a specific time.[8] For example, how quickly is the system expected to produce a report after requested? How quickly will the system dispatch an elevator to a floor after the elevator request button has been pressed? How quickly will it launch the missile after the pilot requests the launch? When the operator asks the system to display an amber light for a duration of x seconds prior to turning a traffic light red, how precisely must the system perform that task? For example, is it acceptable to keep the amber light on for $2x$ seconds? (I think not.) Is it acceptable to keep it on for $x+1$ seconds? (I don't know.) Is it acceptable to keep it on for $x+.01$ seconds? (I think so.)

---

[8]In some systems, if the user (or the environment in general) doesn't do something to the system within a given time period, the system will take some alternative action. That is a pure behavioral requirement and will not be discussed here.

Do you want designers and programmers to make decisions concerning which of these are acceptable? No, the acceptability decision must be made by people intimately involved with the problem and its solution: the requirements team. Here are some examples of some response time specifications:

When the pilot pushes the "launch" button, the system shall launch the missile within one tenth of a second.

When a prospective elevator passenger presses the floor-based elevator request button, the system shall ensure that an elevator arrives at that floor within 2 minutes.

The system shall turn the amber light on and keep it on for the operator-programmed duration ± 1 second.

From a theoretical perspective, *every* response that a system is required to produce *must* include a response time requirement. Take the following requirement, for example:

When the user presses the button, the system shall ring the buzzer.

If a user presses the button and does not hear a buzzer, the system builders can defend themselves by saying something like, "Oh, the requirements document didn't specify how long it would take. Just wait a few more hours. I'm sure it will buzz eventually." You could spend an incredible amount of time defining response times, but my recommendation is to be *reasonable and prudent.* That goes for customers and developers.

Note that response times may be specified as a maximum time, a minimum time, an average time, within a tolerance, with a given distribution across a range, or any combination thereof. Response time is also a function of capacity and degradation.

Capacity: Just about every system will have limits on the number of real-world items it can handle. These are specified as capacity requirements. They include how many items the system can handle over its life span, how many it can handle at one time, and how many arrivals of new items it can handle per time period. For example, how many users can simultaneously ask for reports? How many reports can be produced per hour? How many elevator request button presses can it accommodate per hour? In the one-lane bridge problem, will the system fail if vehicles travel too fast or too slow? You do not want designers and programmers to make decisions concerning the acceptable capacity limits. This decision must be made by members of the requirements team, as they are intimately involved with the problem and its solution. Here are some examples:

The system shall be capable of launching up to 12 missile volleys (where a volley can contain as few as one and as many as four missiles) per 5 minutes.

The elevator system shall handle up to 100 requests for elevator service per hour.

Note that there is an implied "without degradation of the specified response times" at the end of every capacity requirement.

Degradation: Ironically, system builders have very little control over the behavior of the system's environment. If the system is supposed to handle up to x widgets per hour, what should the system do if $x+1$ arrive? An irresponsible development organization would respond with "That's not our problem. The system is only required to meet requirements, and requirements clearly state that no more than x widgets will arrive." A responsible requirements team would make those decisions at requirements time, documenting them with what are typically called "degradation requirements." Degradation requirements define what the system is expected to do when the capacity requirements are violated. Here are two examples:

When more than 12 missile volleys are requested per 5 minutes, the system's response time for all missile-launch requests shall degrade in accordance with this schedule:

Volleys	Degradation
13	10%
14	25%
15	50%
16	80%
17	100%
>17	Unpredictable

All requests for elevator service after the first 100 in any 60-minute period shall be ignored.

Maintainability and adaptability: Maintainability is the ease with which the system can undergo *perfective* and *corrective* maintenance; adaptability is the ease with which the system can undergo *adaptive* maintenance.[9] One could argue that a requirement defining maintainability or adaptability is less about the external behavior of the system and more about its internal structure (and thus perhaps not even an acceptable requirement). On the other hand, if a system is not maintainable, its performance over a period of time is likely to degenerate, and that degeneration will be externally observable. The real motivation for including maintainability and adaptability in the requirements document is to ensure that the development team understands how important these requirements are to customers.

Every software system undergoes a series of enhancements over a period of time (usually between one and twenty years), after which the system accrues too much entropy and must be rebuilt from scratch. The factors that determine whether it survives one year or twenty include: (a) the inherent flexibility of the architecture, (b) the rate of changes to requirements, (c) the type of changes made to the requirements and how they relate to the architectural decisions made during initial construction, and (d) luck.

It is impossible for any group of people, including development and customers, to predict the myriad directions in which requirements will evolve. Some architectures are inherently more adaptable than others, but it is impossible to design and build a system so that any enhancement will be easy. If there were such an approach to design, the costs of construction (or operation) would be prohibitively high.

Personally, I prefer not to include specific maintainability or adaptability requirements in my requirements documents. When I am compelled to do so by customers, I construct the best statements of such requirements as I can, but to me they still seem ridiculously ambiguous.

I have found through experience that the best way to help the development team understand what types of changes are likely to occur in the future is to include in the requirements document all those requirements that have been identified but not included in

---

[9]Perfective maintenance improves the system's performance and/or efficiency. Corrective maintenance repairs errors, fixing the system if it fails to meet its requirements. Adaptive maintenance changes the system to accommodate new or changing requirements.

the current release. At the worst, the development team will get a flavor for the kinds of likely changes. But at the best, the development team can include software hooks in the appropriate places.[10]

Reliability: Reliability is the degree to which the system behaves in a user-acceptable manner. In other words, a reliable system is one that meets its requirements all the time. Software does not spontaneously fail as the result of wearing out, like its sibling technology, hardware. If a software system fails to meet a requirement a year after it was deployed, then one of the following is true:

a. The system never met that requirement, and the system test failed to uncover that fact.
b. The development and test teams interpreted the requirement differently than users.
c. Sometime during that year, a maintainer (while trying to fix another defect or add some new functionality) introduced a defect that made the previously correct software no longer satisfy the requirement.

What can we do during the requirements specification activity to prevent or at least lower the likelihood of these three failures?

- In situation *a,* the correct requirement has already been written and included. Nothing can be done to requirements to make them better. The flaw is in the test planning and/or test execution stages.
- In situation *b,* something can be done. The answer is to work harder to remove ambiguity from critical requirements. The less ambiguous the requirement, the less likely it is to be misunderstood.
- In situation *c,* nothing can be done at requirements time to lower the likelihood of this unfortunate event. The solution lies in more rigorous regression testing.

So, my conclusion is that reliability requirements have a great deal of importance when one is writing a hardware requirements document or a system requirements document, but not so much when writing a software requirements document. Another possibility would be to state reliability in these terms:

---

[10] "Hooks" are slight changes to software that facilitate making later changes.

Requirement Z: 93 percent of the time, the system shall perform requirement A through Y correctly.

But requirements A through Y already say the system must do it correctly 100 percent of the time!

Tailorability: Tailorability is the degree to which users can modify the system's behavior. I consider tailorability requirements *functional* requirements. For example, requirement 1 in Figure 4-9 defines the tailorability of the system—in this case, tailoring the timing of each traffic signal.

Portability: Portability is the ease with which the system can be moved from one host environment to another (hardware, operating system, communications protocol, and so on). As in the case of adaptability, nobody can predict what the future will bring. In this case, nobody can know what types of hosts will exist in the future. And for that reason, it is impossible for any system to be universally portable. Traditionally, standardization efforts for programming languages have given the industry its best hope of achieving portability. However, some of the more recent standards developed by computer manufacturers and software producers have moved us one step closer to being more portable in the short term. For example, the Java, .NET, and C++ communities have all adopted standards that will increase their users' ability to port applications to other platforms.

I do not know how to specify a portability requirement that is externally observable at the time of product delivery. Statements such as the following just don't cut it:

The system shall be able to be ported to environments x, y, and z with a minimum of three person-months of effort.

The best advice I have for readers who need to specify portability requirements is to include a requirement like

The system shall be written for the .NET environment.

Or,

The system shall be written in Java.

These are not valid requirements by the official definition, but they accomplish what we want requirements to accomplish. More importantly, there are no losers, only winners.

User Interface

Most applications offer humans the ability to interact with the system. In fact, the only applications that do not are those termed "deeply embedded." If stakeholders have differing opinions about what the interface should look like, the time to find out is now, not upon product delivery. Many development organizations refuse to include detailed user interface requirements in their requirements documents because they claim that (a) their creativity will be stifled by defining user interfaces "too early"; (b) customers do not understand optimality in user interface definition, so they should not be part of the definition process; and (c) user interface definition is part of design, not requirements.

Yet these claims are faulty. The purpose of building an application is not to exercise the creativity of designers; it is to satisfy a customer need. Optimality is *nice*, but customer satisfaction is *essential*. And one way to increase the likelihood of customer satisfaction is to have no surprises. Avoiding surprises depends on having customer involvement from the beginning. If the designers really have some innovative idea for the look and feel of the application, they should discuss it thoroughly with customers during the requirements definition process. If they cannot convince the customers, then innovation will have to take a backseat to customer satisfaction. And if they do convince the customers, they should document the agreement in the requirements document. If the designers insist that they *will* think of a great new look and feel eventually, but not just yet, then go and find some new designers!

A human interface can be specified in a variety of ways. At the most basic yet most difficult level, you can attempt to enumerate in sentences all the attributes of the user interface, as done below:

A. *The system shall display all error messages to the user in red, in a pop-up box in the center of the screen.*

B. *The system shall provide the user with at least two methods of performing every function: at least one that uses a mouse, and at least one that does not require the use of a mouse.*

C. *All menus shall be provided using the Microsoft File-Edit-View-Insert standard.*

D. *The system shall not allow users to alter the fixed sizes for any windows.*

E. *The system shall display all ocean maps using four colors: color #1 for the water, color #2 for land, color #3 for friendly surface ships, and color #4 for enemy surface ships.*

F. *The system shall allow the user to change any of the four ocean map colors, but they shall default to light blue, brown, dark blue, and red, respectively.*

Writing specifications is so difficult because it is much easier to show a picture of something than to describe every aspect of it.

Another way to specify user interfaces is to refer to any of the numerous user interface standards created by major software vendors, such as

The system shall conform to the user interface requirements set forth in The Windows Interface Guidelines for Software Design *(Redmond, Wash.: Microsoft Press, 1995).*

or

The system shall conform to the user interface requirements set forth in Macintosh Human Interface Guidelines *(Menlo Park, Calif.: Addison-Wesley, 1992).*

Yet another way to record user interface requirements is to provide a user interface prototype as part of the document. Inclusion of a prototype is a double-edged sword. On one hand, users can easily see the look and feel. On the other hand, a prototype never includes everything that the final system will include, and on occasion, includes something that the final system will not possess. For example,

- Will the final system's screen layout be exactly the same as the prototype? If so, what does "exactly the same" mean? Down to the pixel? If not, to what extent will they differ?
- Will the final system's response times be similar to the prototype's?
- Will the error messages, menu items, commands, and reports produced by the final system be identical to those in the prototype (in wording, font, layout, and location)?

- When the prototype displays the words "display map here," will the final system display those words as well? Or will it actually display a real map?

You may think that some of the above issues are silly. However, they all occurred in real life, and in all four cases, I saw disappointed customers whose expectations did not align with development's plans. Don't get me wrong; I am a huge fan of prototyping. Just make sure that everyone's expectations are aligned and that you have the user interface requirements specified in text as well as in the prototype.

You can also define user interface requirements by including a few sample screen shots, a few sample command lines, and a few sample reports to convey the general look and feel of the application. This works when stakeholders have worked together well in the past and trust each other.

Another way to convey user interface requirements is to include a complete set of screens, reports, commands, error messages, and so on as an appendix in the requirements document. This is the safest way to define such requirements while eliminating customer surprises. But it is also quite time-consuming. If this route is taken, I recommend including a map, like the one in Figure 4-19, that shows how the displays relate to each other.

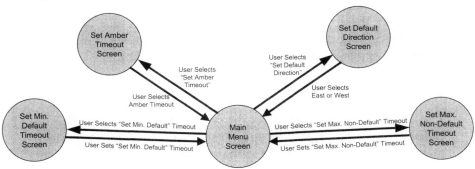

Figure 4-19: User Interface Map.

Hardware Interface

Projects building applications that operate within special-purpose hardware often run into problems with the hardware-software interface. One part of the solution is to write detailed requirements for that interface. Most such system developments proceed from hardware definition to software definition. In that case, the software requirements document should include descriptions of all the protocols, register locations, control techniques, and monitoring techniques. You may define these as software requirements—after all, the software is required to operate the hardware, using these mechanisms. Or you may include these descriptions in appendices to the requirements document. If the hardware and software are being defined simultaneously, hardware definers will need to make clear what can be done, and software definers will need to make clear what they need the hardware to do. The resulting discussions should enable interfaces to be defined precisely, and each party should be able to include details in its own requirements document. In systems where software is sensing events and/or controlling hardware in the real world, as in the case of the one-lane bridge control system described earlier, a picture can be extremely valuable. For example, see how Figure 4-2 helps readers better understand requirements 2, 5, and 6 of Figure 4-9, and how Figure 4-3 helps readers better understand requirements 3 through 6 of Figure 4-9.

Requirements for Reports

Almost all applications have to produce reports. If the reports are all straightforward and little controversy surrounds them, then you can probably get by with just a few natural language requirements that define the general characteristics of the reports. You may want to augment these with one or two samples. However, if the reports risk dissatisfying customers, it's best to include copies of all sample reports as appendices to the requirements document.

THE RESULT OF SPECIFICATION

The activity of specifying requirements results in a document called either a requirements specification or a requirements document. This document should contain a list of all the requirements that stakeholders have agreed to include in the product. To indicate which of the requirements are to be included in the next release, the document is either pruned of excluded ones or annotated according to intended release.

Appendix B shows the final set of requirements for the one-lane bridge problem. In addition to indicating which requirements are to be included in which release, it demonstrates the following:

- Requirements that describe relatively complex situations in which miscommunication could cause a problem are augmented with more formal models. See Models A through H in Appendix B. Requirements are always cross-referenced to models that clarify them.
- Requirements are organized hierarchically. The hierarchy is created as a natural result of (1) earlier elicitation and triage processes, and (2) discussions that ensue as a result of reaching agreement on the exact wording of requirements. In most cases, a resolution is reached by refining the subject requirement into sub-requirements. This refinement process is retained in the final document as a hierarchy. In the list of requirements appearing in Appendix B, note that almost all of the requirements have been refined beyond the levels previously shown.
- The example has been expanded to include nonbehavioral requirements.

Do not expect requirements to be complete, either now or in the future. As described in [DAV04a],

> *The real customer's real needs are in constant flux. Marketing departments know this. Perhaps the reason that developers fail to recognize this is that we [usually describe] requirements activities as a phase in a process model. In reality, it is ongoing, as shown in [Figure 4-20]. Regardless of whether software is being constructed in one large release (as shown in the figure) or in a series of iterations (where the figure represents just one iteration), an organization cannot afford to ever stop eliciting requirements from the customers. This is not an option. Customers' needs change. Our perceptions of their needs change. The problems that customers face are changing. We cannot stop the hands of time. Burying our heads in the sands dooms us to failure. If we ignore the changes we will end up building a useless system. And building a useless system is worse than building no system at all.*
>
> *Let's differentiate for a minute between the customers' actual needs and the documented requirements. As shown in [Figure 4-21], the needs are in constant flux. If we use our original knowledge of those needs to document the requirements at the beginning of the project, and do not allow them to change, we guar-*

antee that the as-built product will fail to satisfy the customers' current needs. The fact that it satisfies the as-documented requirements is a source of satisfaction for some, especially those driven by the "letter of the law" rather than the "spirit of the law." After all, you cannot be sued (at least not successfully) by customers if you meet the as-documented requirements and the contract stipulates that you must do so. However, customers are likely to be more excited with a system that meets their needs than one that prevents them from suing the development group. So what do we do?

If we allow the documented requirements to change every time the needs change, as shown in [Figure 4-22], we have anarchy, and the product will never be completed, let alone on time. So neither extreme is useful. The right answer is moderation, understanding, mutual respect, and common sense. As a guide, Young [YOU01] suggests that requirements change [also called churn] be limited to less than 1/2% per month (or 6% per year).*

Ed Yourdon [YOU00] suggests that churn be limited to 10 percent per year.

When a requirements document is "completed" (in other words, ready for sign-off), it is often signed off on by representatives of management, development, marketing, the customer, and finance. However, I question what it means to simply sign on a page designated the "signature page." I suspect that it means "we the undersigned hereby certify that we have signed this document." What good is this? Instead, I advocate that the parties sign a page with an agreement similar to that shown in Figure 4-23. The objective of this agreement is to capture the spirit under which the document is being signed, not to establish a legally binding contract. Such an agreement works for internal developments as well as it does for external development. The major points of the agreement are as follows:

- Nobody believes that the documented requirements are perfect. So, let us not make any claims to the contrary. Let's agree that they represent a compromise among disparate needs.
- We all agree at the time of signature that the requirements as stated are compatible with the desired schedule and budget.

---

*Alan Davis, "Requirements Are But a Snapshot in Time," *Great Software Debates* (Los Alamitos, Calif.: Wiley–IEEE Computer Society Press, 2004), p. 180. © 2004 IEEE. Used by permission.

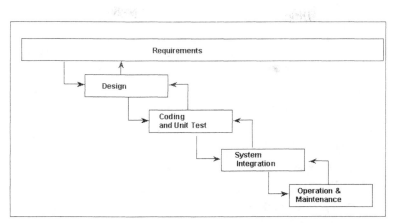

Figure 4-20: Requirements Activities Are Ongoing (from [DAV04a]).*

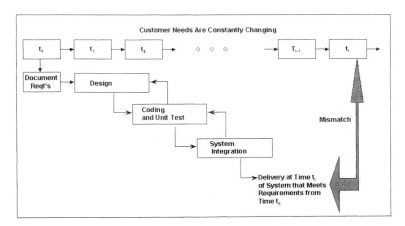

Figure 4-21: Requirements Mismatch (from [DAV04a]).*

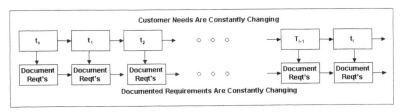

*Figure 4-22: We Cannot Change Requirements
Every Time Needs Change (from [DAV04a]).**

---

*Alan Davis, "Requirements Are But a Snapshot in Time," *Great Software Debates*
(Los Alamitos, Calif.: Wiley–IEEE Computer Society Press, 2004), pp. 180, 181.
© 2004 IEEE. Used by permission.

> **All: We agree that the following list of requirements is the best set of requirements we can now agree to, and it represents the best balance between requirements, schedule, and budget.**
>
> **Marketing (or Customer, or Customer Rep): I agree to not change the requirements prior to product delivery.**
>
> **Development: I agree to deliver this set of requirements with sufficient quality on this date: _____.**
>
> **Source of Financing: I agree to not reduce the total funding of this project below _____.**
>
> **All: We agree to work together to arrive at a new optimal solution in the event that any of us is forced to violate the above clauses.**

Figure 4-23: A Sample Requirements Agreement.

- Requirements are likely to change as we continue to learn more about the customers and the market. And when requirements change, the schedule and resources applied to the project must change accordingly. There is no free lunch.
- If a market condition changes, necessitating a compression of the schedule, then some requirements will need to be removed.
- If resources applied to the project diminish (if a key contributor is pulled off the project to assist in another effort, for example), then some requirements will need to be removed or the delivery date will need to be extended. It is also a good idea to document the development manager's expectation of what a person-month means. Does it mean 174 hours of labor per month? 167? 83?

Much will be learned from individual team members' refusal to sign this document. For example,

- If development refuses to sign it, it becomes clear to everybody on the team that the development manager believes the current schedule is not feasible. In that case, the schedule will *not* be achieved—whether or not it is signed and whether or not it is actually reasonable. This will, of course, result in project failure, and everybody on the team will lose. It is better to know this at the beginning of the project than toward the end.

- If marketing (or the customer) refuses to sign the agreement, it is likely trying to reserve the right to append requirements later without any slippage in schedule or addition of resources. This is blatantly unfair and also dooms the project to failure. Once again, it is better to know this up front.
- If the source of financing (who may also be the customer, in the case of custom development) refuses to sign the agreement, he or she is likely trying to reserve the right to constrict funding without relaxation of any other project variables. Once again, this is bad news.

THE SECRETS OF *JUST ENOUGH* SPECIFICATION

If you pay too little attention to requirements specification, you run the risk of building the wrong system—one based on incomplete and ambiguous requirements. If you spend too much time on specification, you run the risk of never getting around to building the system at all. The secrets of accomplishing *just enough* requirements specification are the following:

- Never lose sight of your goal: to specify the desired behavior of a system, in sufficient detail that system developers, marketing, customers, users, and management are closely aligned in their interpretation.
- Remember that most customers know their own application domain well, but are not especially computer-savvy. Therefore, when you select languages or notations, be sure to select ones that *they* can comprehend easily.
- All stakeholders will understand natural language. It therefore must be the default language for specification.
- Construct models for those parts of the system where natural language introduces intolerable risk. Cross-reference the natural language requirements with the models.
- Use the right model for the right job. Don't follow the advice of requirements pundits who claim that one size fits all. No single notation can be optimal for your job. A notation that attempts to represent everything would be too unwieldy for any customer to comprehend.

- The customer wants his or her problem solved. He or she does not want to take a course on understanding some computer notation.
- Avoiding specification altogether will significantly lengthen the overall development time, not reduce it. The purpose of building systems is to satisfy customer needs, not to satisfy developer desires.
- Include a glossary of terms used in the document. Much of this will be inherited from the glossary produced during elicitation.
- You may want to create an auxiliary list of "bonus" requirements that should be worked on only if all other requirements have been met within budget and schedule. These bonus requirements would likely contain the next most important candidate requirements that did not make the triage cut and the "favorites" of the development team. The items on this list may not be addressed until all other requirements are satisfied to a level demanded by all parties. This list is included for two reasons: It is nice to sometimes deliver more than is expected (I've heard this called "promise a little, deliver a lot"), and developers may be more motivated to do the work if they know their reward is a chance to work on requirements that they think are fun and/or important.
- Stakeholders have the right to change their mind. You may not like this, but it is a fact. The trick is to look at each suggested change as an opportunity, not a threat.

FIVE

Requirements Change

Regardless of how much effort is expended gathering and analyzing requirements, they will still change [LUT93, DAV04a]. Rather than hating the change, embrace it, control it, and make it work for you. Unfortunately, "much of classical engineering literature is based on 'the assumption of fixed requirements,' which leads to the misconception that managers should have unchanging requirements before starting any project" [LAM99].

Here are some of the reasons that requirements *will* change after they are agreed to and baselined:

- A stakeholder will be reviewing the requirements document, and that will trigger the desire for something new.
- A stakeholder will be thinking about what the system will be like to use, and that will trigger something new.
- A stakeholder will be playing with a prototype, and that will trigger something new.
- The situation in which the system is going to be used changes. There may be new types of users, more users, new competitive insight, new business threats, and so on.
- A customer will be using the current version of the system and will think of more things he or she would like it to do.

163

According to a study by Manny Lehman [LEH91], the more requirements you give to customers, the more new requirements they will think of. We can extend this theory to posit that the more requirements customers think of, the more they'll want, and the more they read about, the more they'll want, and the more they discuss, the more they'll want. In general, the spontaneous creation of new requirements is a good sign, not a bad one. It indicates that somebody out there cares and that somebody out there wants to use (or buy) the system. If nobody thinks of new requirements, it is likely that nobody will use the system once it is complete.

So, the real issue is not how to control the flow of new requirements. The real issue is what to do with them when they arrive.

WHERE DO CHANGES COME FROM?

Changes to requirements can come from a variety of sources:

- *Marketing:* the primary source of new requirements for companies selling their products externally. After all, marketing's primary job is to determine the needs of current and potential markets.
- *Analysts:* the primary source of new requirements for companies that build products for internal use. After all, analysts' primary job is to determine the needs of customers and translate them into requirements that the development organization can understand.
- *Sales:* As sales personnel repeatedly attempt to sell the company's products, they will report on patterns they observe. Often called a "loss report," this report describes the reasons behind any failure to convert a serious customer lead into a positive purchase decision. Studying this report enables sales people to alter their sales approaches, recommend to marketing that the product be repositioned, and suggest changes to the product's capabilities to reduce lost sales. It is this third item that makes sales departments so good at suggesting new requirements.
- *Customers and users:* For companies that sell products externally, customers and users generally report their needs to a sales or marketing person, who translates those needs into

requirements in the format expected by the company. For companies that use their products internally, users generally report their needs to the analysts. Regardless of the route, the input from customers and users is not to be treated lightly. They are the most important source of new requirements. Statements such as, "We know our customers' needs better than our customers do," often lead to a company's death. The fact is, you might really know their needs better, but the requirements they suggest are still *requirements*—until you can help them discover alternatives, that is.

- *Developers:* As development personnel continue to make changes to the software, they will regularly conceive of other tasks that the software could accomplish. The trick for managers is to give developers incentives to report those suggestions for the next CCB meeting instead of simply implementing them without authorization.

How to Keep Track of Requested Changes

If the original requirements have been stored in a database, the requested changes should be stored in the same database or in an additional table within the database. If that isn't possible, at least store them in a database that uses the same format. This will make it easy to incorporate new requirements into the existing database of accepted requirements.

When a new requirement appears (or a requested change to an existing requirement), it should be annotated the same way that all earlier requirements were annotated: with an estimate of how much effort will be required to satisfy it (from development) and an indication of how important the requirement is relative to all other requirements. This will enable the CCB to make informed decisions concerning the proper adjudication of the requested changes.

Choices for Handling the Changes

Each suggested change (or set of changes) will undergo careful analysis in order to determine the best course of action. Here are some possible courses of action, some quite conservative and some quite radical. For each of the following examples, assume that Release 2.0 is already in the hands of customers, that Release 3.0 is currently in the development process, and that the subsequent scheduled release is 4.0:

- *Accept the change, incorporate it into Release 3.0, and keep the schedule and budget as is:* This is by far the most common adjudication. Unfortunately, it is also extremely dangerous and should only be attempted after careful analysis of the likelihood of success. As mentioned in Chapter 3, you must analyze the probability of project success before the suggested changes and contrast that with the probability of success after the suggested changes. If the probability decreases insignificantly, say from 83 percent to 81 percent, as shown in Figure 5-1 and Figure 5-2, then perhaps this is the correct route to take. If the probability plunges, say from 83 percent to 47 percent, as shown in Figure 5-1 and Figure 5-3, then this route is guaranteed to produce project failure: delivery of the product later than expected and likely over budget, as well.

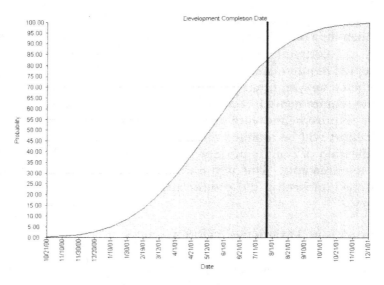

Figure 5-1: Before a Change, 83 Percent Chance of Success.

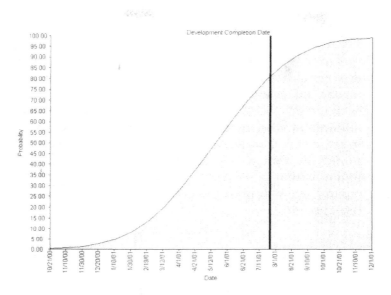

Figure 5-2: After a Change, 81 Percent Chance of Success.

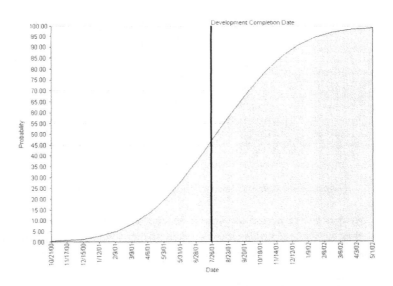

Figure 5-3: After a Change, 47 Percent Chance of Success.

- *Accept the change, incorporate it into Release 3.0, and delay the delivery of the release:* After determining that making the suggested requirements changes will introduce too high a risk of delivering the product late, one alternative is to extend the schedule. In Figure 5-4, we have taken the scenario from Figure 5-3 and simply extended the planned delivery date from July 25 to October 30, in order to accommodate the changed requirements. This route will usually be acceptable to the development group, but it should be followed only when it makes sense for the business overall. In any case, this route will also increase the total cost of the project (in human resources). So, if there are currently seven developers and we extend the schedule by three months, we will need to add at least 21 person-months to the schedule.

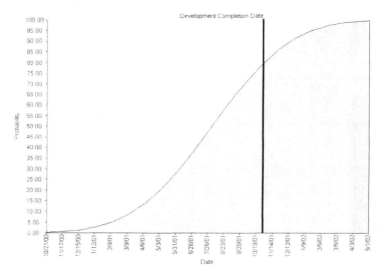

Figure 5-4: After a Change, Extend the Delivery Date.

- *Accept the change and plan to incorporate it into Release 4.0 so that we do not jeopardize the delivery date for 3.0:* If none of the above choices are acceptable, then this becomes the next best alternative. Instead of worrying about the effects on the current release, just announce that you will address the changes in the next full release.
- *Accept the change, create a new point release called 3.1, and plan to incorporate it into that release:* This is actually identical to the previous choice. The only difference is that we are giving the next release a name that is more "friendly" to the

situation (3.1 instead of 4.0). Once this decision is made, you will need to also decide which other features of 3.0 can be delayed to 3.1 and which of the planned 4.0 release requirements should be accelerated to the 3.1 release. Although this is often a best alternative, be a bit careful. There are no free rides. You will experience considerably more overhead by adding a completely new release to your plans. And in any case, make sure you apply cumulative probability graphs, like the one in Figure 5-1, to the analysis of Releases 3.0, 3.1, and 4.0.

- *Accept the change and plan to incorporate it into an unspecified future release (to be determined at the next big triage meeting):* If a requirements change to the current release makes it impossible to meet the delivery date, and the delivery date cannot be extended, you might try this: Simply accept the requirements and address them at the next planning meeting. This works most effectively when the suggested requirements change is of medium to low importance.

- *Reject the change:* If the requirement change is clearly out of scope, just reject it. Of course, make sure you fully understand the business and its politics beforehand. Unhappy customers usually mean an unsuccessful company, layoffs, and so on.

- *Accept the change, incorporate it into Release 3.0, delete less important requirements planned for inclusion in the release, and keep the schedule and budget as is:* This is not a bad alternative. The reason I waited until now to mention it is that many organizations try to do this fairly late in the development life cycle. Deleting a requirement estimated at 40 person-hours of effort to compensate for the addition of a new requirement also estimated at 40 person-hours of effort only works if none of those 40 person-hours have been spent yet! If half have already been used, you will only save 20 person-hours while adding 40, for a net increase in effort (and time). Also, be aware that the implementation of some requirements demands specific types of development talent. Just because you remove 40 person-hours of effort and add another 40 person-hours of effort does not mean you have broken even. If the personnel needed for the new requirement is unavailable, the project is once again doomed.

- *Accept the change, incorporate it into Release 3.0, and add more resources to the development project so that the schedule can remain as is:* When the previous choices are unacceptable, many managers will suggest adding more people to the project in the hope that doing so will enable the project to get completed on schedule. I have never seen this work, and I caution you against attempting it (see [BRO95]).
- *Cancel the current development project and start again from scratch:* Sometimes, the new requirements that surface are so drastic that the old requirements are no longer of any value. In such cases, do not throw good money after bad. Just start all over again.

THE CCB MEETING

The change control board is generally considered part of the process of configuration management (CM). Configuration management is the management of any kind of change that occurs during the life of software. For our purposes, we are only interested in the CCB's role in handling suggested changes to requirements.

The CCB meets on a regular basis, at a rate proportional to the influx of new or changing requirements. For highly volatile environments, the CCB may meet weekly, or even biweekly. For stable environments, it may just meet annually.

The purpose of the CCB is to serve as a decision-making authority for the adjudication of all pending suggested changes to the requirements. To do its job fairly, the CCB needs to include at least the following representatives:

- *Development:* Only the development organization can commit to whether or not it has sufficient or appropriate resources to address a requirement change. Only development can agree to accept more work with no increase in schedule or resources. Only development can agree to the amount of resources or time it needs in order to satisfy additional requirements.
- *Marketing (and/or customers):* Only customers or customer representatives can decide how important it is to include a new requirement or to slip a delivery date. Only they can

establish relative priorities among requirements vying for the same resources.

- *Finance (or management):* Included in the meeting must be somebody authorized to commit additional resources to a new task.
- *Project management:* Usually project managers are the only individuals who can see the really big picture and determine if the project is heading in an appropriate direction.

THE SECRETS OF *JUST ENOUGH* CHANGE

In summary, changes made to requirements after baselining are extremely common. You cannot stem their flow by spending more time on requirements, because real needs are changing; it is not simply that we did not think of them all up front. You cannot stem the flow of changes by deciding to satisfy "all" the known requirements up front—the more requirements you attempt to satisfy, the more requirements changes will arise.

In short, learn how to manage the changes to requirements via the procedures described in this chapter and by building architectures that are more resilient to change.

To perform requirements change management in a *just enough* manner, remember the following:

- Changes to requirements are good, not bad.
- Do not try to retard the flow of requirements change requests.
- Learn to manage the flow of requirements change.
- Meet regularly to decide intelligently which requirements will or will not move into the next software release.
- If you accept requirements changes at a rate greater than 10 percent, you will likely fail.

SIX

Summary

In closing, I need to remind you one more time that

Requirements management is a means *to an end; it is not a goal.*

The goal is to build (or acquire) a system that solves some real problem or leverages some real business opportunity. There is no shortage of ways that we can spend enormous amounts of our time performing requirements management. We need to develop the discipline of avoiding such quagmires. On the other hand, the solution is not the extreme of eliminating requirements management—that dooms us to guaranteed project failure.

Having happy customers and users is the primary indication of a successful product-development project. To increase our chances of creating happy customers, we must

- understand the customers' and users' view of their problems and opportunities
- address only the problems and opportunities that we have time and resources for
- record our understandings so that all parties understand up front what to expect at the end
- remain flexible as customer and user needs evolve

I have applied the terms elicitation, triage, requirements specification, and requirements change management to the activities that contribute to these four oaths. In the sections that follow, I list some of the tricks I've found useful in performing each of these activities in a *just enough* manner.

REQUIREMENTS ELICITATION

The tricks to performing *elicitation* without consuming enormous resources—while still reducing enough of the risk—are as follows (see Chapter 2 for details):

- Never lose sight of your goal: to understand enough of the problem to proceed with minimal risk.
- Never think you understand the problem better than the customer. It is no coincidence that only those with limited experience think this! It is only after you have been burned enough times taking this obviously bad path that you realize just how stupid it is. The fact that more than half the systems we build fail to meet stakeholder needs is *not* going to improve through not trying to understand those needs. If you believe that you know the requirements better than the customer, you are part of the problem, not the solution.
- Never assume that one stakeholder can speak for all stakeholders.
- Maintain a glossary of terms.
- Realize that avoiding elicitation altogether will significantly lengthen the overall development time, not reduce it.
- Prepare for change. The more the stakeholders discuss, the more they will want. Don't solve this "problem" by cutting off the stakeholder. An involved stakeholder is a happy stakeholder.
- Accept that stakeholders have the right to change their mind. You may not like this, but it is a fact. The trick is to look at every suggested change as an opportunity, not a threat. Involve the stakeholders in creating new requirements. Involve them in the decision process to include or exclude new requirements in the next release.
- Prepare for active, explicit, and overt triage.

REQUIREMENTS TRIAGE

The tricks to performing *triage* without consuming enormous resources—while still reducing enough of the risk—are as follows (see Chapter 3 for details):

- Learn to accept that there is no such thing as a perfect solution to the triage dilemma. Compromise is necessary.
- Always annotate your candidate requirements with a relative priority and an estimated cost.
- Record interdependencies between requirements.
- Plan more than one release at a time.
- Plan to replan before each new release.
- If the voices that cry "Add more functionality!" are allowed to overcome the voices of moderation, late delivery is guaranteed.
- If the voices that cry "We can't implement that much functionality!" are allowed to overcome the voices of moderation, a weak product is guaranteed.
- Never lose sight of your goal: to select a subset of all desired requirements so that the product *can* be delivered on time and within budget.
- Triage participants must see themselves as a team trying to solve a business problem, not as separate camps trying to win their own way.
- Development should avoid making absolute statements such as, "We cannot build the system by the delivery date if you add that requirement." Instead, make statements such as, "By adding that requirement, our likelihood of delivering on time reduces from 73 percent to 27 percent." This helps create the environment of teamwork since *nobody* on the team wants to deliver the product late.
- Marketing (and customers) should avoid making absolute statements such as, "We cannot sell (or use) the system if that requirement is excluded." Instead, make statements such as, "By removing that requirement, our expected revenues will be reduced from $20M to $11M." This helps create an environment of teamwork since *nobody* on the team wants to hurt the company's revenues.

- Agreeing to a set of requirements that are impossible to satisfy in the given time constraints guarantees that the company will fail. Why would anybody send a company down such a path?
- Avoiding explicit triage altogether means that triage issues will be addressed through intimidation and politics that will doom the project to failure.
- Prioritization requires flexibility. A requirement that is not important today may become critical tomorrow, and vice versa. Be flexible.

REQUIREMENTS SPECIFICATION

The tricks to performing *requirements specification* without consuming enormous resources—while still reducing enough of the risk—are as follows (see Chapter 4 for details):

- Never lose sight of your goal: to specify the desired behavior of a system, in sufficient detail that system developers, marketing, customers, users, and management are closely aligned in their interpretation.
- Remember that most customers know their own application domain well, but are not especially computer-savvy. Therefore, when you select languages or notations, be sure to select ones that *they* can comprehend easily.
- All stakeholders will understand natural language. It therefore must be the default language for specification.
- Construct models for those parts of the system where natural language introduces intolerable risk. Cross-reference the natural language requirements with the models.
- Use the right model for the right job. Don't follow the advice of requirements pundits who claim that one size fits all. No single notation can be optimal for your job. A notation that attempts to represent everything would be too unwieldy for any customer to comprehend.
- Customers want their problems solved. They do not want to take a course on understanding some computer notation.
- Avoiding specification altogether will significantly lengthen the overall development time, not reduce it. The purpose of building systems is to satisfy customer needs, not to satisfy developer desires.

- Include a glossary of terms used in the document. Much of this will be inherited from the glossary produced during elicitation.
- You may want to create an auxiliary list of "bonus" requirements that should be worked on only if all other requirements have been met within budget and schedule. These bonus requirements would likely contain the next most important candidate requirements that did not make the triage cut and the "favorites" of the development team. The items on this list may not be addressed until all other requirements are satisfied to a level demanded by all parties. This list is included for two reasons: It is nice to sometimes deliver more than is expected (I've heard this called "promise a little, deliver a lot") and developers may be more motivated to do the work if they know their reward is a chance to work on requirements that they think are fun and/or important.
- Stakeholders have the right to change their mind. You may not like this, but it is a fact. The trick is to look at each suggested change as an opportunity, not a threat.

REQUIREMENTS CHANGE MANAGEMENT

The tricks to performing *requirements change management* without consuming enormous resources—while still reducing enough of the risk—are as follows (see Chapter 5 for more details):

- Changes to requirements are good, not bad.
- Do not try to retard the flow of requirements changes.
- Learn to manage the flow of requirements change.
- Meet regularly to decide intelligently which requirements will or will not move into the next software release.
- Remember that if you accept requirements changes at a rate greater than 10 percent per year, you will likely fail.

You have the power to make requirements management help you succeed, but you also have the power to let it bring you to your knees. Choose wisely.

APPENDIX A

Quick Recipes

If you just opened this book and decided to read this section first, I need to warn you: I have included these so-called quick recipes for the professional who has already read and understood the body of this book. Following these quick recipes without an understanding of what you are doing or why you are doing it can lead to bad results and potentially waste millions in an effort to save a few dollars. Please, read the book first, then use these recipes to your advantage.

This chapter contains instructions on how to easily and quickly perform a few of the tasks needed during requirements management. The following recipes are included:

- Brainstorm
- Decide What Is or What Isn't a Requirement
- Decide What to Build
- Produce a Requirements Document
- Assess the Quality of a Requirements Document
- Baseline the Requirements
- Ensure That Everybody Knows the Requirements
- Handle New Requirements After Baselining
- Handle Multiple Customers

BRAINSTORM

Brainstorming is a process of gathering together all the people who have a stake in the success of a product's development, for the purpose of eliciting and recording their needs and concerns. In this recipe, we present one way to gather and prioritize requirements.

Step 1: Identify the Right People. A key component of the long-term success of brainstorming is for the people present during the session to truly represent the most significant stakeholders. If you are responding to the needs expressed by a single customer (whether internal or external to your company), include the key spokespeople for that customer. If you have multiple customers, include key representatives from all customer classes. (If the politics of the situation make it impossible for all of the customer representatives to be present in one room, do not use this recipe.) Try to include

- customers (the people responsible for *buying* the product)
- users (the people who will actually be using the system)
- secondary users (the people who will use the information created by the system)

Other stakeholders to consider include

- your marketing organization (if you are selling the product externally)
- system designers (they may have requirements ideas that could reduce costs, increase long-term maintainability, and so on)
- system testers (they may have ideas that could increase the likelihood that the eventual list of requirements will actually be used as the basis for a system test)
- trainers and manual writers (they know what the system should do to minimize the effort required to train new users)

The actual participants will vary from company to company and from situation to situation. If you are producing shrink-wrapped software and intend to surprise the market with an innovative product, you must be careful to exclude those who could serve as possible leaks. If you are bidding on a government contract, certain laws may prevent you from including the customer in these discussions.

Step 2: Schedule the Brainstorming Session. Usually a full day is required to complete a brainstorming session without counterproductive time-pressure. Contact as many of the key participants as possible in advance to insure their availability. Do *not* just schedule a time and hope everybody will be available. Many people resent being told when a meeting is without being asked about their availability. Notify all participants.

Step 3: Reserve a Room. The ideal room has enough space so that participants do not feel cramped. It has either soft walls (so you can push pins into it without damaging the wall) or flat, painted walls.[1] Tables and chairs should be arranged in a large U shape with an opening toward the front of the room, as shown in Figure A-1. This is to make it easier for everybody to hear each other. If only one wall is soft or painted, make that the front of the room. This insures that all participants can easily see the items posted during the session.

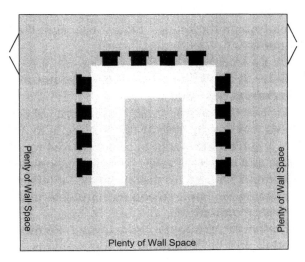

Figure A-1: Ideal Room Arrangement for Brainstorming.

Step 4: Get Supplies. The following items should be acquired well before the meeting:

---

[1]Wallpapered walls generally do not support sticky notes well.

- 5" x 7" index cards (if using soft walls) or 5" x 7" sticky notes (if using painted walls). You should acquire at least 50 per participant.
- Push pins (only if using soft walls). You should acquire at least 50 per participant.
- Thick black markers—one per participant. See Figure A-2 for an example of what the marker should look like when used on a 5" x 7" card or note.
- Thin colored markers—one per participant (preferably a different color for each participant, but this is not absolutely mandatory and not always possible).

Figure A-2: Marker Size on a 5" x 7" Card.

Do not substitute smaller cards or smaller sticky notes. Do not use markers of inadequate thickness.[2] Do not use more than one color for the thick markers.[3]

Step 5: On the Morning of the Session, Place 50 Cards or Notes and One Thick Marker at Every Seat in the Room. Do not distribute the thin-point markers at this time.

Step 6: Explain the Mission to the Participants. Make it clear to the participants that the purpose of the meeting is to determine all the candidate requirements likely to be considered for inclusion in the next release and to surface every participant's opinion on prioritizing the requirements. Insure that everyone understands that we are not determining *the* requirements; we are determining the full range of *candidate* requirements.

Step 7: Explain the Meeting Protocols to the Participants. Explain that the meeting will be conducted in three phases. During the first phase, we will collect all the ideas. During the second phase, we will critique, discuss, prune, organize, and combine the candidate requirements. During the third phase, we will collect opinions about the relative importance of each candidate requirement.

[2] These substitutions will make the notes difficult to read from the participants' seats.

[3] It would be too easy to tell who wrote which ideas. In national cultures where public ownership of ideas is critical, feel free to ignore this advice!

Step 8: Explain the Rules of Phase One. As participants think of ideas, they should say them aloud and write a few words in big letters, with their markers, on the cards or notes, to capture the essence of the idea. The reason for stating the idea aloud is to allow others to piggyback. Also, explain that no criticism or discussion about any particular idea is allowed, not even "Sally already said that." Critical comments may cause the person being criticized to become paranoid and to stop performing spontaneously.

Step 9: Prime the Session. To start the brainstorming, ask a key question, such as, "What do you feel are the key features of our next-generation gizmo?" If this does not start a free flow of ideas, try rewording the question to something like, "Are there things that our current generation gizmo doesn't do but should?" Or, "Are there things that our next generation gizmo absolutely must do?" If this does not work, try seeding the discussion with a few possible ideas of your own.

Step 10: Idea Generation. After a possible slow start, most brainstorming sessions tend to self-perpetuate. The facilitator should walk around every few minutes, collecting the cards and notes and posting them on the wall in front of the room. Some facilitators (including me) like to array them in neat columns and rows, in the order in which they were created (see Figure A-3).

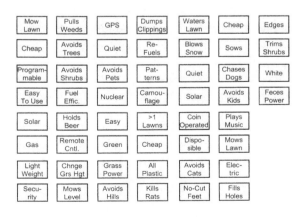

Figure A-3: Typical Wall of Posted Ideas During Brainstorming.

Some facilitators place them in random positions; and others have a preconceived notion of general categories in which the ideas may fit, and place them on areas of the wall according to these categories (see Figure A-4). I avoid the latter technique because it tends to limit subsequent brainstorming to just those categories represented.

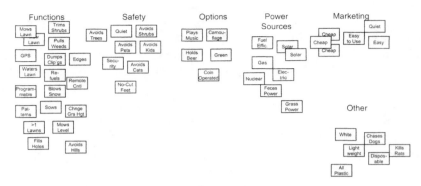

Figure A-4: Typical Categorized Wall of Posted Ideas During Brainstorming.

On occasion, as good ideas are presented (or when a previously quiet member speaks up with a reasonable idea), say, "Great idea!" This encourages participation and sets a positive tone for the entire session. Often, other participants start saying, "Great idea!" as well. That is a good sign. If a participant has a particularly quiet voice, read his or her cards aloud when you pick them up, so everyone can hear them and possibly piggyback.

Step 11: Anomalies. On occasion, a participant may make a negative comment, such as, "That's a really stupid idea" or "That's already been said" or "That idea is out of scope" or "There is no way we can implement that." When such a remark is made, you should quickly remind the group that criticism is not productive at this stage and that there will be plenty of time to discuss particular ideas later.

Step 12: Lulls. As participants express ideas, you (the facilitator) may come up with some of your own. Don't express them right away. Instead, save them for a lull in the session, when the process is slowing down. Then contribute them, to reenergize the group. As an alternative, try to find a posted idea that is very different from the rest, repeat it aloud, and ask the participants if they have any similar ideas.

Step 13: The Second Phase—Visiting the Ideas. Visit each idea on the wall. Read each concept aloud and ask if the group would like any clarification on it. Ask if it is the same as or closely related to an earlier idea (in which case, move it next to the earlier idea). If there is disagreement, just leave the idea where it is. Do not allow a discussion of any idea to last more than five minutes or so. If strong disagreements arise, remind the group that you are just trying to enumerate the *candidate* requirements at this point, not the *final* requirements.

Step 14: The Third Phase—Collecting Relative Priorities. The goal now is to find out how much support exists for each candidate requirement. If there are eight or fewer participants, follow alternative *a*. Otherwise, follow alternative *b*.

a. Distribute the colored markers. Tell each participant that he or she has $100 to distribute among the ideas posted on the wall. Ask each participant to go to the wall and write on each card or sticky note how much of the $100 he or she would spend on that requirement. The distributions show each participant's perspective of each requirement's relative importance. It may be a good idea to ask participants to write down their $100 distribution on a separate piece of paper first, so they won't forget how much they've spent.

b. Point to each candidate requirement. Ask the participants to vote with a show of fingers: two fingers up, one finger up, no fingers, one finger down, or two fingers down, to show their strong support, mild support, apathy, mild dissent, or strong dissent, respectively. Write the total votes on each card or sticky note.

Step 15: Capture Electronically. Soon after the meeting, have somebody enter all the ideas into a database or spreadsheet, one idea per record or row. Record the votes, as well.

DECIDE WHAT IS OR ISN'T A REQUIREMENT

Step 1: Review the Definition of a Requirement. Remember that a requirement describes an externally observable characteristic of a desired system. The term *externally observable* implies that the presence of the characteristic can be sensed in some way from a perspective that's external to the system. The term *desired* implies that some stakeholders believe the final system should exhibit this characteristic.

Step 2: Understand the Types of Valid Requirements. Requirements include the following:

- description of inputs into the system, including those coming from users (such as commands and menu selections), hardware (especially sensors and other input devices), and other software systems
- description of outputs from the system, including those being given to users (such as reports, screens, and error messages), hardware (especially controllable devices and other output devices), and other software systems
- relationships between inputs and outputs, especially the conditions under which outputs are generated
- models that show more complex interrelationships among inputs and outputs (such as scenarios, finite state machines, or decision tables)
- descriptions (including pictures) of real-world items and events that need to be tracked, followed, controlled, interfaced, or otherwise known by the system
- classes of users, and their characteristics
- characteristics of the environment in which the system will reside
- response times, which define how quickly (or how slowly) the system must respond to its environment, for each class of output
- expected levels of reliability, adaptability, maintainability, and the like
- user interface
- any other need expressed by the customers or users

Step 3: Understand the Correct Level of Detail. There is *no* predefined "right" level of detail for a requirement. Especially at elicitation time, almost any level is acceptable as long as it falls into one or more of the requirement categories listed above. In general, the requirement is too detailed if it eliminates choices that *customers or users* would find acceptable.[4] At elicitation time, no requirement is too vague. As requirements activities progress toward specification, the requirements will naturally become more detailed.

Step 4: Understand What Is Not a Valid Requirement. Requirements do not include the following:

---

[4]Note that I deliberately omitted designers and developers from this.

- Descriptions (or even mentions) of components to be built in the software system are not requirements. Exception: If the requirements being gathered are for a noninitial version of a software system, it is not a terrible crime to add parenthetical comments to otherwise acceptable requirements, referring to the components that will likely be affected.
- Descriptions of algorithms to be used by the software to perform its task are not requirements. Exception: When software is being built specifically because a new algorithm has been invented, a description may be acceptable.
- Plans to achieve any of the requirements (such as for schedules, resources, people, and milestones) are not requirements.
- Business goals—such as market, market window, pricing, marketing strategies, sales scripts, and so on—are not requirements. Exception: Some of these goals may end up in the *introduction* of the requirements document, to help define the product's context.

Step 5: Visit Every Requirement. Go through every candidate requirement in the list and analyze it relative to the above criteria. Move those that do not meet the criteria to an alternative document (a draft design document, a draft project plan, a draft business case, and so on). It is highly unlikely that any will simply be discarded.

DECIDE WHAT TO BUILD

Step 1: Create the Annotated List of Requirements. From elicitation, create a single list of the candidate requirements. If a requirement is clearly subsumed within another, indent it below that requirement. In a column beside the requirements, capture the results of the stakeholder voting (see Step 14 of the brainstorming process described above). Ask the development team to generate approximate values for the efforts associated with the requirements. Capture these estimates in yet another column, to the right of the requirements.

Step 2: Determine Desired Schedule. This is usually driven by the marketing department or the customer.

Step 3: Determine Desired Budget. Usually defined in terms of person-months (or person-days), the budget is often determined by the customer-supplier relationship (when a bid has been generated), by the development organization (when it has a specific budget), or by finance or corporate executives (when a business case has determined that the product is economically viable only when n dollars are spent on research and development).

Step 4: Are We Close? Using historic data from past projects, determine how likely it is that you can satisfy *all* the requirements within the desired budget and schedule. If you do not have such data, then you will have to use the opinions of the development team or external consultants; you will also have to start collecting such data now, for use on future projects. Answer the question, "Are we close?" in terms of two percentages: First, the probability of completing the entire set of candidate requirements by the desired date (as shown in Figure A-5), and second, the probability of completing the entire set of candidate requirements within the desired budget (as shown in Figure A-6). Do not fret if these percentages are woefully low. You have a great deal of company. If the probability is reasonable, you are done.[5] Go ahead and complete the requirements document, and get on with the development.

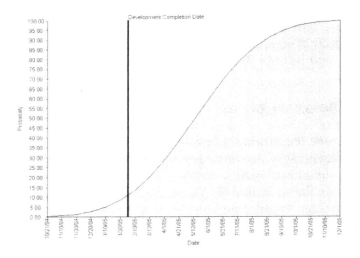

Figure A-5: Probability of Completing On Schedule, 11 Percent.

---

[5]I cannot tell you what is "reasonable." That depends on the risk tolerance of your organization.

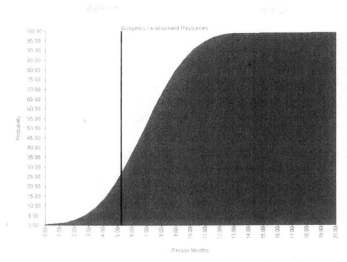

Figure A-6: Probability of Completing Within Budget, 27 Percent.

Step 5: Back to Realism. Now, tentatively "delete" all the require-ments.[6] Once again, examine the probabilities of completion within budget and on schedule. Both should now be close to 100 percent likely. After all, no matter what the schedule and budget, you should be able to complete zero work within those constraints. This is not just a blind exercise; it is to create the mind-set among all participants that the "right answer" lies in a balance between the two extremes.

Step 6: Start Adding Requirements. Sort the requirements from highest to lowest priority (based on the votes). One by one, starting with the most important, reintroduce the requirements. As you do so, watch the probability of success. As soon as it reaches a tolerable level, stop. If the resulting set of requirements makes an acceptable product, then you are done. Go ahead and complete the requirements document, and get on with the development. If the set of requirements flagged for inclusion does not make an accept-able product (to marketing, the customer, or the strategic plan of the company), then try Steps 7 and/or 8.

Step 7: Try Adding a Follow-On Point Release. Let's say you are planning Release 2.0 and you have just determined that the requirements that can be satisfied are unacceptable given the schedule and budget constraints. Try planning Release 2.1 at the

---

[6]Don't actually delete them! In the database, just move the flag next to the requirement to the TBD position (see Chapter 3).

same time. Perhaps 2.1 can be released soon after 2.0, with a more acceptable set of features. If this is feasible, think about what you can do with the "poor" Release 2.0. For example, can it be sold at a much lower price? Can it be used for training? Can it be given away to potential customers to sell them on your superior approach? Can it be sold to potential customers, with a coupon good for a free upgrade to 2.1? And so on.

Step 8: Try Adding an Earlier Partial Release. Another possibility is to decide to build Release 1.5 (assuming 1.4 has already been sold). This release might roll out earlier, with fewer requirements than are planned for the 2.0 release. If so, schedule the 2.0 release for a later date that has a more acceptable probability of success. So, for example, if the goal is to deliver Release 2.0 in April, you can try delivering Release 1.5 in February and the real Release 2.0 in June. As in Step 7, a variety of marketing possibilities exist. For example, can the 1.5 release be sold at a much lower price? Can it be given away to potential customers to sell them on the superior approach delivered in the 2.0 release? Can 1.5 be sold to potential customers, with a coupon good for a free upgrade to 2.0? Will the earlier 1.5 release be sufficient to deter potential customers from going to competitors? And so on.

PRODUCE A REQUIREMENTS DOCUMENT

Step 1: The Easiest Approach. By far, the easiest, most effective way to produce a requirements document is to just print the database of requirements. Use a standard as a checklist to insure that all possible requirements are included—this could be a government, corporate, or otherwise publicly available standard (such as Volere [ROB99]) or an industry standard (such as IEEE Standard 830).

Step 2: Determine Customer Documentation Demands. If the customer demands a more formal requirements document, try to create one of the following (in order of preference):

- Create a word-processed document that contains four sections: an introduction (which you will need to write), detailed requirements (which contain a simple printing of the database of requirements), a glossary, and an index.
- Create a word-processed document that conforms to some applicable standard for organizing a requirements document. For most sections, you will need to start from

scratch. But for the section on detailed requirements, try to get by with a simple printout of the requirements database.

Step 3: Corporate Standards. If your company has a long tradition of writing long-winded textual requirements documents, you have three choices:

- Declare that your project is going to be an experiment. Use just the database of requirements and dispense with the documentation standard. Collect data about past projects to see how often their outcomes have resulted in satisfied customers (or markets). Do the same for your project. Thus, demonstrate that a database is all you need for project (and corporate) success.
- Redefine the standard, and then start your project.
- Follow the standard (see Step 2), but immediately after you complete your project, initiate a task force to redefine that standard.

Step 4: Preserve the "Deleted" Requirements. When you performed triage, you eliminated some of the candidate requirements from the currently planned release. What should you do with these? You have three choices:

- Include them in the requirements document. Clearly mark them as excluded or, better yet, when you print the database of requirements, print the column that indicates the target release for each requirement. The advantage of this is that developers can see the features that are likely to be built next, and can thus include "hooks" for them at little to no additional cost. The disadvantage is that some developers may decide to just go ahead and implement those features anyway, risking the entire project's success.
- Exclude them from the requirements document. The advantage of this is that developers cannot be tempted or sidetracked into implementing the unnecessary requirements. The disadvantage is that developers may end up satisfying an included requirement in a manner that precludes the eventual incorporation of one of the excluded requirements.
- Since the requirements document is just a printing of the requirements database, print two versions of the document:

one that contains only the included requirements and one that presents the entire picture.

Whatever you do, do not remove the "deleted" requirements from your database completely!

ASSESS THE QUALITY OF A REQUIREMENTS DOCUMENT

Step 1: Print the Requirements.[7]

Step 2: Check for Ambiguity, Correctness, and Organization. Read the list of requirements from top to bottom. Read it for meaning. As you do this, make notes in the margins, marking any requirements that seem suspicious, unclear (mark these with "AM," for ambiguous), incorrect or in need of further analysis (mark these with "CR," for possible incorrectness), or not co-located with closely related requirements (mark these with "OR," for organization).

Step 3: Check for Completeness, Inconsistency, and Achievability. Now that you know the requirements are where they should be and that they make general sense, read them again. This time, look at the whole. Look for requirements that conflict with other requirements (mark these with "CF," for conflict, and add a reference to the page number of the conflicting requirements; do the same in the margin beside the conflicting requirement itself). Look for cases that not being addressed (mark these with "CM," for incompleteness). Look for individual requirements and for sets of requirements that simply cannot be satisfied (mark these with "AC," for lack of achievability). The easiest way to find inconsistencies and incompleteness is to construct some type of model. Here are some possibilities:

- Construct a two-dimensional table: Label the columns with the names of various inputs into the system (including events). Label the rows with names for conditions or states of the system. Within each intersection, make a note of what the system is expected to do and add a cross-reference to the unique requirement number. Whenever you find you need to enter conflicting responses into a single intersection, you may have found an inconsistency. Do not

---

[7]Thanks to Tsuyoshi Nakajima of Mitsubishi Electric for many of the ideas contained in this recipe [NAK94].

rush to judgment, though; think about it. It is also possible that there is really no conflict and something that differentiates the two situations is missing (you have found an incompleteness). When you have finished filling in the table, look at the remaining empty intersections. These also may indicate incompleteness in the requirements.

- Examine your models: Do the requirements describe most of the situations described by the models and diagrams? And vice versa?

Step 4: Check for Traceability and Annotation. Do all the requirements have a unique identifier (name or number)?[8] Mark those that don't with "TR," for lack of traceability. Are all the included requirements annotated by their relative level of importance and estimated effort? Mark those that aren't with "AN," for lack of annotation.

Step 5: Check the Spelling and Grammar. Mark errors with "SP" for spelling and "GR" for grammar. Spelling and grammar errors are not likely to contribute to a project's success or failure per se, but the reason we have spelling and grammar rules is to improve our communication; such errors are likely to add to the ambiguity of the requirements (and should be marked "AM," as well). The fact is that a document that is edited for these errors will appear more professional and will increase confidence in the team.

Step 6: Score the Requirements. Scan the entire document, looking for each of the errors found in Steps 1 through 5. A count of the errors will give you some measure of the general quality of the document. However, some types of errors guarantee failure, some have just a strong influence on failure, and some are just minor issues. So, if you want to assign a real score to the document's quality, taking into account the degree to which it will interfere with your ability to develop a successful project, use a scale such as the following[9]:

---

[8]If the requirements are stored in a database, every record (and thus every requirement) will have a unique identifier called the *primary key.*

[9]I have used a range of 50 points, with 50 points for errors that will guarantee project failure and 1 to 2 points for errors that will mildly interfere with the project's success.

AC	50 points
CF	50 points
CR	50 points
AM	10 points
CM	10 points
AN	2 points
OR	2 points
TR	3 points
SP	1 point
GR	1 point

BASELINE THE REQUIREMENTS

Step 1: Print the Requirements. If the database represents the requirements, print it, along with all pertinent columns of annotation. If you have a traditional word-processed requirements document, print that.

Step 2: Sign-Off on the Requirements. After the requirements are agreed to, make sure you get all major stakeholders to sign-off on them. Stakeholders include

- the development organization
- management representatives, especially those in charge of resources
- marketing (only if selling the product externally)
- customers (only for custom-built products for internal or external use)

Rather than just signing a blank page in the document, stakeholders should sign a statement of agreement like the one shown in Chapter 4.

ENSURE THAT EVERYBODY KNOWS THE REQUIREMENTS

Step 1: Identify the Concerned Stakeholders. Although you contacted many stakeholders during the elicitation stage, there are many more who need to know and understand what is in the agreed-upon set of requirements. The following is a more comprehensive list of stakeholders and an explanation of why they need to know the requirements:

- developers, so they know what to build
- system testers, so they can construct system test plans in plenty of time to conduct system testing as soon as the development organization finishes building the system
- user-manual writers, so they can write the user manuals in plenty of time to ship the product
- trainers, so they can start preparing training material (training is often initiated prior to product delivery)
- managers, so they can allocate appropriate resources to all aspects of the project
- marketing people (only if selling the product externally), so they can refine their target market, develop marketing communications materials, identify beta customer sites, find and negotiate distribution channels, identify and negotiate with other business partners, create initial databases of potential leads, and so on
- sales people (only if selling the product externally), so they can start to synthesize sales scripts for use before and after product release, to identify hot leads, close orders, and so on
- customers (usually only for custom-built products, but occasionally for beta sites, also), so they can start planning the implementation process, assured that the product being built is indeed the product they need and expect
- users (usually only for products to be used in-house, but occasionally for beta sites, also), so they can be assured that the product being built is indeed the product they need and expect

Step 2: Distribute the Database. Make sure the document is clearly marked with one of the following:

- "DRAFT. NOT YET APPROVED." For distribution (generally for comment) prior to baselining.
- "FINAL APPROVED DOCUMENT." For distribution after baselining.

Step 3: Create a Change Request Process. Develop a means for all stakeholders to suggest changes to the approved requirements database. Promulgate the process to all the above stakeholders.

HANDLE NEW REQUIREMENTS AFTER BASELINING

Step 1: Schedule Regular Change Control Board Meetings. A CCB meeting gathers key stakeholders to make decisions about what to do with each suggested change to the requirements. Schedule these meetings well in advance. It is not uncommon to schedule them monthly, a year in advance. In highly volatile situations, CCB meetings could occur weekly, while in relatively stable situations, once per year may suffice.

Step 2: Collect Proposed Requirements Changes. Proposals for changes to requirements originate from a variety of sources: current or future customers, marketing personnel who identify new opportunities, developers who identify possible new features they believe could be useful, and so on.

If practical, allow customers and users to enter their proposed changes electronically, as this will greatly facilitate entry into a database. Ideally, stakeholders will be able to enter the proposed changes directly into the database. At a minimum, the proposed changes should be recorded with the following:

- unique identifier (usually created automatically by the database)
- name of the proposer (sometimes entered automatically by the database)
- date of the request (usually entered automatically by the database)
- proposed change to the requirements (the main body of the request)
- urgency level as assessed by proposer

Step 3: Make a Preliminary Assessment. Before the CCB can make any decisions, it needs some additional information about each proposed requirements change:

- estimated level of effort required to address the requested change: Usually supplied by developers or their management, this can be measured in terms of dollars or person-hours.
- impact on other requirements: The CCB will need to understand how this proposed change will affect other requirements, whether implemented, baselined, or just

proposed. For example, would the satisfaction of a newly proposed change be greatly facilitated by satisfying some other proposed requirement first? Or, is the satisfaction of this requirement incompatible with an existing baseline or implemented requirement? Usually, this information is supplied by the development team, but it may also require input from customers or marketing.

- impact on release schedule: Often, a proposer will make a statement such as, "We need to add this to the current baseline" or "This must be included before we convert to Release 3.6." In such cases, development should add information about how much of a delay is likely (if any) if this requirement change is approved.

Step 4: Prioritize the Proposed Changes. Taking into consideration the sense of urgency recorded in the proposer's original request, the estimated effort, the likely effect on schedule, and the impact on other requirements, representatives of the organization responsible for satisfying the requirement should add their assessment of the relative priority.

Step 5: The CCB Makes the Decision. The CCB should examine each of the proposed requirements changes that it has not yet addressed. It should contrast the urgency and priority of each change with the requirements already approved for the current and later releases. It should pay close attention to how each proposed change will affect other requirements. It must categorize each proposed change in one of the following categories:

- Approve . . .
    - for inclusion in the release currently under development
    - for inclusion in a specific later release
    - for inclusion in an unspecified later release
- Reject

Step 6: Notify All Stakeholders. After a decision is made, the following individuals must be so informed:

- original requestor
- managers, so it can start allocating resources appropriately if the change affects the current release

- development, so it can start working on the change if it affects the current release
- document control, so it can make appropriate changes to all aspects of documentation, including updates to the official requirements database—after these revisions are made, document control usually notifies many other parties (see the list in the previous recipe) so they can respond accordingly

HANDLE MULTIPLE CUSTOMERS

When trying to satisfy just one customer (or even one class of customer), the problems of gathering, organizing, pruning, and satisfying requirements are often challenging. Other stakeholders (marketing, management, sales, development, and so on) have their own opinions about what the system should do (opinions that will likely differ from those of the customers), and your customer may not be able to describe all of the requirements in the first place. However, when you try to satisfy multiple customers, the problem can become almost impossible.

In this recipe, be extremely careful! Often, considerable politics are involved, and by following the recipe too closely, you may find yourself ignoring the politics and the critical, sensitive issues related to caring about and communicating with people. The recipe provides only the *mechanics* for handling multiple customers. It is an adaptation of quality function deployment [MIZ94].

Step 1: Rank the Customers. On a scale of 1 to 10, with 10 being the most important, rank each customer or class of customer. Use this scale to capture the relative ranking. For example, if customer A is twice as important as customer B, then give customer A a ranking that is double the ranking of customer B. If you have five customers named A through E, your rankings might look like Figure A-7.

Customer:	A	B	C	D	E
Ranking:	8	4	8	2	10

Figure A-7: Ranking of Multiple Customers.

Step 2: Record How Each Customer Prioritizes the Requirements. For each customer, ascertain how he or she rates the relative priority of each requirement, following the "prioritizing candidate requirements" procedure given in Chapter 3. You will now have a two-dimensional table like the one shown in Figure A-8. In that particular example, I have normalized the ratings of all requirements by all customers on a 10-point scale, so the lowest ranked requirements are numbered "0" and the highest are numbered "9."

Customer:	A	B	C	D	E
Ranking:	8	4	8	2	10
Requirement					
1	0	2	6	7	3
2	7	2	5	7	6
3	9	2	9	7	8
4	9	5	2	9	0
5	7	6	0	7	7
6	6	8	6	9	7
7	9	3	4	9	9
8	4	2	5	2	5
9	2	1	6	2	7
10	8	0	1	2	2
11	2	0	2	1	2
12	1	0	1	6	0

Figure A-8: Ratings of Requirements by Multiple Customers.

Step 3: Compute Weighted Customer Priorities for Requirements. In the table, multiply every requirement rating by the relative ranking of the customer (recorded at the top of the column, just below the name of the customer). The result will look like the table in Figure A-9.

Customer: Requirement	A	B	C	D	E
1	0	8	48	14	30
2	56	8	40	14	60
3	72	8	72	14	80
4	72	20	16	18	0
5	56	24	0	14	70
6	48	32	48	18	70
7	72	12	32	18	90
8	32	8	40	4	50
9	16	4	48	4	70
10	64	0	8	4	20
11	16	0	16	2	20
12	8	0	8	12	0

Figure A-9: Weighted Ratings of Requirements by Multiple Customers.

Step 4: Compute the Relative Importance of Each Requirement. Add up the rows to find out how important each requirement is, as a sum of the weighted ratings by customer, as shown in Figure A-10.

Customer: Requirement	A	B	C	D	E	Weighted Sum
1	0	8	48	14	30	100
2	56	8	40	14	60	178
3	72	8	72	14	80	246
4	72	20	16	18	0	126
5	56	24	0	14	70	164
6	48	32	48	18	70	216
7	72	12	32	18	90	216
8	32	8	40	4	50	136
9	16	4	48	4	70	142
10	64	0	8	4	20	96
11	16	0	16	2	20	54
12	8	0	8	12	0	28

Figure A-10: Sums of Weighted Ratings of Requirements.

Step 5: Normalize the Results. Find the requirement with the highest score—in this case, 246. Next, divide each of the weighted sums by one tenth of the highest score—in this case, 24.6. Round each answer to the nearest whole number. Thus, when you divide 100 (the weighted sum for requirement 1) by 24.6, you get 4. When you divide 178 (the weighted sum for requirement 2) by 24.6, you get 7. And so on. The results should be recorded as shown in Figure A-11.

Requirement	Priority
1	4
2	7
3	10
4	5
5	6
6	9
7	9
8	6
9	6
10	4
11	2
12	1

Figure A-11: Final Relative Priority of Requirements.

APPENDIX B

A Set of Documented Requirements

In this appendix, I provide you with a list of requirements for the traffic control system used repeatedly throughout the book. Models A through H, most of which appeared earlier, follow immediately after the database of requirements.

Reqt. No.	Requirement Text	Priority	Person-Hours	Release	Risk	Cross-Ref. to Model
1	The system shall be programmable by the operator.	10	120	2.0	10%	See Models A and B
1.1	The system shall be programmable by the operator to set the default for the green direction to be "East" or "West."	8	20	2.0	10%	See Model B
1.1.1	When the operator has programmed the system for "East" being the default, the system shall provide a green signal to the westbound traffic whenever no cars are waiting eastbound.		0	2.0	5%	
1.1.2	When the operator has programmed the system for "West" being the default and no cars are waiting westbound, the system shall provide a green signal to the eastbound traffic.		0	2.0	5%	
1.2	The system shall be programmable by the operator to set the maximum duration for the light to remain green in the non-default direction.	12	20	2.0	10%	See Model B
1.2.1	If the operator attempts to set the maximum duration to a number greater than 999 seconds, the system shall sound a 1 second buzzer within .5 seconds, and return to the initial mode, where a function button press is expected.		0	2.0	10%	
1.3	The system shall be programmable by the operator to set the minimum duration for the light to remain green in the default direction.	12	20	2.0	10%	See Model B
1.3.1	If the operator attempts to set the minimum duration to a number greater than 999 seconds, the system shall sound a 1 second buzzer within .5 seconds, and return to the initial mode, where a function button press is expected.		0	2.0	10%	

Reqt. No.	Requirement Text	Priority	Person-Hours	Release	Risk	Cross-Ref. to Model
1.4	The system shall be programmable by the operator to set the duration of the amber light prior to it changing to red.	7	15	2.0	10%	See Model B
1.4.1	If the operator attempts to set the duration to a number greater than 20 seconds, the system shall sound a 1 second buzzer within .5 seconds and return to the initial mode, where a function button press is expected.		0	2.0	10%	
1.5	For all programming operations, the operator will be expected to first select a function, then (if applicable) enter a time (in seconds), and then press the "set" button.	7	10	2.0	10%	See Models A and B
1.5.1	If the operator presses any button out of order, the system will ignore the button press and the system shall sound a 1 second buzzer within .5 seconds.		0	2.0	10%	
1.5.2	When the operator presses the "set" button at the proper time, the system shall generate two .25 second beeps, .25 second apart, within 1 second of the button press.		0	2.0	10%	
1.6	When the operator has completed the programming, and wishes to start the operation of the traffic lights, he/she must press the "done" button.	7	0	2.0	10%	See Model B
1.6.1	When the operator presses the "done" button at the proper time, the system shall generate three .25 second beeps, .25 second apart, within 1 second of the button press.		0	2.0	10%	See Model H
2	The system shall provide safe access to a one-lane east-west bridge via green/amber/red traffic lights.	20	200	2.0	30%	See Model C

Reqt. No.	Requirement Text	Priority	Person-Hours	Release	Risk	Cross-Ref. to Model
2.1	Two sets of traffic lights shall be controlled by the system.	11	0	2.0	10%	See Model F
2.1.1	The "East" traffic lights will be located at the east end of the bridge and control westbound traffic.		0	2.0	10%	
2.1.2	The "West" traffic lights will be located at the west end of the bridge and control eastbound traffic.		0	2.0	10%	
2.2	When either set of lights is "green," the other set of lights shall be set to "red."	20	0	2.0	10%	See Model C
2.3	When the system determines that it is time to switch the direction of traffic, it shall do so in a safe manner.	20	0	2.0	30%	See Model C
2.3.1	When the system determines that it is time to switch of the direction of traffic, it shall change the green light to amber, and then to red.		0	2.0	10%	
2.3.2	After the green light has been turned to red, the other direction shall remain red until the same number of vehicles have egressed as have ingressed.		0	2.0	30%	
2.3.3	The system shall never allow the light in the non-default direction to remain green longer than the maximum duration programmed by the operator.		0	2.0	10%	See Model D
2.3.4	The system shall never allow the light in the default direction to remain green less than the duration programmed by the operator.		0	2.0	10%	See Model E
2.3.5	The system shall advise oncoming traffic of an up-coming change of light from green to red by first changing to amber for the appropriate length of time.		0	2.0	10%	

Reqt. No.	Requirement Text	Priority	Person-Hours	Release	Risk	Cross-Ref. to Model
3	The system shall control eastbound traffic coming from northwest and southwest converging roads.	8	150	2.1	40%	See Model G
3.1	During the period while the eastbound traffic is authorized to be green, the system shall provide equal time (+/- 2 seconds) for the traffic coming from the southwest and the northwest.		0	2.1	15%	
3.2	Four sets of traffic lights shall be controlled by the system.		0	2.1	15%	
4	The system shall control westbound traffic coming from northeast and southeast converging roads.	8	150	2.1	40%	See Model G
4.1	During the period while the westbound traffic is authorized to be green, the system shall provide equal time (+/- 2 seconds) for the traffic coming from the southeast and the northeast.		0	2.1	15%	
4.2	Four sets of traffic lights shall be controlled by the system.		0	2.1	15%	
5	The system shall interface to vehicle sensors capable of determining if there is a vehicle waiting at either of the two entrances.	10	40	2.0	10%	See Models F and G
5.1	One sensor shall be provided for each incoming road.	10	0	2.0	5%	
6	The system shall interface to vehicle counters capable of counting vehicles as they pass through each of the two entrances.	15	120	2.0	60%	See Models F and G
6.1	Two counters shall be provided, one at the east and one at the west entrances/exits for the bridge.	-2	10	2.0	10%	

Reqt. No.	Requirement Text	Priority	Person-Hours	Release	Risk	Cross-Ref. to Model
6.2	The vehicle counters can be reset to zero by the system.	12	10	2.0	25%	
6.3	The system can inquire of a vehicle counter the number of vehicles that have passed that counter since last reset.	9	25	2.0	60%	
7	The system shall sense the weight of vehicles on the road and not allow either light to turn to green while a vehicle remains on the bridge.	3	200	3.0	75%	
8	If a vehicle is disabled on the bridge, the system shall automatically contact a tow truck.	1	200	TBD	80%	

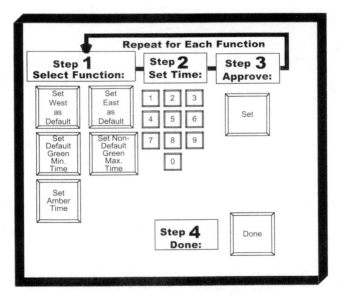

Model A: Operator Console.

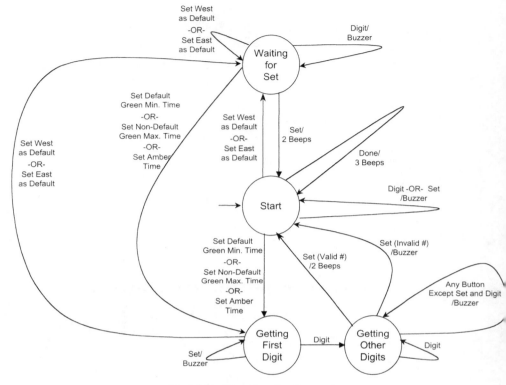

Model B: User Interface Interaction.

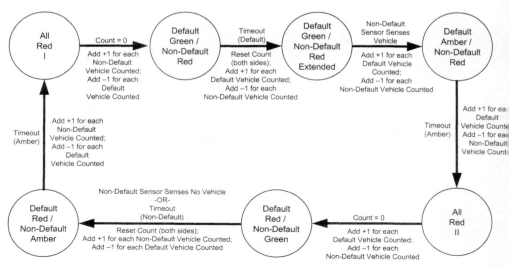

Model C: Operation of Traffic Signals.

Step 1.   Vehicle arrives from the east.
Step 2.   If the light is green for westbound traffic, vehicle proceeds over the bridge.
Step 3.   If the light is red for westbound traffic, then
    Step 3a.   Vehicle stops.
    Step 3b.   After minimum-duration-for-default-green expires, light for westbound traffic turns green.
    Step 3c.   Vehicle proceeds over the bridge.

Model D: Typical Scenario for Arriving Westbound Vehicle (Default Direction).

Step 1.   Vehicle arrives from the west.
Step 2.   If the light is green for eastbound traffic, vehicle proceeds over the bridge.
Step 3.   If the light is red for eastbound traffic, then
    Step 3a.   Vehicle stops.
    Step 3b.   After maximum-duration-for-non-default-green expires, light for eastbound traffic turns green.
    Step 3c.   Vehicle proceeds over the bridge.

Model E: Typical Scenario for Arriving Eastbound Vehicle (Non-Default Direction).

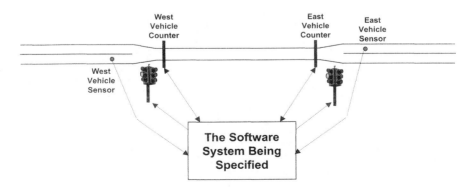

Model F: Basic Configuration.

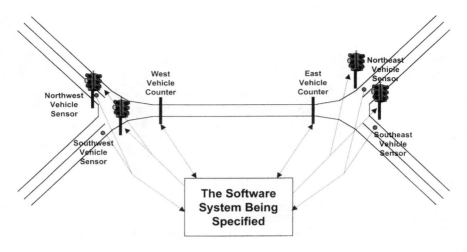

Model G: Extended Four-Road Configuration.

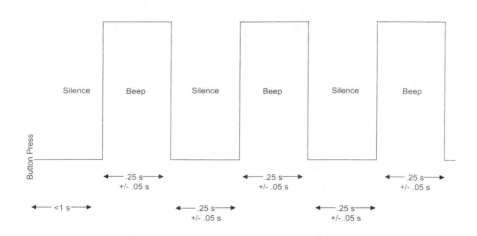

Model H: Beep Timing.

References and Additional Readings

For a regularly updated listing of readings on the subject of requirements, visit http://web.uccs.edu/adavis/reqbib.htm.

[ALE02]   Alexander, I., and R. Stevens. *Writing Better Requirements.* Harlow, Eng.: Addison-Wesley, 2002.

[ALE03]   Alexander, Ian. "Misuse Cases: Use Cases with Hostile Intent." *IEEE Software,* 20, 1 (January/February 2003), pp. 58–66.

A nice discussion of how one can combine failure analysis with use cases to elicit and specify nonbehavioral requirements.

[AMB02]   Ambler, Scott. *Agile Modeling.* New York: John Wiley & Sons, 2002.

See especially Chapters 24 and 25.

[AMB00]   Ambriola, V., and V. Gervasi. "Process Metrics for Requirements Analysis," *Software Process Technology: 7th European Workshop, EWSPT 2000, Kaprun, Austria, February 21–25, 2000: Proceedings* (Lecture Notes in Computer Science, 1780), Reidar Conrad, ed., pp. 90–95. Berlin: Springer-Verlag, 2000.

[AND91]   Andrews, Dorine C. "JAD: A Crucial Dimension for Rapid Application Development." *Journal of Systems Management,* 42, 3 (March 1991), pp. 23–31.

The classic paper that introduced the first proprietary version of brainstorming: the Joint Application Development (JAD) approach.

[AND92]   Andriole, Stephen J. *Rapid Application Prototyping.* Wellesley, Mass.: QED, 1992.

Although this book received relatively little attention when published, it remains in my opinion one of the best collections of ideas in the literature on how to construct user interface prototypes. It is full of real case studies.

[AND94]   ———. "Fast, Cheap Requirements: Prototype, or Else!" *IEEE Software*, 11, 2 (March 1994), pp. 85–87.

Stephen and I have been debating for many years the issue of whether prototypes are always appropriate (his view) or are often appropriate (my view). Here he justifies his position in his usual eloquent manner.

[AND96]   ———. *Managing Systems Requirements*. New York: McGraw-Hill, 1996.

Describes in detail one company's approach to writing requirements.

[ANT01] *   Antón, A., et al. "Deriving Goals from a Use-Case-Based Requirements Specification." *Requirements Engineering Journal*, 6, 1 (February 2001), pp. 63–73.

After applying use cases and scenarios to a case study, Annie and her team discovered some advantages and disadvantages. Although the use cases and scenarios were extremely helpful in surfacing needs and goals, they found that the notations were insufficient replacements for an actual requirements document. They also found that maintaining manual traces between requirements introduced intolerable overhead.

[ANT03]   Antón, Annie. "Successful Software Projects Need Requirements Planning." *IEEE Software*, 20, 3 (May/June 2003), pp. 44–47.

A brief summary of four requirements principles: Understand the problem before documenting requirements, involve the users, work on the critical requirements, and spend as much time understanding and documenting the nonbehavioral requirements as the functional requirements.

[ARM01] *   Armour, F., and G. Miller. *Advanced Use Case Modeling*. Reading, Mass.: Addison-Wesley, 2001.

[AUS03]   Austin, R., and L. Devin. "Beyond Requirements: Software Making as Art." *IEEE Software*, 20, 1 (January/February 2003), pp. 93–95.

Presents an excellent argument in favor of the agile community, specifically claiming that theater production is a lot like software development. I am not personally convinced, but this essay is well worth reading so that you can make your own judgment.

[BEC99] *   Beck, Kent. *Extreme Programming Explained*. Reading, Mass.: Addison-Wesley, 1999.

[BEL76] *   Belady, L., and M. Lehman. "A Model of Large Program Development." *IBM Systems Journal*, 15, 3 (March 1976), pp. 225–52.

Reports on an excellent study performed at IBM to discover if a relationship existed between the number of enhancements released with each delivery of IBM OS/360 and the subsequent requests for more features.

[BER95]   Berry, Daniel M. "The Importance of Ignorance in Requirements Engineering." *Journal of Systems and Software*, 28, 2 (February 1995), pp. 179–84.

This little article is so easy to read, I recommend that everybody in the practice take a look at it. Dan describes two projects on which he worked. In both cases, he, the analyst, was completely ignorant of the application domain. He hypothesizes that perhaps his ignorance explains why the projects were so successful. I cannot agree more![1] He even goes so far as to suggest that analysts include on their résumés a list of application domains in which they are ignorant.

---

[1] Not that Dan is ignorant; he is one of the smartest people I know. But that ignorance of the application domain can make the requirements elicitation effort more successful.

*Asterisks indicate works cited within the text of this book.

[BER99]   ———. "Software and House Requirements Engineering: Lessons Learned in Combating Requirements Creep." *Requirements Engineering Journal*, 3, 3 & 4 (1999), pp. 242–44.

A wonderful description of the similarities and differences between the practices of home construction and software construction, with particular emphasis on how differently they handle requirements and requirements changes. Well worth reading!

[BER01] * Berry, T., and D. Wilson. *On Target: The Book on Marketing Plans.* Palo Alto, Calif.: Palo Alto Software, 2001.

[BEY95]   Beyer, H., and K. Holtzblatt. "Apprenticing with the Customer." *Communications of the ACM*, 38, 5 (May 1995), pp. 45–52.

[BEY98]   ———. *Contextual Design: Defining Customer-Centered Systems.* San Francisco: Morgan Kaufmann, 1998.

[BIC93]   Bickerton, M., and J. Siddiqi. "The Classification of Requirements Engineering Methods," *Proceedings of IEEE International Symposium on Requirements Engineering*, pp. 182–86. Los Alamitos, Calif.: IEEE Computer Society Press, 1993.

In our quest to improve our understanding of requirements elicitation techniques, we try to find ways of classifying them. This short paper presents one such taxonomy, based on the assumptions we make about the social structure of our environment.

[BOE76] * Boehm, Barry. "Software Engineering." *IEEE Transactions on Computers*, 25, 12 (December 1976), pp. 1226–41.

From the title alone, you can figure out that this paper was written in the very early days of the field. It is now regularly referenced as the source of data concerning the escalating costs associated with software defects as their discovery and repair is delayed to later phases of software development.

[BOE86] * ———. "A Spiral Model of Software Development and Enhancement." *ACM Software Engineering Notes*, 11, 4 (August 1986), pp. 16–24. Reprinted in *IEEE Computer*, 21, 5 (May 1988), pp. 61–72.

Introduces the spiral model of software development.

[BOE99]   ———, et al. "Requirements Engineering, Expectations Management, and the Two Cultures," *Proceedings of IEEE International Symposium on Requirements Engineering*, pp. 14–22. Los Alamitos, Calif.: IEEE Computer Society Press, 1999.

Describes a complex solution to the requirements triage problem.

[BOE00] * Boehm, B., et al. *Software Cost Estimation with COCOMO II.* Englewood Cliffs, N.J.: Prentice Hall, 2000.

This is the second edition of the classic book that serves as the bible of software cost estimation for most practitioners in the industry.

[BOO94]   Booch, Grady. *Object-Oriented Analysis and Design with Applications.* Redwood City, Calif.: Benjamin/Cummings, 1994.

The classic book that introduced the world to an integrated approach to object-oriented analysis and object-oriented design.

[BRA02]   Bray, Ian. *An Introduction to Requirements Engineering.* Reading, Mass.: Addison-Wesley, 2002.

[BRE96]   Brereton, P., et al. "Requirements Elicitation for Software-Based Systems." *Software Engineering Journal*, 11, 3 (May 1996), p. 148.

[BRO95] * Brooks, Frederick P., Jr. *The Mythical-Man Month.* Reading, Mass.: Addison-Wesley, 1975.

The classic book, updated in 1995 for its 25th anniversary, describes all the project management ideas that Brooks learned as the result of being a project manager for the IBM OS/360 operating system development project. An easy and educational read. Highly recommended.

[BRO01]   Browne, G., and M. Rogich. "An Empirical Investigation of User Requirements Elicitation: Comparing the Effectiveness of Prompting Techniques." *Journal of Management Information Systems,* 17, 4 (Spring 2001), pp. 223–49.

[CAR00a]   Carlshamre, P., and B. Regnell. "Requirements Lifecycle Management and Release Planning in Market-Driven Requirements Engineering Processes," *Proceedings of Eleventh IEEE International Workshop on Database and Expert Systems Applications,* pp. 961–65. Los Alamitos, Calif.: IEEE Computer Society Press, 2000.

Compares two companies' disparate approaches to performing requirements triage. Emphasis is placed on who performs each unique role during triage and how the two approaches are similar or different.

[CAR01] *   Carlshamre, P., et al. "An Industrial Survey of Requirements Interdependencies in Software Product Release Planning," *Proceedings of Fifth International Symposium on Requirements Engineering,* pp. 84–91. Los Alamitos, Calif.: IEEE Computer Society Press, 2001.

[CAR02] *   Carlshamre, Pär. "Release Planning in Market-Driven Software Product Development: Provoking an Understanding." *Requirements Engineering Journal,* 7, 3 (May 2002), pp. 139–51.

I only started reading Pär's writings recently. I wish I had discovered them sooner. He and his team are by far the most knowledgeable in the industry on the subject of relationships between requirements.

[CAR00] *   Carroll, John M. *Making Use: Scenario-Based Design of Human–Computer Interactions.* Boston: MIT Press, 2000.

John has provided us with a wealth of information about the practical use of scenarios in the requirements and design phases of software development in this and his earlier book, Scenario-Based Design.

[CHA96]   Chatzoglou, P., and L. Macaulay. "Requirements Capture and Analysis: A Survey of Current Practice." *Requirements Engineering Journal,* 1, 2 (1996), pp. 75–87.

[CHE02]   Chen, K., et al. "Visual Requirements Representation." *Journal of Systems and Software,* 61, 2 (March 2002), pp. 129–43.

[CHE99]   Chen, P., et al., eds. *Conceptual Modeling: Current Issues and Future Directions* (Lecture Notes in Computer Science, 1565). Berlin: Springer-Verlag, 1999.

[CHU00]   Chung, L., et al. *Non-Functional Requirements in Software Engineering.* Norwell, Mass.: Kluwer Academic Publishers, 2000.

[COA91]   Coad, P., and E. Yourdon. *Object-Oriented Analysis.* Englewood Cliffs, N.J.: Prentice Hall, 1991.

This was the first published book to introduce the concept of applying object-orientation to the requirements phase. Well written, its approach has been superceded in popularity by other object-oriented analysis approaches.

[COC01] *   Cockburn, Alistair. *Writing Effective Use Cases.* Reading, Mass.: Addison-Wesley, 2001.

[COC02] *   ———. *Agile Software Development.* Reading, Mass.: Addison-Wesley, 2002.

[COH95] *   Cohen, Lou. *Quality Function Deployment: How to Make QFD Work for You.* Reading, Mass.: Addison-Wesley, 1995.

[COO98]   Cooper, Robert G. *Product Leadership.* Cambridge, Mass.: Perseus Books, 1998.

[COS95]   Costello, R., and D. Liu. "Metrics for Requirements Engineering." *Journal of Systems and Software,* 29, 1 (April 1995), pp. 39–63.

[COU73] *   Couger, J. Daniel. "Evolution of Business Systems Analysis Techniques." *ACM Computing Surveys,* 5, 3 (September 1973), pp. 167–98.

               One of the earliest studies of how companies perform requirements elicitation. A mandatory read for anybody doing research on elicitation techniques.

[COU02]   Coughlan, J., and R. Macredie. "Effective Communication in Requirements Elicitation: A Comparison of Methodologies." *Requirements Engineering Journal,* 7, 2 (June 2002), pp. 47–60.

[CYS01]   Cysneiros, L., et al. "A Framework for Integrating Non-Functional Requirements into Conceptual Models." *Requirements Engineering Journal,* 6, 2 (2001), pp. 97–113.

[DAM00]   Damian, D., et al. "Using Different Communication Media in Requirements Negotiation." *IEEE Software,* 17, 3 (May/June 2000), pp. 28–36.

               Presents the results of an experiment to determine the most effective means of communication during a requirements negotiation session (during triage). In particular, this study showed that some computer-supported cooperative work environments were actually more productive than live, face-to-face meetings.

[DAV79] *   Davis, A., and T. Rauscher. "Formal Techniques and Automatic Processing to Ensure Correctness in Requirements Specifications," *Proceedings of IEEE Specifications of Reliable Software Conference,* pp. 15–35. Los Alamitos, Calif.: IEEE Computer Society Press, 1979.

               An early paper that introduced the expression "stimulus-response sequences" to describe a recommended style of documenting requirements. That term has since been replaced by "scenario" in common use.

[DAV93] *   Davis, Alan. *Software Requirements: Objects, Functions, and States.* Englewood Cliffs, N.J.: Prentice Hall, 1993.

               A compendium of detailed information on how to use models during the elicitation and specification phases of software development.

[DAV93a] *   ———, et al. "Identifying and Measuring Quality in Software Requirements Specifications," *Proceedings of IEEE-CS International Software Metrics Symposium* (May 1993), pp. 141–52.

               Provides the richest set of quality metrics for evaluating requirements specifications.

[DAV95] *   Davis, Alan. *201 Principles of Software Development.* New York: McGraw-Hill, 1995.

               Two-hundred and one pages long, this "airplane book" presents 201 of the most basic principles guiding software developers today. Each one is supported by a reference to the original source of the principle.

[DAV95a] *   ———. "Software Prototyping." *Advances in Computers, Vol. 40,* M. Zelkowitz, ed. New York: Academic Press, 1995.

[DAV97] *   ———. "Why Build Software?" *IEEE Software,* 14, 1 (January/February 1997), pp. 4, 6. Reprinted in A. Davis, *Great Software Debates.* Los Alamitos, Calif.: Wiley–IEEE Computer Society Press, 2004.

It might seem obvious that we build software to solve the problems of the intended users or to leverage a business opportunity. Unfortunately, many software developers do not realize this. This article makes developers painfully aware of this reality.

[DAV98] *   ———. "The Harmony in Rechoirments." *IEEE Software*, 15, 2 (March/April 1998), pp. 6, 8. Reprinted in A. Davis, *Great Software Debates*. Los Alamitos, Calif.: Wiley–IEEE Computer Society Press, 2004.

This article argues that the primary qualities an analyst should possess are from the right brain—not the left, as so many methodologists would like us to believe. It pours cold water on people who proclaim that if you use a particular notation, your elicitation problems will disappear.

[DAV99]   ———. "Achieving Quality in Software Requirements." *Software Quality Professional*, 1, 3 (June 1999).

Discusses what "quality in requirements" really means. Deemphasizes the use of false metrics that are easy to quantify but have no bearing on real quality. Emphasizes the measurement of attributes that relate directly to customer satisfaction.

[DAV00]   ———, and A. Zweig. "Requirements Management Made Easy." *PM Network Magazine*, 14, 12 (December 2000).

One of the first articles to suggest that less time, not more time, should be spent on the requirements process by adopting a smarter process, not a more complex one.

[DAV00a]   ———. "Editor's Corner: The Missing Piece of Software Development." *Journal of Systems and Software*, 53, 3 (September 2000), pp. 205–6. Reprinted in A. Davis, *Great Software Debates*. Los Alamitos, Calif.: Wiley–IEEE Computer Society Press, 2004.

Introduces the subject of requirements triage. An early paper, it uses the term "product planning" instead of "requirements triage."

[DAV03] *   Davis, Alan. "The Art of Requirements Triage." *IEEE Computer*, 36, 3 (March 2003), pp. 42–29.

The first treatise written to explore the subject of requirements triage.

[DAV03a]   ———. "System Phenotypes." *IEEE Software*, 20, 4 (July/August 2003). Reprinted in A. Davis, *Great Software Debates*. Los Alamitos, Calif.: Wiley–IEEE Computer Society Press, 2004.

[DAV04] *   ———. "Thoughts on Software Estimation," *Great Software Debates*. Los Alamitos, Calif.: Wiley–IEEE Computer Society Press, 2004.

Presents this author's relatively controversial opinions concerning estimating schedules and budgets for software development.

[DAV04a] *   ———. "Requirements Are But a Snapshot in Time," *Great Software Debates*. Los Alamitos, Calif.: Wiley–IEEE Computer Society Press, 2004.

Presents the argument that requirements can never be completely known.

[DEL92]   Delugach, Harry. "Specifying Multiple-Viewed Software Requirements with Conceptual Graphs." *The Journal of Systems and Software*, 19, 3 (November 1992), pp. 207–24.

[DEM79] *   DeMarco, Tom. *Structured Analysis and System Specification*. Englewood Cliffs, N.J.: Yourdon Press/Prentice Hall, 1979.

One of two classic books (the other by Gane and Sarson) that introduced to the world the methodology called structured analysis. Even though this book was written more than twenty years ago, it is still a strong seller.

[DEN01]   Dennis, A., et al. *Systems Analysis and Design: An Object-Oriented Approach with UML.* New York: John Wiley & Sons, 2001.

[DEU01]   van Deursen, Arie. "Customer Involvement in Extreme Programming, XP2001 Workshop Report." *ACM Software Engineering Notes,* 26, 6 (November 2001), pp. 70–73.

[DÖM98] *   Dömges, R., and K. Pohl. "Adapting Traceability Environments to Project-Specific Needs." *Communications of the ACM,* 41, 12 (December 1998), pp. 54–62.

[DOR90] *   Dorfman, M., and R. Thayer. *Standards, Guidelines, and Examples of System and Software Requirements Engineering.* Los Alamitos, Calif.: IEEE Computer Society Press, 1990.

            Merlin and Dick did a great job with this volume. They collected and reprinted the requirements documentation standards from more than a dozen different standardization bodies. They appended to the end a few simple examples of what a requirements specification would look like using each standard.

[DUN01]   Duncan, Richard. "The Quality of Requirements in Extreme Programming." *Crosstalk* (June 2001), pp. 19–22, 31.

            Describes how traditional XP deals with requirements. Users are present with the development team. They record the requirements using stories. They prioritize stories. If a developer deems that any story will take more than two weeks to implement, the story is rejected, and returned to the user to be divided into two separate stories. If you want to see how XP should implement a requirements process, read [NAW02].

[EAS95]   Easterbrook, S., and B. Nuseibeh. "Managing Inconsistencies in an Evolving Specification," *Proceedings of Second International Symposium on Requirements Engineering,* pp. 48–55. Los Alamitos, Calif.: IEEE Computer Society Press, 1995.

            Describes an approach that monitors inconsistencies that develop as a consequence of evolving needs. This approach was designed to work in an environment where stakeholders have independently defined their requirements and inconsistencies develop between sets of stakeholders.

[ELE95]   El Emam, K., and N. Madhavji. "Measuring the Success of Requirements Engineering," *Proceedings of Second International Symposium on Requirements Engineering,* pp. 204–11. Los Alamitos, Calif.: IEEE Computer Society Press, 1995.

[ELE95a]   ———. "A Field Study of Requirements Engineering Practices in Information Systems Development," *Proceedings of Second International Symposium on Requirements Engineering,* pp. 70–77. Los Alamitos, Calif.: IEEE Computer Society Press, 1995.

            This paper presents the results of a survey of sixty cases to discover how people in internal IT organizations and their customers perform requirements activities. The authors make some terrific, unbiased recommendations concerning what companies should do to improve their requirements processes: (1) Consider using COTS packages as part of the solution system, (2) manage the level of detail on writing requirements, (3) examine the current system, (4) require user participation, (5) manage uncertainty through effective use of prototyping, (6) use CASE tools when it makes sense, but don't overestimate what they will do, and (7) make sure the project manager has appropriate skills. However, the experimental method of how they derived these recommendations from the survey is unclear.

[ELE96]   El Emam, K., et al. "User Participation in the Requirements Engineering Process: An Empirical Study." *Requirements Engineering Journal,* 1, 1 (1996), pp. 4–26.

[END75] *   Endres, Albert. "An Analysis of Errors and Their Causes in Systems
             Programs." *IEEE Transactions on Software Engineering*, 1, 2 (June 1975),
             pp. 140–49.

[END03]   ———, and D. Rombach. *A Handbook of Software and Systems Engineering:
             Empirical Observations, Laws, and Theories.* Harlow, Eng.: Pearson
             Addison-Wesley, 2003.

[FAI97]   Fairley, R., and R. Thayer. "The Concept of Operations: The Bridge from
             Operational Requirements to Technical Specifications." *Annals of Soft-
             ware Engineering, Vol. 3,* N. Mead, ed., 1997, pp. 417–32.

             *These two authors are on a path that's similar to mine. They believe that the
             requirements process should be made simpler and that the terminology and
             orientation of the requirements must remain in the domain of the user.*

[FEA02] *   Feather, M., and T. Menzies. "Converging on the Optimal Attainment of
             Requirements," *Proceedings of Tenth Joint International IEEE Conference on
             Requirements Engineering.* Los Alamitos, Calif.: IEEE Computer Society
             Press, 2002.

             *Combines two experimental tools—the requirements interaction model and the
             summarization tool—to do cost-benefit analysis and arrive at an optimal selec-
             tion of requirements for inclusion in the next baseline. In other words, the tech-
             nique performs triage. Uses a scatter plot to visually determine the optimality of
             the solution.*

[FER01]   Ferdinandi, Patricia L. *A Requirements Pattern.* Reading, Mass.: Addison-
             Wesley, 2001.

[FIR93]   Firesmith, Donald G. *Object-Oriented Requirements Analysis and Logical
             Design.* New York: John Wiley & Sons, 1993.

[FLA81]   Flavin, Matt. *Fundamental Concepts of Information Modeling.* Englewood
             Cliffs, N.J.: Yourdon Press/Prentice Hall, 1981.

[FLE02] *   Fleisher, C., and B. Bensoussan. *Strategic and Competitive Analysis:
             Methods and Techniques for Analyzing Business Competition.* Upper Saddle
             River, N.J.: Prentice Hall, 2002.

[FLY03]   Flynn, Doral J. *Information Systems Requirements: Determination and
             Analysis.* New York: McGraw-Hill, 2003.

[FOR97] *   Forsberg, K., and H. Mooz. "System Engineering Overview," *Software
             Requirements Engineering,* eds. M. Dorfman and R. Thayer. Los Alamitos,
             Calif.: IEEE Computer Society Press, 1997.

[FOW93] *   Fowler, Floyd J., Jr. *Survey Research Methods,* 2nd ed. Newbury Park, Calif.:
             Sage Publications, 1993.

[GAN79]   Gane, C., and T. Sarson. *Structured Systems Analysis: Tools and Techniques.*
             Englewood Cliffs, N.J.: Prentice Hall, 1979.

             One of the first books written to describe the structured analysis process.

[GAU89] *   Gause, D., and G. Weinberg. *Exploring Requirements: Quality Before
             Design.* New York: Dorset House Publishing, 1989.

             *Don't miss this one. The world's experts in elicitation via the interview wrote
             this book to help practitioners improve how they do elicitation.*

[GAU90] *   ———. *Are Your Lights On?* New York: Dorset House Publishing, 1990.

             *Another one not to be missed. Classic Gause and Weinberg, with lots of illus-
             trations and random (but fascinating) thoughts. This book presents a wake-up
             call to the readers. Elicitation is not just following some prescription; it is
             instead all about caring.*

[GLA00]   Glass, Robert L. "Software Requirements Success Predictors—Behavioral Factors Beat Technical Ones." *Journal of Systems and Software*, 51, 2 (April 2000), pp. 85–86.

[GLI00]   Glinz, Martin. "Problems and Deficiencies of UML as a Requirements Specification Language," *Proceedings of Tenth International Workshop on Software Specification and Design*, pp. 11–22. Los Alamitos, Calif.: IEEE Computer Society Press, 2000.

               Using a medical system as a case study, the author reports on some of the problems he experienced using UML as a requirements language. The problems include: an inability to model situations where the system initiates an action (as opposed to an external actor); an inability to model complex interactions among actors (this is an interesting observation; UML was built to ease the development of a computer system, not to model a real world); the fact that use cases can have their own states, but UML does not recognize that the system itself can be in a state quite independent of the cross-product of the states of its objects; and the modeling of information flow is awkward (that is why we have both use cases and data flow diagrams in the modeling world).

[GOG93]   Goguen, Joseph. "Social Issues in Requirements Engineering," *Proceedings of IEEE International Symposium on Requirements Engineering*, pp. 194–95. Los Alamitos, Calif.: IEEE Computer Society Press, 1993.

               A brief summary of the social issues that are present within the customer community, the analyst community, the development community, and between each pair of them.

[GOG93a]   ———, and C. Linde. "Techniques for Requirements Elicitation." *Proceedings of IEEE International Symposium on Requirements Engineering*, pp. 152–64. Los Alamitos, Calif.: IEEE Computer Society Press, 1993.

               A terrific survey of the wide range of techniques available for conducting requirements elicitation.

[GOG94] *   Goguen, J., and M. Jirotka, eds. *Requirements Engineering: Social and Technical Issues*. Boston: Academic Press, 1994.

               The best collection of ideas anywhere dealing with the use of ethnomethodologies (especially observation) to learn about the problems experienced by potential system users.

[GOT94]   Gotel, O., and A. Finkelstein. "An Analysis of the Requirements Traceability Problem," *Proceedings of IEEE International Conference on Requirements Engineering*, pp. 94–101. Los Alamitos, Calif.: IEEE Computer Society Press, 1994.

               Describes the confusion in the industry today concerning requirements traceability, starting with the wide variation in the definition of the term. In a survey of 100 practitioners, the authors discovered that the single biggest traceability problem experienced is the inability to find the origin of requirements.

[GOT00] *   Gottesdiener, Ellen. *Requirements by Collaboration*. Reading, Mass.: Addison-Wesley, 2000.

               Gottesdiener is to facilitated group sessions as Gause and Weinberg are to interviews. Everything you will ever need to know about how to conduct such sessions for requirements elicitation can be found in this book.

[GRA98]   Graham, Ian. *Requirements Engineering and Rapid Development*. Reading, Mass.: Addison-Wesley, 1998.

               Advocates a specific way to do requirements using facilitated group sessions for elicitation and objects for requirements specification.

[HAD97]   Hadden, Rita. "Does Managing Requirements Pay Off?" *American Programmer*, 10, 4 (April 1997), pp. 10–12.

[HAL02] * Hall, T., et al. "Requirements Problems in Twelve Software Companies: An Empirical Analysis." *IEEE Proceedings—Software*, 149, 5 (October 2002), pp. 153–60.

An easy-to-read report of an experiment to ascertain the types of problems twelve companies are experiencing with respect to their requirements processes.

[HAR87] * Harel, David. "Statecharts: A Visual Formalism for Complex Systems." *Science of Computer Programming*, 8, 3 (June 1987), pp. 231–74.

The original article that presented Harel's ideas on how finite state machines can be extended to make them much more expressive when specifying requirements for real-time systems.

[HAR88] ————. "On Visual Formalisms." *Communications of the ACM*, 31, 5 (May 1988), pp. 8–20.

In this paper, Harel extends the concept of statecharts to encompass a wider range of formal models useful during requirements specification.

[HAR98] ————, and M. Politi. *Modeling Reactive Systems with Statecharts*. New York: McGraw-Hill, 1998.

A great compendium of ideas on how to model systems (during both requirements and design activities) using statecharts.

[HAY96] * Haywood, E., and P. Dart. "Criteria Used for the Evaluation of Software System Requirements Models," *Proceedings of First Australian Workshop on Requirements Engineering*, pp. 3.0–3.10. Los Alamitos, Calif.: IEEE Computer Society Press, 1996.

Independent of the techniques used to create them, this paper surveys a wide array of requirements modeling notations, including use cases, narrative (with hyperlinks), formal logic, domain networks, statecharts, goal hierarchies, and conceptual state machines. Each is analyzed according to a redefined set of criteria relating to its ease of use, degree of formalism, and so on. A nice, easy read.

[HEI96] Heimdahl, M., and N. Leveson. "Completeness and Consistency in Hierarchical State-Based Requirements." *IEEE Transactions on Software Engineering*, 22, 6 (June 1996), pp. 363–77.

Includes a nice definition of theoretic completeness (in the spirit of "mathematical closure") and goes on to describe every possible type of violation that can occur.

[HIC02] * Hickey, A., and A. Davis. "The Role of Requirements Elicitation Techniques in Achieving Software Quality," *Proceedings of Workshop on Requirements Engineering: Foundations for Software Quality*. Essen, Germany, September 2002.

Presents an argument that shows how doing requirements elicitation poorly (or not at all) will result in dismal project failure.

[HIC03] ————. "Elicitation Technique Selection: How Do the Experts Do It?" *Proceedings of International Joint Conference on Requirements Engineering (RE03)*, pp. 169–78. Los Alamitos, Calif.: IEEE Computer Society Press, 2003.

Reports on the result of a survey of the some of the most famous consulting analysts concerning how they actually perform elicitation.

[HIG01] * Highsmith, J., and A. Cockburn. "Agile Software Development: The Business of Innovation." *IEEE Computer* (September 2001), pp. 120–22.

Provides a great overview of the spirit of all types of agile development. Very little is actually said about requirements other than "changes to feature priorities and requirements are handled within the context of a team and the customer partners." This assumes that the customer is generally co-located with the development team.

[HOO00] Hooks, Ivy. "Requirements Engineering: Is It Mission Impossible?" *Requirements Engineering Journal*, 5, 3 (2000), pp. 194–97.

[HOO01] ———, and K. Farry. *Customer-Centered Products: Creating Successful Products Through Smart Requirements Management*. New York: AMACOM, 2001.

[HUB84] * Huber, G. "Issues in the Design of Group Decision Support Systems." *MIS Quarterly*, 8, 3 (Fall 1984), pp. 195–204.

[HUL02] Hull, M., et al. *Requirements Engineering*. Berlin: Springer-Verlag, 2002.

A nice survey of a wide range of practical modeling techniques. It contains a nice mix of both elicitation modeling techniques and the use of the DOORS tool for recording requirements.

[IEE98] * Institute of Electrical and Electronics Engineers. *IEEE Recommended Practice for Software Requirements Specifications, IEEE-STD-830-1998*. New York: IEEE Press, 1998.

A commercially available standard for organizing the contents of a software requirements document.

[IEE98a] * Institute of Electrical and Electronics Engineers. *IEEE Standard for Software Project Management Plans, IEEE-STD-1058-1998*. New York: IEEE Press, 1998.

A commercially available standard for organizing the contents of a software project plan.

[IN01] * In, H., et al. "A Requirements Negotiation Model Based on Multi-Criteria Analysis," *Proceedings of Fifth International Symposium on Requirements Engineering*, pp. 312–13. Los Alamitos, Calif.: IEEE Computer Society Press, 2001.

A brief summary of how the WinWin project performs requirements triage.

[IOW57] * *The Diffusion Process*, Agriculture Extension Service, Iowa State University, Special Report No. 18, Ames, Iowa, 1957.

[JAC95] Jackson, Michael. *Software Requirements and Specifications*. Harlow, Eng.: Addison-Wesley, 1995.

[JAC97] ———. "The Meaning of Requirements." *Annals of Software Engineering*, *Vol. 3*, N. Mead, ed., 1997, pp. 5–21.

[JAC01] ———. *Problem Frames*. Harlow, Eng.: Addison-Wesley, 2001.

[JAC92] * Jacobson, I., et al. *Object-Oriented Software Engineering: A Use-Case Driven Approach*. Reading, Mass.: Addison-Wesley, 1992.

The book that introduced to the industry the expression "use case."

[JAH94] * Jahanian, F., and A. Mok. "Modechart: A Specification Language in Real Time Logic." *IEEE Transactions on Software Engineering*, 20, 12 (December 1994), pp. 933–47.

Just as Harel's statecharts extended finite state machines to improve their ability to describe requirements, Jahanian and Mok take this one step further by introducing their modecharts.

[JON96] * Jones, Capers. "Strategies for Managing Requirements Creep." *IEEE Computer*, 29, 5 (May 1996), pp. 92–94.

In order to reduce requirements creep, Capers recommends that you (a) perform requirements inspections, (b) use joint application development, (c) build prototypes, (d) perform rapid application development, (e) use cost-per-function-point contracts, (f) use quality function deployment, and (g) use change control boards.

[JON98] * ———. *Estimating Software Costs.* New York: McGraw-Hill, 1998.

Classic Capers, here you will find data on anything you ever wanted to know about the software industry, with particular emphasis on the use of feature points to do schedule and cost estimation.

[KAM02] Kamsties, E., et al. "Requirements Engineering in Small and Medium Enterprises: State of the Practice, Problems, Solutions and Technology Transfer," *Proceedings of Conference on European Industrial Requirements Engineering,* pp. 40–50. London: British Computer Society, 2002.

[KAR96] * Karlsson, J., and K. Ryan. "Supporting the Selection of Requirements," *Proceedings of Eighth International Workshop on Software Specification and Design,* pp. 146–49. Los Alamitos, Calif.: IEEE Computer Society Press, 1996.

Using a series of pair-wise comparisons of candidate requirements, the authors demonstrate (on a very small test case) that 20 percent of the candidate requirements represented 80 percent of the importance, and a different 20 percent of the candidate requirements represented 80 percent of the effort required for satisfaction.

[KAR97] ———. "A Cost-Value Approach for Prioritizing Requirements." *IEEE Software,* 14, 5 (September 1997), pp. 67–74.

An updated version of [KAR96] that applies the pair-wise method to two small cases.

[KAR97a] Karlsson, Joachim. "Managing Software Requirements Using Quality Function Deployment." *Software Quality Journal,* 6, 4 (January 1997), pp. 311–26.

[KAR97b] ———, et al. "Improved Practical Support for Large-Scale Requirements Prioritizing." *Requirements Engineering Journal,* 2, 1 (January 1997), pp. 51–60.

[KAR98] Karsai, G., et al. "An Evaluation of Methods for Prioritizing Software Requirements." *Information and Software Technology,* 39, 14–15 (February 1998), pp. 939–47.

[KEN01] * Kendall, K., and J. Kendall. *Systems Analysis and Design.* Englewood Cliffs, N.J.: Prentice Hall, 2001.

[KIL98] Kilov, Haim. *Business Specifications: The Key to Successful Software Engineering.* Englewood Cliffs, N.J.: Prentice Hall, 1998.

[KNA97] Knapp, M., and J. Hall. *Nonverbal Communication in Human Interaction.* Austin, Tex.: Holt, Rhinehart, and Winston, 1997.

[KOT96] Kotonya, G., and I. Sommerville. "Requirements Engineering with Viewpoints." *Software Engineering Journal,* 11, 1 (January 1996), pp. 5–18.

[KOT98] * ———. *Requirements Engineering: Processes and Techniques.* New York: John Wiley & Sons, 1998.

Very similar coverage to my 1993 book. Nice survey of problem modeling and specification modeling.

[KOT99] Kotonya, Gerald. "Practical Experience with Viewpoint-Oriented Requirements Specifications." *Requirements Engineering Journal,* 4, 3 (1999), pp. 115–33.

[KOV99] Kovitz, Benjamin L. *Practical Software Requirements: A Manual of Content and Style.* Greenwich, Eng.: Manning, 1999.

Primarily covers the breadth of traditional systems analysis techniques useful for elicitation.

[KOW92] * Kowal, James A. *Behavior Models.* Englewood Cliffs, N.J.: Prentice Hall, 1992.

[KRU00] *   Krueger, R., and M. Casey. *Focus Groups: A Practical Guide for Applied Research.* Newbury Park, Calif.: Sage Publications, 2000.

[KUL00] *   Kulak, D., and E. Guiney. *Use Cases: Requirements in Context.* Reading, Mass.: Addison-Wesley, 2000.

[KUU00] *   Kuusela, J., and J. Savolainen. "Requirements Engineering for Product Families," *Proceedings of International Conference on Software Engineering,* pp. 61–69. Los Alamitos, Calif.: IEEE Computer Society Press, 2000.

   By organizing all the requirements in a hierarchy, the authors are able to show what the requirements are for each member of a family of products, and how they relate.

[LAM98]   Lam, W., et al. "Managing Requirements Change: A Set of Good Practices," *Proceedings of Fourth International Workshop on Requirements Engineering: Foundations for Software Quality.* Pisa, Italy, June 1998.

[LAM99] *   Lam, W., et al. "Requirements Changes: A Dissection of Management Issues," *Proceedings of Fifth International Workshop on Requirements Engineering: Foundations for Software Quality,* Heidelberg, Germany, June 1999; also appears in *Proceedings of 25th Euromicro Conference, Vol. 2,* pp. 244–51. Los Alamitos, Calif.: IEEE Computer Society Press, 1999.

   A nice summary of the reasons for our misconceptions about requirements change, it makes a series of recommendations on what management should do to reduce the changes and their impact. Includes some measures of success.

[LAU02]   Lauesen, Soren. *Software Requirements: Styles and Techniques.* Reading, Mass.: Addison-Wesley, 2002.

[LEF00] *   Leffingwell, D., and D. Widrig. *Managing Software Requirements—A Unified Approach.* Reading, Mass.: Addison-Wesley, 2000.

   An excellent survey book that covers almost every aspect of requirements management.

[LEH91] *   Lehman, M. "Software Engineering, the Software Process, and Their Support." *Software Engineering Journal,* 6, 5 (September 1991), pp. 243–58.

[LOU95]   Loucopoulos, P., and D. Karakostos. *System Requirements Engineering.* London: McGraw-Hill International, 1995.

[LUT93] *   Lutz, Robyn R. "Analyzing Software Requirements Errors in Safety-Critical, Embedded Systems," *Proceedings of IEEE International Symposium on Requirements Engineering,* pp. 126–33. Los Alamitos, Calif.: IEEE Computer Society Press, 1993.

   Lutz is to requirements errors as Carlshamre is to requirements relationships. Robyn has an uncanny ability to write. Every reader will easily understand the results of her numerous surveys concerning the classes of requirements errors prevalent in the industry today.

[MAC96]   Macaulay, Linda A. *Requirements Engineering.* London: Springer-Verlag, 1996.

[MAC01]   Maciaszek, Leszek A. *Requirements Analysis and System Design: Developing Information Systems with UML.* Harlow, Eng.: Pearson Education, 2001.

[MAI98]   Maiden, N., and M. Hare. "Problem Domain Categories in Requirements Engineering." *International Journal of Human-Computer Studies,* 49, 3 (September 1998), pp. 281–304.

[MAR98]   Martin, Charles F. *User-Centered Requirements Analysis.* Englewood Cliffs, N.J.: Prentice Hall, 1998.

[MAS70] *   Maslow, Abraham H. *Motivation and Personality.* New York: Harper and Row, 1970.

[MCL01] *   McLeod, R., and G. Schell. *Management Information Systems.* Englewood Cliffs, N.J.: Prentice Hall, 2001.

[MCM84] *   McMenamin, S., and J. Palmer. *Essential Systems Analysis.* Englewood Cliffs, N.J.: Yourdon Press/Prentice Hall, 1984.

As far as I know, this is the first book to present a means to create data flow diagrams during structured analysis in a bottom-up manner. And it even seems to work.

[MIL82]   Miller, T., and B. Taylor. "A Requirements Methodology for Complex Real-Time Systems," *Proceedings of Symposium on Current Issues in Requirements Engineering Environments,* pp. 133–41. Amsterdam, The Netherlands: North Holland Publishers, 1982.

[MIZ94] *   Mizuno, S., and Y. Akao. *QFD: The Customer-Driven Approach to Quality Planning and Deployment.* Portland, Oreg.: Productivity, Inc., 1994.

[MOO91] *   Moore, Geoffrey A. *Crossing the Chasm.* New York: HarperBusiness, 1991.

If you are an entrepreneur (or a wannabe entrepreneur) in the software industry, you must read this book. It presents product life cycles in a way that anybody can understand, and it offers a new explanation for why so many companies grow to a moderately small size and then fail to make it big.

[MOR97]   Moreno, Ana M. "Object-Oriented Analysis from Textual Specifications," *Proceedings of Ninth IEEE International Conference on Software Engineering and Knowledge Engineering,* pp. 48–55. Skokie, Ill.: Knowledge Systems Institute, 1997.

Based on the author's Ph.D. thesis, this paper offers an innovative approach to deriving object models automatically from natural-language requirements specifications.

[MYL01]   Mylopoulos, J., et al. "Exploring Alternatives During Requirements Analysis." *IEEE Software,* 18, 1 (January/February 2001), pp. 92–96.

An excellent discussion of goals analysis, emphasizing the need to think before diving into documentation of requirements. Specifically, the authors describe a method to fully explore what the users really want out of the system.

[NAK94] *   Nakajima, T., and A. Davis, "Classifying Requirements for Improved SRS Reviews," *Proceedings of International Workshop on Requirements Engineering: Foundations for Software Quality (REFSQ)* (June 1994), pp. 88–100.

[NAW02] *   Nawrocki, J., et al. "Extreme Programming Modified: Embrace Requirements Engineering Practices," *Proceedings of Tenth Joint International IEEE Conference on Requirements Engineering.* Los Alamitos, Calif.: IEEE Computer Society Press, 2002.

This paper is a great attempt at modifying standard XP so that it collects, records, and evolves requirements in a sensible manner. I'm not convinced that mainstream XP adherents will buy this. After all, the ideas here help to empower customers and hold the developers implicitly responsible if things go awry.

[NUN91] *   Nunamaker, J., et al. "Electronic Meeting Systems to Support Group Work." *Communications of the ACM,* 34, 7 (July 1991), pp. 40–61.

[OCK97]   Ocker, R., et al. "An Exploratory Comparison of Four Modes of Communication for Determining Requirements: Results on Creativity, Quality, and Satisfaction," *Proceedings of 30th Hawaii International Conference on System Science, Vol. 2,* pp. 568–77. Los Alamitos, Calif.: IEEE Computer Society Press, 1997.

Compares the results of an experiment that contrasted requirements elicitation using face-to-face communication with a variety of computer-supported cooperative work environments. Results are compared relative to creativity and quality, and the data sources are both the participants themselves (their own opinion of their own creativity and quality) and a third party.

[PAR76] * Parnas, David L. "On the Design and Development of Program Families." *IEEE Transactions on Software Engineering*, 2, 1 (March 1976), pp. 1–9.

[PAU93] * Paulk, M., et al. "Capability Maturity Model 1.1." *IEEE Software*, 10, 4 (July 1993), pp. 18–27.

An early description of how the CMM works, and what it includes.

[POH94] * Pohl, Klaus. "The Three Dimensions of Requirements Engineering: A Framework and Its Application." *Information Systems*, 3, 19 (June 1994), pp. 243–58.

[POH96] ———. *Process-Centered Requirements Engineering*. Chichester, Eng.: John Wiley & Sons, 1996.

[PUT78] * Putnam, Lawrence H. "A General Empirical Solution to the Macro Software Sizing and Estimation Problem." *IEEE Transactions on Software Engineering*, 4, 4 (July 1978), pp. 345–61.

[RAM78] * Ramamoorthy, C.V., and H. So. *Software Requirements and Specifications: Status and Perspectives*. University of California at Berkeley Electronics Research Laboratory Report #M78/44. Berkeley, Calif.: June 1978.

[RAM98] * Ramesh, Balasubramanium. "Factors Influencing Requirements Traceability Practice." *Communications of the ACM*, 41, 12 (December 1998), pp. 37–44.

[REG95] Regnell, Björn. "Improving the Use Case Driven Approach to Requirements Engineering," *Proceedings of Second International Symposium on Requirements Engineering*. Los Alamitos, Calif.: IEEE Computer Society Press, 1995.

[REG98] * ———, et al. "A Market-Driven Requirements Engineering Process." *Requirements Engineering*, 3, 2 (February 1998), pp. 121–29.

An excellent paper that offers an alternative approach to requirements elicitation, triage, and specification to the one presented in this book, it emphasizes the entire requirements process for independent software vendors. Contains a lot of good ideas that can complement this book, including, a format for a requirements record in a forms view, a method of performing triage, a nice chart showing the evolution of a specific requirement, and so on.

[REI03] * Reifer, Donald J. *Making the Software Business Case*. Reading, Mass.: Addison-Wesley, 2003.

[REI97] * Reinertsen, Donald G. *Managing the Design Factory: A Product Developer's Toolkit*. New York: The Free Press, 1997.

One of the best sources I have found for information about market windows.

[ROB99] * Robertson, S., and J. Robertson. *Mastering the Requirements Process*. Harlow, Eng.: Addison-Wesley, 1999.

Delivers Volere to the community. Volere is an extensively researched standard for documenting requirements. Serves as an excellent checklist for all requirements.

[ROB00] ———. "Requirements Management: A Cinderella Story." *Requirements Engineering Journal*, 5, 2 (March 2000), pp. 134–36.

Packed full of observations and advice like, (a) business requirements and the final product often have little in common, (b) elicitation can disrupt the stakeholders' work, (c) stakeholders are often left out, (d) natural language works, (e) use a "fit criterion" for every requirement, (f) elicitation is fundamentally a human-oriented activity, and—the best one of all—(g) tools most often omitted from elicitation: pencil, paper, and two ears. I wish I could write like this.

[ROB01]   Robertson, Suzanne. "Are We Afraid of the Dark?" *IEEE Software*, 18, 4 (July/August 2001), pp. 12–15.

            A wonderful and brief wake-up call. The author observes that we are expending too much effort looking at requirements tools and techniques when what we really need is something entirely different.

[ROY98] *   Royce, Walker. *Software Project Management: A Unified Framework.* Reading, Mass.: Addison-Wesley, 1998.

            Walker (Winston Royce's son) wrote this book to show how to be a project manager when building systems iteratively. I have been using it for many years as a textbook in my project management course.

[ROY70] *   Royce, Winston. "Managing the Development of Large Software Systems," *WESCON 70, 1970.* Reprinted in *Proceedings of 9th International Conference on Software Engineering,* pp. 328–38. Los Alamitos, Calif.: IEEE Computer Society Press, 1987.

            The original source of the waterfall model.

[RUH03]   Ruhe, G., et al. "Trade-Off Analysis for Requirements Elicitation." *International Journal on Software Engineering and Knowledge Engineering,* 13, 4 (August 2003), pp. 345–66.

[SAI00]   Saiedian, H., and R. Dale. "Requirements Engineering: Making the Connection Between the Software Developer and Customer." *Information and Software Technology,* 42, 6 (April 2000), pp. 419–28.

[SHE92] *   Sheldon, F., et al. "Reliability Measurement: From Theory to Practice." *IEEE Software,* 9, 4 (July 1992).

            Provides an overview of the entire field of software reliability. At the end of the paper, the authors provide data concerning the distribution of error types (including "requirements" and "requirements incompleteness," which I combined in my pie chart in Figure 1-27 into just one category: requirements) found on a U.S. Air Force project.

[SID96]   Siddiqi, J., and C. Shekaran. "Requirements Engineering: The Emerging Wisdom." *IEEE Software,* 13, 2 (March 1996), pp. 15–19.

[SOM97]   Sommerville, I., and P. Sawyer. "Viewpoints: Principles, Problems, and a Practical Approach to Requirements Engineering." *Annals of Software Engineering,* 3 (January 1997), pp. 101–30.

[SOM97a]   ———. *Requirements Engineering: A Good Practice Guide.* New York: John Wiley & Sons, 1997.

            A wonderful compendium of best requirements practices. Organized similarly to my 201 Principles of Software Development [DAV95], it contains a three-to-four-page description of each principle.

[SPR82] *   Sprague, R., and E. Carlson. *Building Effective Decision Support Systems.* Englewood Cliffs, N.J.: Prentice Hall, 1982.

[STA95] *   Standish Group. *The Chaos Report.* www.standishgroup.com, 1995.

[STA98]   Stark, G., et al. "An Examination of the Effects of Requirements Changes on Software Releases." *CrossTalk* (December 1998).

            Presents the results of a study of a series of forty releases of a software product, with detailed analyses of the types and sources of requirements changes for each release. One of the few studies I have seen that reports on which stakeholders introduce the most requirements changes: the development organization!

[SUT98]   Sutcliffe, A., et al. "Supporting Scenario-Based Requirements Engineering." *IEEE Transactions on Software Engineering,* 24, 12 (December 1998), pp. 1072–88.

One of the very few papers that offers step-by-step advice concerning how to create and document scenarios as part of a requirements methodology. Although a lot of the paper is typical IEEE Transactions-type read-only text, many parts of this paper are quite readable and understandable—even to the layperson.

[SUT99]   Sutcliffe, A., et al. "Tracing Requirements Errors to Problems in the Requirements Engineering Process." *Requirements Engineering Journal*, 4, 3 (1999), pp. 134–51.

[SUT02]   Sutcliffe, Alistair. *User-Centered Requirements Engineering*. London: Springer-Verlag, 2002.

[TAY80] *   Taylor, Bruce. "A Method for Expressing Functional Requirements of Real-Time Systems." *IFAC Real-Time Programming*, pp. 111–20. Oxford, Eng.: Elsevier, 1980.

[THA97]   Thayer, R., and M. Dorfman, eds. *Software Requirements Engineering*. Los Alamitos, Calif.: IEEE Computer Society Press, 1997.

A collection of essays from many of the best authors of requirements management articles. Reading this volume is a great way to understand the primary issues and opinions in the field circa 1997.

[USA97] *   *Requirements Generation System*. U.S. Army, Memorandum of Policy, CJCSI 3170.01, 1997.

[WAS86] *   Wasserman, A., et al. "Developing Interactive Information Systems with the User Software Engineering Methodology." *IEEE Transactions on Software Engineering*, 12, 2 (February 1986), pp. 326–45.

[WEI88] *   Weinberg, Gerald M. *Rethinking Systems Analysis and Design*. New York: Dorset House Publishing, 1988.

[WHI98]   Whitten, Neal. "Meet Minimum Requirements: Anything More Is Too Much." *PM Network*, 12, 9 (September 1998), p. 19.

[WIE03] *   Wiegers, Karl E. *Software Requirements, 2nd ed.* Redmond, Wash.: Microsoft Press, 2003.

[WIE96]   Wieringa, Roel J. *Requirements Engineering: Frameworks for Understanding*. Chichester, Eng.: John Wiley & Sons, 1996.

Primarily covers the breadth of traditional systems analysis techniques that are useful for elicitation. Also addresses the use of formal models for requirements specification.

[WIN03]   Windle, D., and L. Abreo. *Software Requirements Using the Unified Process*. Upper Saddle River, N.J.: Prentice Hall, 2003.

Dedicated to the use-case approach, one of many practical techniques.

[WIT01] *   Wittgenstein, Ludwig. *Tractatus Logico-Philosophicus*. Oxford, Eng.: Routledge, 2001.

[WOO95] *   Wood, J., and D. Silver. *Joint Application Development*. New York: John Wiley & Sons, 1995.

[YOU01] *   Young, Ralph R. *Effective Requirements Practices*. Reading, Mass.: Addison-Wesley, 2001.

[YOU00] *   Yourdon, Ed. "A New Perspective on Metrics." *Total Metrics*, 1, 4 (September 2000), pp. 1, 6.

[YUE87]   Yue, Kaizhi. "What Does It Mean to Say That a Specification Is Complete?" *Proceedings of Fourth International Workshop on Software Specification and Design*, Monterey, Calif., 1987.

[ZOW02] *   Zowghi, D., and V. Gervasi. "The Three C's of Requirements: Consistency, Completeness, and Correctness," *Proceedings of Eighth International Workshop on Requirements Engineering (REFSQ'02)*. Essen, Ger.: Foundation for Software Quality, 2002.

[ZOW04] *   ———. "Erratum to On the Interplay Between Consistency, Completeness, and Correctness in Requirements Evolution." *Information and Software Technology*, 46 (2004), pp. 763–79.

Index

Boeing 777, 9
burglar alarm, 43
cherry soda manufacturing, 101
cover dependency, 81
decision tables, 143–44
decision trees, 145
degradation, 149
effort dependency, 79
elevator, 59, 132, 143–45, 147, 148, 149
finite state machines, 140–42
heating, ventilation, and air-conditioning (HVAC), 44
hotel, 4
lawn mower, 49, 50, 51, 60
London stock traders, 48
manufacturing laser printers, 101
mass storage device, 93–97
missile, 56, 147, 148, 149
necessity dependency, 78–79
one-lane bridge, 59–61, 72–73, 74–75, 84–86, 98–99, 123–24, 137–39, 141–42, 147–48, 156, 200–208
remote mouse, 5
robot, 6, 43
scenarios, 56–57, 137, 138, 207
subset dependency, 80–81
traffic signal, 59–61, 72–73, 74–75, 84–86, 98–99, 123–24, 137–39, 141–42, 147–48, 156, 200–208
user interface map, 155
Expenses. See Cumulative expenses.
Externally observable, 3–5, 145, 152, 183
Extreme programming, 43, 210, 215, 222

Facilitated group meeting, 47, 48–52
validating with question-naires, 54–55
Fagan, Michael, 36
Fairley, Richard, 216
Farry, K., 219

Feather, Martin, 65, 84n., 216
Feature points, 74
Features. See also Requirements.
abstract requirements, 26
adding, 103, 104, 109
removing, 104, 109
Ferdinandi, Patricia L., 216
Finance department, 31, 32, 158, 160, 171
Finite state machine, *xi*, 59, 140–42, 206
Finkelstein, Anthony, 132, 217
Firesmith, Donald G., 216
Five-way priority scheme, 69, 71–72
Flavin, Matt, 216
Fleisher, Craig, 41, 216
Flynn, Doral J., 216
Focus group. See Facilitated group meeting.
Formal specification, 123, 128–29
Forsberg, Kevin, 19, 216
Fowler, Floyd J., 54, 216
Function points, 74
Fuzzy problems, 19

Gane, Chris, 214, 216
Gause, Donald C., 43, 44, 47, 216, 217
GDSS. See Computer-supported cooperative work (CSCW).
Gervasi, Vincenzo, 130, 209, 226
Glass, Robert L., 217
Glinz, Martin, 217
Glossary, 46, 62, 162, 173, 176
Goguen, Joseph, 48, 54, 217
Gotel, Olly, 132, 217
Gottesdiener, Ellen, 46, 49, 217
Graham, Ian, 217
Grammar, 191
requirements and, 191
Group decision support systems (GDSS). See Computer-supported cooperative work (CSCW).
Group session. See Facilitated group meeting.
Guiney, Eamonn, 57, 221

About the Author

Alan M. Davis is a professor of information systems at the University of Colorado at Colorado Springs. He also serves as president of The Davis Company, a consulting firm dedicated to helping organizations define, acquire, and construct systems that address actual needs. He has consulted for many corporations since 1975, including Boeing, British Telecom, Cadence Design Systems, Cigna Insurance, Federal Express, Flight Dynamics, Fujitsu, Great Plains Software, IBM, Loral, MCI, Mitsubishi Electric, NEC, NTT, Rockwell, Schlumberger, Sharp, Software Productivity Consortium, Storage Tek, and Sumitomo. He has consulted for many corporations since 1975.

Previously, he was

- chairman and CEO of Omni-Vista, a software company in Colorado Springs that assisted companies in selecting the right features to include in products in order to maximize their return on investment
- member of the board of directors of Requisite, which was acquired by Rational Software in 1997 and by IBM in 2003
- vice president of engineering services at BTG, a Virginia-based defense contractor that went public in 1995 and was acquired by Titan in 2001

- a director of R&D at GTE Communication Systems in Phoen Arizona
- director of the Software Technology Center at GTE Laboratories in Waltham, Massachusetts

He has held academic positions at George Mason University, University of Tennessee, University of Illinois at Champaign-Urbana, and the University of the Western Cape, South Africa.

Dr. Davis is the author or coauthor of more than 100 papers on software and requirements engineering. From the IEEE Computer Society, he has received the Core Member Award, in 1999; the Meritorious Service Award, in 1999; and Certificate of Appreciation Awards, in 1984 and 1998. He received Recognition of Service Awards in 1990 and 1992 from the Association of Computing Machinery.

He served as editor-in-chief of *IEEE Software* from 1994 to 1998, and as co-columnist of that publication's Manager Column from 1992 to 1994. He has been an associate editor for the *Journal of Systems and Software* since 1987, and he was an editor for *Communications of the ACM* from 1981 to 1991. He is the author of *Software Requirements: Objects, Functions and States* (Prentice Hall, 1990 and 1993), the best-selling *201 Principles of Software Development* (McGraw-Hill, 1995), and *Great Software Debates* (Wiley and IEEE Computer Society Press, 2004).

He is the founder of the *IEEE International Conferences of Requirements Engineering* and served as general chair of its first conference, in 1994. He has been a fellow of the IEEE since 1994.

Dr. Davis earned his B.S. in mathematics from the State University of New York at Albany, in 1970, and his M.S. and Ph.D. in computer science from the University of Illinois, in 1973 and 1975, respectively.

Waltzing with Bears

Managing Risk on Software Projects

by Tom DeMarco *and* Timothy Lister

ISBN: 978-0-932633-60-6   ©2003   208 pages   softcover
$27.95 (plus shipping)*

Just Say No to Slam Dunk Projects— If There's No Risk, Don't Do It

Greater risk brings greater reward, especially in software development. A company that runs away from risk will soon find itself lagging behind its more adventurous competition. Conversely, ignoring the threat of negative outcomes—in the name of positive thinking or a can-do attitude—software managers drive their organizations into the ground.

In *Waltzing with Bears*, Tom DeMarco and Timothy Lister—the best-selling authors of *Peopleware*—show readers how to identify and embrace worthwhile risks. Developers are then set free to push the limits.

The authors present the benefits of risk management, including that it • makes aggressive risk-taking possible • protects management from getting blindsided • provides minimum-cost downside protection • reveals invisible transfers of responsibility • isolates the failure of a subproject.

Readers are armed with strategies for confronting the most common risks that software projects face: • schedule flaws • requirements inflation • turnover • specification breakdown • and under-performance.

Waltzing with Bears will help you mitigate the risks—before they turn into project-killing problems.

"In the past, you may have looked at . . . a slam dunk and thanked your lucky stars to be given an easy project for a change. We've had the same reaction. What dummies we were. Projects with no real risks are losers."
—from Chapter 1

". . . destined to become the Bible for serious IT professionals and project managers. . . .

"Pearls of wisdom like 'It's okay to be wrong, but not okay to be uncertain' are, by themselves, worth the price of this book—for they remind us of how childishly unrealistic our risk management culture really is."
—**Edward Yourdon,** www.yourdon.com

"The seminal work on managing software project risk. . . . Explosive insights, practical advice. Finally we have a guide to risk management that we can implement and use."
—**Rob Austin,** Professor Harvard Business School

"Bold, provocative yet coolly pragmatic . . ."
—**Michael Schrage,** Co-Director of MIT Media Lab's e-Markets Initiative Author of *Serious Play*

Read more about WALTZING WITH BEARS *at www.dorsethouse.com/books/waltz.html*

Order Today! • (800) 342-6657 • (212) 620-4053 • fax (212) 727-1044
Phone, fax, or mail with credit card information, check, or money order. *Prices subject to change without notice.
DORSET HOUSE PUBLISHING 3143 BROADWAY, SUITE 2B NEW YORK, NEW YORK 10027 USA
info@dorsethouse.com • www.dorsethouse.com

Peopleware

Productive Projects and Teams, 2nd ed.

by Tom DeMarco *and* Timothy Lister

ISBN: 978-0-932633-43-9   ©1999   264 pages   softcover
$33.95 (plus shipping)*

A Project Management Best-Seller
—Now Updated and Expanded

Two of the computer industry's most popular authors and lecturers return with a new edition of the software management book that started a revolution.

With humor and wisdom drawn from years of management and consulting experience, DeMarco and Lister demonstrate that the major issues of software development are human, not technical—and that managers ignore them at their peril.

Now, with a new preface and eight new chapters—expanding the original edition by one third—the authors enlarge upon their previous ideas and add fresh insights, examples, and potent anecdotes.

Discover dozens of ingenious tips on how to

- put more quality into a product
- loosen up formal methodologies
- fight corporate entropy
- make it acceptable to be uninterruptible

Peopleware shows you how to cultivate teams that are healthy and productive. The answers aren't easy—just incredibly successful.

Read more about Peopleware *at www.dorsethouse.com/books/pw.html*

Order Today! • (800) 342-6657 • (212) 620-4053 • fax (212) 727-1044
Phone, fax, or mail with credit card information, check, or money order. *Prices subject to change without notice.
DORSET HOUSE PUBLISHING 3143 BROADWAY, SUITE 2B NEW YORK, NEW YORK 10027 USA
info@dorsethouse.com • www.dorsethouse.com